THE HISTORY OF EASINGWOLD
AND THE FOREST OF GALTRES

The History of Easingwold and the Forest of Galtres

GEOFFREY C. COWLING, M.A.

Introductory Note December 2001

Cowling's *History of Easingwold* has long been out of print and over the years G. H. Smith & Son have often been asked to produce a reprint. This is it, and it was decided to reproduce the work as a facsimile of the original. Sometime in the future it is hoped that Cowling's work will be brought up to date with an additional chapter. Meanwhile this reprint will be welcomed by many.

A. J. Peacock

Addendum to pp 80, 117, 122
William Lockwood 1725 - after 1752
Wine Merchant, Leeds
his son:- William Lockwood 1752-1821
Attorney, Leeds then Easingwold
his son:- William Lockwood 1778-1836
Attorney, Easingwold
his son:- William Lockwood, 1804-1854
in Holy Orders

G. H. Smith & Son, THE PRINTERS
The Advertiser Office,
Market Place, Easingwold, York, YO61 3AB.
Tel: 01347 821329 www.ghsmith.com

December 2001

ISBN N° 0 904775 18 6

TABLE OF CONTENTS

LIST OF ILLUSTRATIONS

PREFACE

This book has developed from notes made over the past ten years. Though written primarily for my fellow townspeople, I hope it may be of interest to others, including the teaching profession. A great deal of the material is from original sources and the section on the Forest of Galtres is, I think, the first attempt to give a historical account of this very interesting (and probably typical) royal forest. I hope indeed that it will lead to the further research which Galtres deserves.

I owe a particular debt to the librarians of the Yorkshire Archaeological Society and Leeds and York City Libraries, as well as to Captain and Mrs. V. M. Wombwell for permission to study the archives at Newburgh Priory. I offer them my grateful thanks. In addition I have been helped with information and material by W. Bannister Esq., G. R. Drake Esq., Mrs. L. Foster, J. E. Gollifer Esq., the Rev. R. S. Hawkins, the Rev. A. C. A. Smith, Miss M. M. Smith, Miss Hilda Sturdy and many other residents or former residents of Easingwold. These and all others who have helped, not least of course, the subscribers listed elsewhere, have put me under a considerable obligation. Special thanks are due to Allan Green Esq. for his photographic skill, generously put at my disposal in the preparation of the illustrations, and to Mrs. J. C. Warner, Secretary, and to the other members of the Forest of Galtres Society for their help and support. I should finally like to thank most sincerely Mrs. Joan Thirsk, MA., Ph.D., Reader in Economic History in the University of Oxford, editor of the "Agricultural History Review" and of volume IV of "The Agrarian History of England" (C.U.P., 1967), who has found time among her many other commitments to write the Foreword.

Since the text was printed I have found references which indicate that a number of flatts disappeared from the open arable fields of the town at some date between 1625 and 1797 — probably towards the beginning of that period. They included in the Church Field a flatt on the south side of the Church of at least five roods, and the Stockell Mires "goinge to Toft Ings"; and in the Crayke Field two flatts $12\frac{1}{2}$ acres in extent called the Hall Flatts and held by the parson (rector) as part of the Archdeaconry Manor. A reference to "the Elisker headland" in 1677 may also disclose another such flatt. Finally a flatt known as "Lones Dailes" had existed in Church Field prior to 1625, apparently on the south side of Church Hill. Enclosure by agreement of these flatts with the approval of the manor court would parallel similar improvement in adjoining townships (Crayke, Raskelf, Thormanby and probably other places) during the Seventeenth century.

GEOFFREY C. COWLING

Allerton House,
Easingwold,
York.

FOREWORD

No country in Europe, apart from Ireland, possesses a smaller area of forest than Britain. A fifth of France and more than a fifth of Switzerland are still given over to forest, a quarter and more of east and west Germany, and more than a third of Austria. In Sweden forests occupy more than half the land surface, and in Finland more than three-quarters. In Britain — once as thickly forested as any other European country — no more than seven per cent of the land is forest. The chronology and pace of this unique clearance is still not altogether clear. The process was rapid in prehistoric times, and went quickly forward in the centuries of Anglo-Saxon conquest and rule. Piecemeal assarting continued steadily during the Middle Ages. But the forests remained numerous, and were surprisingly densely clustered in some areas, particularly in southern and eastern England. One could still have walked from Northhampton to Southampton with only brief escapes from the shadow of the trees. In the early sixteenth century, the Italian, Polydore Vergil, estimated that a third of the kingdom was still occupied by parks and forests. The final phase of destruction took place between the seventeenth and nineteenth centuries, most of it, one suspects, in the seventeenth century, by the disafforestation of the royal forests, by the destruction of timber for industrial uses, and by the labour of farmers urged on by exhortations about the improvement of wastes. Because of this three-pronged attack on our woods, the traditions of forest life do not pervade our culture or our literature as they do the culture of many other countries of Europe. The story of Robin Hood stands alone, preserving the flavour of the outlaw's life, but hardly that of the more law-abiding peasant, pursuing a routine of stock-keeping and woodland crafts.

Mr. Cowling's history of Easingwold draws our attention to one of these forests that has now all but disappeared. Galtres was disafforested in 1630, and by this regal act all restraint upon land

13

clearance was removed. It was the beginning of the end. But the transformation of the landscape was more rapid than the transformation of the communities inhabiting it. Forest villages had a personality of their own which could not be destroyed overnight. The district around Easingwold remained the home of small farmers into the early nineteenth century. Dairying and pig-keeping — the ideal pursuit on small family farms, when the felling of trees put an end to more strictly woodland pursuits — enabled the inhabitants to supply London with butter and bacon in the late eighteenth century, as did the similarly-placed inhabitants of the former forests of north-west and south-west Wiltshire. The forest tradition of horse-breeding lingered on in the annual horse races. Thus memories of the old woodland economy persisted into the nineteenth century, though not, it would seem, into the twentieth.

Mr. Cowling's portrait of Easingwold and Galtres forest is built upon an ideal combination of recollections by his neighbours and documents. The former particularly enrich his history of Easingwold; without the latter, the study of Galtres forest could not have been written. Together they illuminate a chapter in that history of England's forest communities, which must one day be written to supplement the brave and lonely study by J. C. Cox on "The Royal Forests of England" (1905).

JOAN THIRSK, Ph.D.
St. Hilda's College,
OXFORD

I

EASINGWOLD UP TO THE 16th CENTURY

As with many other places in England, there is no written record of Easingwold before Domesday Book in 1086. Its name, which is usually translated as "the high land of the Esingas (or people of Esa)," is Anglican and this suggests that the original settlement was made by a group of Angles during the 5th or 6th century A.D.[1] The district itself had then long been occupied by a settled population of which there are many remains on Grimston and Yearsley Moors and elsewhere on the high ground to the North. It had been developed to some extent in Roman times. There was a major road from Lincoln to Newcastle, by way of the Humber ferry at Brough, Stamford Bridge, Easingwold, (along Long Street) Thirsk and Northallerton, and a road of somewhat less importance from Malton to the Roman town of Isurium of the Brigantes, which is now Aldborough. The latter ran along the ridge of the Howardian Hills through the "street villages" near Malton to Hovingham and across Grimston Moor to Newburgh and Husthwaite. Its course can still be traced along modern roads, except for the section diverted to the south of his park of Newburgh by Sir Henry Belasyse in 1606. The former of these roads would certainly be metalled and the latter probably also. A deed of 1201 relating to land at Oulston contains a place name "Haresteingate" which could refer to the old Roman road, and the last two syllables may mean "the stone road". It is now called Malton Street. There was a third road directly from York through what later became the Forest of Galtres, joining the road from Stamford Bridge at about Easingwold. This may not have been a metalled road.

Romans or Romanised Britons are known to have established a number of farms or villas on the higher ground, the nearest to Easingwold so far discovered being on Oulston Moor, but there is no evidence of any settlement at Easingwold earlier than the one which may be inferred from its Anglian name.

The northern part of the town, Uppleby, bears a Danish name and since Danish settlement in the area probably did not precede the assignment of lands made by Halfdan in 876 A.D. in the valleys of the Derwent, Rye, Ouse and lower Ure and in Birdforth Wapentake, it seems fair to infer that this was an addition made by a group of Danes in the ninth or tenth century to the already long established Anglian settlement. Such "twin" settlements are found in several places in Yorkshire — Thirsk and Sowerby; Brafferton and Helperby; and Wrelton and Aislaby being other examples.

The first definite information about Easingwold is given in the national taxation survey made in 1086 known as Domesday Book. From this we know that it was held as a manor by the King himself. Prior to the Norman Conquest in 1066 it had been held by Morcar, Earl of Northumbria. Morcar had replaced Tostig as earl in October, 1065, and it seems likely that Easingwold had been previously held by Tostig. Tostig was earl from 1055 and his predecessor, Siward Digera, from about 1041, but exactly when Easingwold became a manor of the Earls of Northumbria is not known.

In 1086 there were twelve carucates of taxable land. A carucate in theory is as much land as can be ploughed by one team in a year, but it is not an exact measure and varies from about 120 to 180 acres, depending on the type of soil, which would make the twelve carucates at Easingwold in modern terms anything from 1,440 to 2,160 acres. It is known that a lesser unit, the oxgang or bovate, had a value of eight acres at Easingwold, as against, for example, nine at Heslington, nine and a half to ten and a half at Ampleforth, twelve at Huby, fourteen at Ricall, twenty at Newbald, South Newbald and Pickering and no less than twenty four at Bole, near Gainsborough. This indicates that the carucate at Easingwold had a comparatively low value.

There was enough land for seven ploughs, but only four were actually working in 1086. There were ten villeins, that is tenants who were not freeholders and who could not convey their land or receive it by inheritance without the permission of the lord of the manor. In addition (though this could apply to freeholders too) they had to perform services for the lord, usually in the form of agricultural labour. In most manors the villeins were unable to leave the manor for any length of time without the lord's consent, but this did apply to land which was part of "the ancient demesne of the Crown". The ancient demesne consisted of land which had been the property of the Crown prior to the Conquest or had been owned by William I or II. Tenants of the ancient

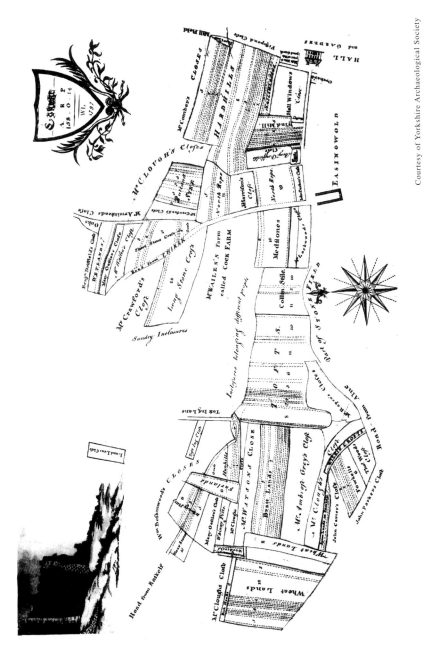

A plan of the Church Field in 1797

A plan of the Mill Field about 1800

demesne had a number of special privileges including the right to leave the manor without consent and exemption from tolls and similar payments throughout the realm. Easingwold was, of course, ancient demesne.

There was wood pasture in the manor two leagues long and two leagues broad. A league is said to have been one and a half miles at this date, but no doubt this is another variable measure.

In the time of Edward the Confessor (1042-66) the manor was worth thirty-two pounds, but by 1086 its value had dropped to twenty shillings, very probably in consequence of damage caused by reprisals following the 1069 rebellion.

The number of free tenants is not known, but the population cannot have been confined to the villeins and their families. It is perhaps fair to think of Norman Easingwold as a village of a couple of hundred souls, or something of that order. It is known that there was a church and a priest, the former no doubt on the site of the present parish church. In Edward the Confessor's time the manor was of some local importance since its lord was entitled to exercise jurisdiction over other lands in the district, which therefore were said to be in the "soke" of Easingwold. These soke lands consisted of thirty-nine carucates, four of which were at Huby, three at Moxby. six at Sand Hutton, one and a half at Thormanby and five at Sowerby. The rest of the land seems to have been either in the Forest of Galtres, around Sutton-on-Forest, or at Cold Kirby on Blackamoor. The tenants of the soke land had to attend the court of the lord of Easingwold. There were probably not many of them in 1086 — there were only two villeins and four borders (a sort of inferior villein) on the whole of the soke land.

The Manor of Easingwold was within the bounds of the royal Forest of Galtres. This originally covered most of the Wapentake of Bulmer though its bounds were considerably contracted in Henry II's reign. The area had been renowned for hunting long before the Conquest as its Danish name "boars' "brushwood", indicates. One of the Norman kings, William I, William II or Henry I, made Galtres a royal hunting preserve, subject to special laws for the preservation of the game and timber, but giving the inhabitants of the townships in and near it many common and similar rights. Easingwold seems always to have been a place for the holding of forest courts and the head of one of the bailiwicks or major divisions of the forest. Up to 1630, when Galtres ceased to be a forest, its history is closely bound up with that of Easingwold, though for the sake of clarity it is dealt with in Chapter 5.

The physical appearance of Easingwold at this date and indeed during any part of the medieval period is entirely a matter for conjecture, but Long Street and Uppleby were perhaps streets of small thatched cottages of timber and plaster, interspersed with garths, with the church at the head of the town. Eventually there were four common arable fields, but all this land was probably not brought under cultivation at once. It is perhaps appropriate to digress a little here to consider what is known of the medieval system of communal agriculture at Easingwold, though it must be stressed that the evidence is all from a much later period. It cannot be said that all the features which existed in the 18th century did so in the 11th. The typical history of community agriculture in England consists of a pioneering period in which new ground is successively broken, a period of maximum communal use and a period of gradual division into individual holdings. Final enclosure in modern times has normally been of an area much reduced from the maximum area. This last certainly seems to have been the case at Easingwold.

Four open fields seems to have been a usual number for the district. There were for example four large fields at Stillington (though some small areas of arable had been added to these) and again at Bulmer. The Easingwold fields were named respectively the Crayke Field, lying to the east of the town; the Mill Field, lying north of Church Hill and Uppleby; the Church Field to the north and north-west; and the Stone or Suskers Field to the south. The fields were subdivided into long narrow strips known as "field lands" or simply "lands". Groups of lands in a field were known as "flatts", a field being subdivided into a number of flatts. In each flatt all the lands would lie more or less parallel to each other though they were by no means all of the same size, the chief variation being in the width. There was a well recognised division into "broad" and "narrow" lands. The lands in a flatt might lie parallel to those in the adjoining flatts or they might lie at any angle to them. At first, perhaps, the division into flatts marked successive stages in bringing the waste of the manor under cultivation. It no doubt also had a connection with what appears to have been an original element in the open field system, that is that all inhabitants should share alike the good and the bad land. The working of the open field system in its early days may also have attempted to ensure this by annual re-allotment, but by the end of the Middle Ages, and probably long before that, owners acquired continuous occupation of their strips.

The earliest extant plans of the town fields of Easingwold were made about 1797, at a time when there had been considerable reduction of their original areas by enclosure. Their total area was then something like 550 acres. The number of field-lands in the Crayke Field was 229, in the Mill Field 327, in the Church Field 547 and in the Stone Field 321. When the fields were at their greatest extent there were probably at least two thousand lands. A terrier made by the vestry clerk about 1801, at the very end of the system so far as Easingwold was concerned, specifies several different classes of tenure for the field lands — "King's" or "Kinghold". "Archdeacons", "Asserts", "Dear Land", "Free Land", "Good Cheap" and copyhold. There was comparatively little copyhold. Exactly what the remaining tenures were can only be guessed, but "Kinghold" and "Archdeacons" were presumably part respectively of the King's and the Archdeacon of Richmond's manors, "Asserts" is probably a corruption of "assarts" (newly cultivated parts of the waste), while the other three names may refer to the rents paid. In 1801 Kinghold rent was a shilling an acre, Dear Land $8^1/_2$d. an acre, Asserts $6^1/_2$d. Free Land 5d. and Good Cheap $2^1/_2$d.

The flatts of the Easingwold town fields each bore a distinctive name, as for example the Wranglands flatt, the Hallikeld flatt or the Oxenby flatt, and a man who had a strip or strips in a flatt was said to hold one or more Wranglands, Hallikelds or Oxenbys. The size of his strip was often indicated by the adjective "broad" or "narrow", for example "one Broad Oxenby". Thus in 1801 in the Church Field a broad land was 1 $^1/_2$ roods and a narrow $^3/_4$ of a rood. This distinction between broad and narrow lands varied somewhat from flatt to flatt — in Hall Windows a narrow land seems to have been a rood. It appears from documents from Jacobean times that all flatts then bore the names under which they were enclosed in 1812, but clearly some are of earlier origin than others. Quite a large group is distinctively Scandinavian and these may be taken as the earliest. They include the Wranglands, the Matmires and the Gate Grains in the Stone Field; the Thorn Rains, the Barns Wray, the Busk Ings and the Hows Carrs in the Mill Field; the Fulkells or Foulkells (later the Spaw Lands) in the Church Field; and the Wandales in the Crayke Field. "Wrang" meaning "crooked" or "out of line"; "mire", a marshy place;

"grain", a branch; "rain", a headland or verge; "wray", a corner; " busk", a bush; "ing", a meadow; "ful", foul (smelling); "keld" or "kell", a spring; and "wandale", a piece marked off by wands or hurdles, are some of the elements of these names and they are evidence (if proof was needed) that the early speech of Yorkshire was a Scandinavian language.

Other flatt names seem to be of medieval origin — Wilkin Crofts and Mallisons for example — while others seem to be post-medieval, such as the Hall Windows in the Church Field and the Tay or Tea Crofts in the Mill Field. Probably the last group was exceptional and most of the names had a life of five hundred years and upwards.

The Easingwold Inclosure Act of 1808 was passed to deal with the then remaining open fields and waste grounds of the township, but in fact it dealt scarcely at all with any of the lands beyond the open fields which in former times had been the common meadows and pastures. Directly to the east of the town were Lady Carr and the Hurns, both enclosed during the reign of James I. To the north lay the hilly ground known as the Howe, which was the subject of a tremendous battle between enclosers and anti-enclosers in the same reign and that of Charles I, while to the south-east were the Lessimers, Penny Carr and Ox Moor. West of the town were Lund Leys, Toft Ings and Lund Moor, or the Lund as it is more generally called. All these were probably enclosed by the mid-seventeenth century. Ox Moor and at least part of the Lund were allotted and enclosed on the disafforestation of Galtres in 1630.

It seems likely, in fact, that at Easingwold by 1660 or there abouts, common of pasture was chiefly exercised over grass in lanes and on field balks and headlands or sike edges, and in the parts of the arable fields which were not in cultivation, in partic- ular the "faugh" or fallow field, rather than over any wide expanses of heath or rough pasture such as are traditionally associated with the term "common". The manorial court, the court leet, had apparently permitted enclosure of practically everything except the arable fields and the roadside waste. One of its court books, starting in 1667, is at Newburgh Priory, but while this shows a great deal of light on the operation of the open field system in its decline, the light is a flickering one at best. It would be pleasant to find a clear and comprehensive account of the complete system, but this of course is unlikely to happen. The suitors of the court and the steward were quite familiar with

20

it and there was no need for anyone to set it down, much less to explain it for posterity.

A complete working example of an open field system has been preserved, perhaps somewhat artificially, at Laxton in Nottinghamshire and this gives many pointers to its operation elsewhere. There were, of course, many local variations and probably the greater the number of fields, the greater the flexibility in cropping. Within a field however each occupier of a land was required to grow a particular crop or one of a particular range of crops. Under a traditional four course system each field might grow in rotation winter or bread corn (which might be wheat or in the North rye or some such mixture as maslin), spring corn and peas for a year. In 1669, for example, the Easingwold fields included a barley field, a winter corn field and a fallow field. A rye field is mentioned at Huby in 1678. The manorial court might permit considerable variation in cropping over some of the area. A field which was nominally growing spring corn might actually have strips of barley, oats, beans, peas, vetches (tares), hemp or clover intermingled. It is interesting to note that a plan of the Crayke Field from the end of the 18th century has pencilled on a number of the lands in the Oxenby Flatt the word "clover". Two narrow lands in the Hall Windows Flatt of the Church Field seem to have carried flax in April, 1801.

At certain seasons the court required each field land to be enclosed by a temporary fence. At other seasons, after harvest, or during the whole year in the case of fallows, stock might be permitted to graze on the arable land.

The making of hay in the common meadows usually took place in June and July, the grass being allotted in strips or doles in a manner resembling the division of the arable fields. A survey of the Manor of Easingwold and Huby in 1617 refers to "swaths" or "swaythes" of meadow on North Moor and at a place called Fordenbrooks. After haytime the meadows were thrown open to grazing usually until the beginning of November.

Other sources of grazing were the eatage of lanes and of the cartroads and balks of the arable fields. Balks were left along the edges of fields and between some of the constituent flatts to afford access to the individual lands and avoid as far as possible any necessity for a man crossing his neighbour's land. An example of a common balk at Easingwold was that which ran down the west side of the Crayke Field within the hedge which enclosed the whole field. The part of this balk south of the Back Lane survives as the Kell Balk footpath. Grazing for horses and cows, at any rate on the balks and lanes, would no doubt be tether grazing. Frequently the numbers of each kind of stock which a person might graze on land over which he had rights of pasture were defined, in which case the rights were said to be "stinted".

"Farthing goose lands" which seem to have been lands reserved for feeding geese, are mentioned in the court book of the manor of Easingwold-cum-Huby in the late seventeenth and early eighteenth centuries.

The manorial court drew up rules for the regulation of the open fields and common lands and appointed officers to see that they were enforced. At Easingwold four such officers, known as "the byelawmen", were appointed each year during the seventeenth century and no doubt for many generations before that. The office of pinder, theoretically annual, but often continuing in the same person for many years, was also filled by the court. The pinders duty was to impound straying animals and look after them until they could be restored to the owner. A small enclosure known as the pinfold was often used as a place of impounding, or parts of the open fields might from time to time be allotted as "pinder grass", as was done at Easingwold in the 18th Century.

After Domesday Book the next appearance of Easingwold in the records seems to be in the reign of King Stephen (1135-54). He gave to the parish church twelve acres of assarts or land enclosed from the Forest of Galtres, and also presented an incumbent to the living, Master Mainard, described as "the King's Chaplain". This donation is thought to be the origin of the second manor in the township of Easingwold, later vested in the Archdeacons of Richmond.[2]

Master Mainard is the earliest inhabitant of Easingwold whose name is known. The next are Ingelram who owed King John two marks in 1199 for a forest offence and Anketill, who seems to have been the parish clerk, and who owed King John ten marks in the same year for another forest offence. In 1200 Ingelot of Easingwold was fined twenty shillings, of which he still owed forty pence in 1207.[3] In 1208 a man named Ralph was reeve of Easingwold. The reeve was an officer of the manor, chosen from among the villein tenants, whose duty it was to ensure that all services owed to the lord by way of labour, rents in kind or money, were duly rendered. In the same year William Brune or Brown was a tenant at Easingwold.[4] Villeins at Easingwold in 1218 were Nigel and Simon the sons of Gilbert.[5]

The Pipe Roll for 1201 refers to King John as having an "ospicium" at Easingwold.[6] Exactly what the status and purpose of this property was is not clear — the word usually means a guest house, but may here mean a manor house. Henry III is believed to have had such a manor house at Easingwold in 1220.[7]

In 1221 the men of Easingwold are recorded as owing a palfrey for the privilege of having a market in the manor every Saturday until the King's majority. Henry III attained his majority in 1227.[8]

Limited grants of the manor were made by the King in 1219 to Robert former Abbot of Tournai in Flanders, pending his preferment in the church[9], and in 1230 to one of the King's servants, Henry de Helyon or Heliun. The latter was a grant to Henry and his heirs at a rent of £5 per annum of the town of Esingwaud with 300 acres of heath, wood and waste between it and the manor of Thorniton (Thornton Hill), the land to be taken out of the forest jurisdiction, with leave to cultivate if he wished. De Helyon seems to have fallen into arrears, leading to forfeiture of the grant. In the Pipe Roll for 1241-2 he is down as owing £26 and one mark of the farm (rent) of Easingwold for several years. His lease had probably ended before that, since in 16th November, 1236, orders were sent to a Crown official to cause 200 acres of the lands and woods which he formerly held in the forest of Esingwaud to be cultivated as an extension of the King's own estate there.

It does indeed appear that another farm or letting of the King's manor to Robert Bon and others as joint tenants commenced about 1237 and was still subsisting in 1247 and probably in 1249.[10]

The King had a mill at Easingwold in 1244, let to Robert de Ayville.[11] This was apparently the mill known as Waneless Mill, mentioned several times in the 13th and 14th centuries, and situated somewhere on the north side of the town, on the Kyle.

The names of quite a number of Easingwold people from the mid-thirteenth century are known from a record made in the latter part of 1249. Some are still Scandinavian. Gamel sounds Danish, while Ragenild the daughter of Matilda may bear a Norwegian name. Others again definitely derive from the church, as Adam, Jordan and Basil. The majority seem to have been without surnames, so that we get William son of Hugh, Alan son of Ingelot, Hugh son of Henry. William son of Uctred and Oda daughter of Ralph among others. Surnames were emerging however, as witness the names of Ralph Hert, William Kempe, Robert

May, Gerard Bosse and John Fem. Roger Chaplain may have been the parish priest or an assistant. Simon of Esyngwald was reeve of the manor in 1254.[12]

Exactly when the Archdeaconry Manor at Easingwold was created is not known, but in 1247 Master John Romain, Archdeacon of Richmond from 1246 to 1256. received ten oaks from the Forest of Galtres for repairing the Chancel of "his" church at Easingwold,[13] so that he must then have been its rector. He certainly was in 1269 when he received permission from the Archbishop to let the rectory for three years.[14] Perhaps therefore the Archdeaconry Manor was created in the first half of the 13th century when the parish church and its property were transferred to the Archdeaconry. This would include the twelve acres given by King Stephen as mentioned above, but there was probably other land. An extent in 1317 shows that this manor then had four bovates (about thirty-two acres) of arable land in demesne (i.e. in hand), with at least as much let to free tenants. There were also about sixteen acres at Raskelf with a tithe barn, and a piece of enclosed land at Cold Kirby. The King presented to the living of Easingwold as late as 1266, after which the Archdeacons presented.

The Manor House of the Archdeaconry Manor was at the foot of Church Hill, on the North side of the road leading into Uppleby. It was described as being in good condition in 1281, though by 1317 it seems to have fallen into disrepair. It may have been the manor house which had belonged to the King in 1201.

On 27th July, 1259 Henry III assigned the Crown Manor of Easingwold to his sister Countess Eleanor of Leicester and her husband Simon de Montfort, Earl of Leicester. This was part of a series of transactions arising out of Eleanor's first marriage to William Marshal, Earl of Pembroke. When the latter died in 1231 his brother Richard sold Eleanor's dower lands, mostly in Ireland, to pay the debts of the estate. She called on the King to intervene and in 1233 it was arranged that Richard should pay £400 a year, which the King was to convert into English land for her. This payment was not duly made and from 1249 it appears that the King was forced to find the money himself. In 1259 he assigned a number of his manors, including Easingwold, to Eleanor and Simon, to be held until the King had provided other land to the value of five hundred marks for them.[15] In 1265 Earl Simon exchanged the manor for other land granted by the King and on

16th May, 1265, the latter granted it during his pleasure to his second son Edmund, First Earl of Lancaster from 1267 to 1296.[16] Curiously enough, when Edward I challenged his brother's title to the manor in about 1280, Earl Edmund relied on a general charter of his father granting him the estates of Earl Simon forfeited after the latter's death at Evesham in 1265. No mention was made of the grant of 16th May, 1265.[17] However, Earl Edmund retained the manor and in 1271 granted it by way of security to Sir John de Oketon,[18] later redeeming it from the latter's son and heir for a payment of £300.[19]

In 1283 there is the first mention of a yeoman family long connected with Easingwold and the Forest of Galtres in a record of a debt owed by William Gryvel.[20] A taxation account of 1301 names Elizabeth Grivill[21] of Easingwold, while Hugh Grevell is named in 1327[22] and 1333.[23] In 1335 Hugh Gryvel of Easingwold and Margaret his wife took a conveyance of land at Myton and Easingwold from Richard de Becbank, chaplain.[24] In October of the same year Roger and William Gryvel of Easingwold were pardoned of various offences in the Forest of Galtres and any other of the King's forests, whether in the time of Edward II or Edward III.[25]

At about this time in fact can be seen the emergence of several families prominent at Easingwold in medieval times. The Paynots are first noticed in the person of John Paynot in 1301.[26] William Paynot, reeve of Easingwold in 1313 and 1314, seems to be named again in 1327[27] and 1333[28] and to have died in 1349. His wife Emma, who died in 1346, the year of Crecy, made a long and remarkable will printed in the first volume of the Surtees Society's "Testamenta Eboracensia". Apparently, though this seems hard to believe, she had thirty sons and at least two daughters. The Paynots, or Pannetts as they later spelt their name, did not die out at Easingwold until the beginning of the 18th century.

Other Easingwold families of long duration were the Pacockes, the Becbanks, the Goderykes, the Lovels and the Peitevins or Paytfines, all appearing at about the beginning of the 14th century. Of somewhat less duration were the Serjeaunts, the Prynces and the Kingsmans. Surnames were coming into general use at this time and many of them seem to show that the population of England, though doubtless less mobile than at present, was by no means stagnant. Thus William de Raskelf became a burgess of Berwick on Tweed and in 1317 was granted a safe conduct for a voyage to Gascony in the wineship la Trinité.[29] John de Hustwyt took holy orders and made a career for himself as a royal clerk. He was the treasurer of the Agénois district of Gascony from about 1308 to 1312. Robert de Hoby (Huby) was one of the men accused by John Chaundler, Citizen of London, in 1334 of assembling in boats to steal the cargo and tackle of his ship, Le Leonard, stranded near Fyvele (Filey) in the County of York.[30] William de Wyncestre (Winchester) was living at Yearsley in 1301[31] and John de Maincestre or Mainchester (Manchester) settled at Easingwold in the early part of the century. In 1291 John de Bockingham (Buckingham) was an inhabitant of Easingwold.[32] There is admittedly seldom any certain way of telling whether a man, who at this period was named as "of such-and-such a place" actually came from there. One may guess that in the 13th and early 14th century he very often did, but that later it was much more likely to be his father or grandfather who was the native.

On this basis perhaps Easingwold may claim the monk John de Esyngwald, who in 1281 had to be removed from Marton Abbey for indiscipline,[33] the William de Esyngwald, who was one of the bondmen of the prebendary of Ampleforth at Fulford in 1295 or thereabouts,[34] the Robert de Esingwald, who was a cottar (or cottage tenant) at Stillington at the same date,[35] the John de Esingwald, who was excommunicated for a trespass in the Archbishop's park at Beverley about the beginning of 1308[36] and the Walter de Esingwald, who was in holy orders in York in 1343. The fourteenth century in fact saw the establishment of one or more families named de Esyngwald or Esyngwald at York and later in the Ouse and Derwent Wapentake. Originally no doubt founded by natives of Easingwold, they later seem to have lost all connection with the place. Many of the York Esyngwalds made careers in the church, for example John de Esyngwald, Doctor of Theology, Prior of St Mary's Abbey, York in 1390;[37] Thomas and William de Esyngwald, who were both rectors of Everingham at about the same period;[38] Master Nicholas de Esyngwald, procurator of St. Mary's Abbey, York, from 1390 to 1398;[39] and John Esyngwald who was prior of Newburgh at the end of the 14th and the beginning of the 15th century. Most of the York Esyngwalds seem to have been well to do. No less than twenty were admitted as members of the fashionable religious guild of Corpus Christi at York in the 15th century.[40] Thomas de Esyngwald was sheriff of York in 1410 and Lord Mayor in 1422. He may in fact have been born at Easingwold, since his brother is said to have lived there.[41] Master Robert Esyngwald, a notary public, was an officer of the ecclesiastical court of York as well as Rector of Burneston in Richmondshire. He acted as an executor of the Will of Stephen Le Scrope or Scrope, Archdeacon of Richmond, who died in 1418. Master Robert himself died in 1446, surviving his wife Hawisia by twenty-six years, and was buried in York Minster. As he left a bequest to Thomas Smyth of Esyngewald it is possible that he had kept up a family connection with the place.[42] John Esyngwald was Rector of St. Mary, Castlegate, York in 1427;[43] a namesake was a moneyer at the York Mint in 1431;[44] while another namesake of the same period was a well to do mercer. Roger Esyngwald, bachelor of laws, appeared in a York heresy case in 1426,[45] while William Esyngwald was one of the vicars Choral of York Minster from at least as early as 1458 to his death in 1498.[46] A man named William Essyngwald, probably not the same man, was granted administration of the estate of Henry Percy Earl of Northumberland, killed at the Battle of St. Albans in 1455.[47]

Master Alan de Esyngwald, a cleric who acted from 1281 to 1291 as the official of Antony Bek, Bishop of Durham and was very much involved in the latter's struggle with the Archbishop of York, owned property in Easingwold and was probably born there. He seems to have died at some date between 1301 and 1313.

We also know for certain that Nicholas Browne or Brown, clerk, who practised as a notary public from at least 1361 to 1393, was an Easingwold man.[48]

Some of the early surnames of Easingwold are curious. They include the Faderles (Fatherless) family in the 1290s, the Folenfaunts or Folyfants in the early 1300's, the Chattes of the same period, a man named Coldcole and a family called "in le Wra", which means "in the corner".

Archbishop le Romeyn visited Easingwold on 18th September, 1286, and again on 27th April, 1291,[49] at which time the parish priest may have been called John. A vicarage was established in about 1293, the first vicar being Thomas de Walorilafe, whose name may perhaps really have been Warlollay or Varlollay, a name met with in the district in the first half of the 14th century, possibly of French origin. At the date of his institution he was a deacon. He held the living for some twenty-eight years.

In 1291 Edward I granted to his brother, Earl Edmund, the right to hold an annual fair at Easingwold on the eve and Festival of Our Lady.[50]

It is possible to some extent to reconstruct the life of Easing-wold at the beginning of the fourteenth century. At this time the manorial system in the district can be generally regarded as mature and well established. Although there was a good deal of variation from place to place, the system was essentially the same every-where. There were generally in Yorkshire three classes of villien tenant - the bondmen, the gresmen and the cottars in descending order of status. The bondmen held the most land and rendered the largest services: the gresmen (who appear to derive their name from the payment of a small sum on inheritance known as a "gressum" or "gersum") seem generally to have held a toft and croft for which they paid a small money rent and rendered smaller services than the bondmen; while the cottars held a toft or a "small toft" or "small domicile", for which they might give a cock and hen at Christmas and twenty eggs at Easter, or perhaps a very small money rent.

The services varied from manor to manor and tenant to tenant, but usually included mowing; making and stacking the lord's hay; weeding and hoeing the lord's corn; ploughing, sowing, harrowing, reaping and ricking; carting corn, provisions, fuel, building materials and turves; repairing the lord's buildings and fences; and finding additional men to do these things. The times and periods at and for which the lord was entitled to call for the services were usually well established by the custom of the manor and also the extent to which the lord had to provide food during the work. Some of the services were known as "boonworks" or "beneworks" (precaria) and seem to have originated in special work over and above the tenant's normal obligations, done for the lord at particularly busy periods such as seed time or harvest. Theoretically done "as a favour", they seem to have become as obligatory and fixed as the other services.

Less usual manorial services included sheepwashing and shearing; collecting and carting reeds for thatch; finding a mate for the mason and thatcher; carting materials for the repair of the lord's mills; making malt for the lord's mills; scouring the mill-stream; or carrying the lord's letters. Blacksmiths usually held on condition of mending the lord's implements. Thus Robert Smith of Ampleforth, a gresman, held a toft and croft by the service of making the lord's implements and plough-shares throughout the year, using the lord's iron.

The lord was entitled to various dues, monetary or in kind. They usually included "merchet", a payment due on the marriage of a daughter (perhaps in most manors if the daughter married a stranger); "leyrwite", a customary payment for a child born out of wedlock; and reliefs on succession to land on the death of a parent or husband. The normal rate of relief at Easingwold in 1313 and 1314 seems to have been three shillings and fourpence for each oxgang. Part of the deceased's estate was also sometimes paid to the lord by the successor. This was known as "heriot". Other dues might include payments for newly cleared land; on the sale of bullocks or colts bred by the tenant; a "gift" of two shillings or a pig of the same value at Christmas; or a "strak" (strike or bushel)[51] of nuts at Martinmas.

Money rents had become quite normal. The account of William Paynot, the reeve of Easingwold, from 30th September, 1313, to 30th September, 1314, shows rents totalling £4. 8s. 8d. payable from Easingwold and Huby on St. Andrews Day and at Midsummer and of £37. 5s. 1d. at Easter and Michaelmas. The latter figure includes a payment for exercising the office of weaver. The rates of rent vary considerably according to the character of the property. William de Engeland paid 13s. 4d. for a toft, while Robert Brown only gave 12d. for a toft and three and a half acres of land. William son of Robert, Thomas the Vicar and Thomas de Briddeford (Birdforth) between them paid 6d. for three places taken out of the waste, while at Huby Walter Tarcis paid what must have been a nominal rent of 1d. for a piece of land taken out of the waste to build a common oven. Shortly before 1322 two hundred and sixty acres of waste on North Moor were let at 8d. an acre.

The lord at Easingwold was entitled to receive the goods and chattels of felons and fugitives; fines for trespass; and payments in respect of stray bees. The King from time to time by custom levied a special due known as a "tallage", on his own lands. The assessment for Easingwold and Huby in 1313-4 was £10. 13s. 4d., or £5 for respiting the tallage (no doubt a discount for prompt payment).

The tenants at Easingwold would also be under obligations to have their corn ground at the lord's mill, unless this for some reason was not available to them, and to attend the lord's court.

The reeve of Easingwold accounted to the Bailiff and Receiver of Pickering and the manor was for almost three centuries considered part of the Honour of Pickering.[52]

The Archdeaconry Manor had six free tenants at Easingwold in 1317. Of these the Widow Beatrix, who held a croft and two oxgangs of arable land, paid a money rent of 4/- and gave a cock and three hens at Christmas and forty eggs at Easter. She was also obliged to find a man to mow the lord's meadow for one day and to make hay and carry and house it in the grange within the lord's court (i.e. in the farm buildings of the Archdeacon's Manor house), receiving one meal per day. Robert in le Wra held a toft and one oxgang at a rent of 2/-, while Robert Folyfant paid 12d. per annum for a toft and croft, and helped with the lord's hay, receiving one meal in the day.[53]

The general impression is of orderly machinery running smoothly. Trouble, however, was not far off. The King's Scottish War recoiled on him after the disaster of Bannockburn in 1314. Yorkshire had already been heavily drawn on for manpower before the battle, all able bodied men in the Wapentake of Bulmer between sixteen and sixty having been (in theory at any rate) arrayed for service.[54] There seems to have been a fresh muster at Easingwold on 11th December, 1314.

The district was also called upon for supplies from time to time, as in September, 1316, when Bulmer Wapentake was required to provide twenty quarters of wheat and one hundred of oats.[55]

Far worse than these, the normal burdens of a country at war, must have been the large scale raids carried out by the Scots in 1318, 1319 and 1322. In 1318 destruction included the firing of the towns of Boroughbridge, Knaresborough, Northallerton, Skipton and Scarborough. In 1319 the Scots raided up to the walls of York and soon afterwards destroyed the pursuing county forces at Myton-on-Swale on 12th October, 1319, with heavy loss of life, including the Lord Mayor of York and many clergy. In 1322 King Robert Bruce himself outflanked and routed an English force posted on "Blakehoumor" under the Earl of Richmond. The battlefield in fact is thought to have been at Sutton Bank and Roulston Scar. Douglas and Moray led their men up the steep track or path, while the highlanders and islesmen scaled the cliffs on the flank. Wherever the Scots won their battle, they almost succeeded in exploiting it by capturing the King who was lodging at Rievaulx Abbey. He escaped with difficulty to York and the Scots ravaged across the Wolds to Beverley, causing heavy damage to Moxby Nunnery, among other places, on the way. The Scots also seem to have visited Easingwold at the same time and in 1323 the King respited the previous, as well as the current, years rents on account of the destruction of lands and chattels there by the Scots "rebels" [56] The rental of the manor went down by

£20 16s. 4d., including a "decay of the toll of the mill" calculated as £2. 13s. 4d. and rents which could not be levied because the tenants could not be found amounting to £5. 13s. 8¹/₂d.[57]

The reason why the King, and not the Earl of Lancaster, respited the rents in 1323 was because the Manor had been for feited to the Crown in 1322, following Thomas Earl of Lancaster's rebellion, defeat at Boroughbridge and execution. It was in the King's hands until 23rd April, 1327, when Edward III restored it to Henry, Third Earl of Lancaster, the brother of Earl Thomas.[58] Earl Thomas's rebellion must have played its part in disrupting the life of the district.

Though the Bannockburn war terminated in favour of Scotland in 1328, it was not long before there was fresh fighting. The Halidon Hill campaign in 1333, a Scots expedition in 1336 and a threatened Scots invasion in 1345, among other events, kept Yorkshire's memories alive and Yorkshiremen employed. A muster roll of hobilars and archers guarding Perth in 1340 is full of Yorkshire names. One of the horse hobilars (paid 6d. a day) was John of Helperby, and Thomas Aalne (Alne), John Crayk (Crayke) and John Cukwald (Coxwold) were horse archers at 4d. a day. (A hobilar was a lightly armed spearman, mounted on a "hobby", a light horse. When he served dismounted the hobilar was paid 4d. a day, so that 2d. a day of his normal wages was for the keep of his horse. The hobilar may have had a certain amount of armour to keep, perhaps a helmet and a back and breast, whereas the horse archer, who received only 4d. a day for himself and horse, probably had nothing better than a steel cap and a leather jacket).[59]

At least one Easingwold man fought in the French wars. He was Thomas Russel and he may well have been at Crecy. The battle took place on 26th August, 1346, and on 14th September from his camp at Calais the King granted a general pardon to a number of his soldiers for their good service. Russel was one of these. What he had done to require a pardon is not known, but a later appearance in the records gives a clue. In 1359 he beat and wounded William Clyst of Easingwold for which he was eventually fined 40d. by the new Justices of the Peace, sitting at Birdforth in 1361. He was also, at about the same time, one of a large number of Easingwold men, who forcibly broke into an enclosure of Thomas Darell at Thornton Hill, pastured their beasts and cut wood there.[60]

The granting of pardons for service in the Kings wars was quite a common practice. In 1327 Thomas de Thormodby (Thormanby) was pardoned of the killing of a Skelton man, on condition of serving against the Scots.[61]

The will of Emma Paynot who died in 1346 gives a good many pieces of information about Easingwold at that time, albeit rather a miscellaneous collection. The parish church contained a crucifix and an image of the Virgin, and probably a light known as the light of St. Katherine. The Vicar was assisted by Sir Robert the parish Chaplain and the parish clerk was named John. Mrs. Paynot specified that twelve pounds of wax candles were to be burned round her body in the church and that at her funeral money should be given to the poor and to any friar of the mendicant orders who should attend. Bequests made include one of 3d. to each widow of Easingwold, the estimated number being forty-three widows. Her property included at least five beasts (which may mean cattle), at least twenty-nine sheep, a "kymelyn" or brewing tub, twenty-eight ells of linen, forty-eight handfuls of flax, two overtunics with hoods, five coats, three "courtebyes" or short coats, a mantle, six kerchiefs, a shift, a feather bed, two tapestries, a coverlet, a blanket, three sheets, two brooches, and a "remenant" of russet cloth sufficient for a coat. Some of the material of the clothing is strange to modern eyes. One overtunic is described as of "burnet", which seems to have been a brown woollen cloth, and the other as of green "melle", a name which may perhaps derive from the word "melé", meaning a mixed cloth of some kind. A kerchief is described as of better "serico", which may mean either silk or serge — the latter seems more likely — and a coat is furred with "grys", which is a grey fur. Two of her kerchiefs were of "crisp", a light crinkly material which was often used for kerchiefs, and a coat was of "vyolet". Altogether Mrs. Paynot's will shows that villein tenants and their families were not always among the poorest members of the community.[62]

Mrs. Paynot left 12d. for the maintenance of Raskelf Bridge on the Thirsk road. Raskelf Bridge was kept in repair by the inhabitants of Easingwold and in 1255 the King had allowed them two oaks from the Forest of Galtres for this purpose.[63]

In the spring of 1349 the terrible "Black Death", which seems to have been a type of bubonic plague, started to hit Yorkshire and was well into its stride by summer. On 23rd March, 1349, Pope Clement VI, writing to Archbishop Zouche, granted certain

Easingwold parish church before its restoration in 1858

Thirteenth century North door (The Raskelf door) of Easingwold parish
church

faculties and indulgences in response to a petition declaring that the pestilence had begun to afflict the city, diocese and province of York. One would think, therefore, with due allowance for the speed of medieval communications, that the disease had appeared at least as early as the very beginning of 1349.

Of 141 vacancies in West Riding livings in 1349, ninety-six were caused by death and in the East Riding sixty-five incumbents died. It has been calculated that at least half the Yorkshire clergy succumbed.[64] Among them may have been John de Huntyngton, the Vicar of Easingwold, named by Mrs. Paynot as "Sir John the Vicar". His successor John Deyvill was instituted on 20th March, 1349.[65] William Paynot, the reeve, also seems to have died in 1349, as no doubt did many other laymen.

An old Easingwold name is first met with in 1357 when instructions were recorded for the investigation of a complaint of forcible entry, robbery, deer stealing, malicious damage and assault at Kilburn against Thomas de la Ryvere, parson of Brandsby, his brother and a number of men from the district. Among the latter was John Reynald. The Reynalds are frequently named up to at least the end of the 17th century and may be the ancestors of the present Reynard family. John son of Robert Raynald, who may be the same man, was one of a large number of persons charged in 1361 with a forcible entry at Thornton Hill.[66]

One of the other Easingwold men named on this occasion was William Frost, who was outlawed in 1361 by the justices of the peace at Northallerton for a larceny.[67]

Easingwold men in the 1360's included William de Driffield, Robert and William Lyght, Robert, Thomas and William Haymryk, John and William Malleson, William Hamson, John Bosse, Robert Abbott, John Raufson and Geoffrey Barker. Occupational surnames include William Lockesmith, Peter Piper, John Plummer, John Walker and Walter Carpenter. John Vickerman made his living as a wheelwright at Easingwold in 1361.[68]

William de Driffield is probably an early member of the Driffields of Easingwold who by the 17th century had become the principal family of the town. Plummer is a very well known name at Thormanby. John Walker, first named in 1361, later killed William Pacock of Easingwold and stood his trial at the assizes, but was granted a pardon on 16th May, 1367, it having been found that he acted in self defence.[69]

By this stage of the Middle Ages it seems likely that the "frankpledge" system of law enforcement by mutual responsibility for each others acts was in decline. Life was no doubt normally peaceful for the ordinary person, but no very effective steps were taken to prevent crime or disorder. Any local dispute might easily lead to a riot, as when thirty-six Easingwold men, among others, forcibly pastured their cattle in Thomas Darell's close at Thornton Hill in 1361.[70] It is easy to infer that they thought they were acting in exercise of some right — possibly Darell had enclosed land previously subject to common of pasture, or something of that sort. More habitual criminals robbed on the highways or worse. In 1342 some of the King's men are said to have been killed or maimed by deerstealers in Galtres.[71] In about 1351 John le Wodeward of Raskelf, a forester, had his eyes put out and his tongue and fingers cut off by malefactors when on duty in the forest. The unfortunate man was still alive in 1378.[72]

Then there are what may be termed feuds. In 1362 for example a Husthwaite man wounded a Raskelf man on the road between Rawcliffe and Clifton. The following day eleven friends of the wounded man forced their way into the Husthwaite man's house in the night and beat him.[73]

Robert del Wood, forester of Crayke, was charged in 1361 with two woundings, a rape, forcible entry of Newburgh Priory, intimidation of its tenants and holding up the Abbot of Byland on the King's highway. He did not appear and was outlawed.[74]

In 1391 Hugh Gardyner of Esyngwald was charged with a robbery at Balk, with harbouring a murderer from the West Riding, and with being one of a number of men who had lain in wait at Thornton Hill to murder Sir Thomas Colvill.[75] In 1398 John Gyrsyngton, "dwelling with the Vicar of Esyngwald", was alleged to have stolen a ram in a wood by Raskelf and in the following year to have stolen a horse.[76] It is true that both the two men last named were pardoned, but a pardon does not usually imply innocence.

When a sum of £4,000 in coin was transported from York to Scotland in 1304 it was felt necessary to provide an escort of six carriage guards and twelve archers for the cart and its five carters and the two officials in charge.[77] This indicates that traditions of robbers in the Forest of Galtres may not be without foundation. The record also underlines the poor state of the roads through the Forest, since it took all day for the party to reach Easingwold. Adam de Quenby (Whenby), hermit of the Chapel of St. Helen

34

at Shupton (Shipton) is known to have tried to improve a road through the forest at a place called "Les Polles", and as Shipton is on the main road from Easingwold to York, in all probability that was the road concerned. Prior to the mid-17th century the Fleet beck on West Moor was traversed by a ford at the place where Blue Bridge now stands and this may have been the site of "Les Polles", or it may have been another marshy place on Shipton Moor or West Moor. Significantly enough the latter seems to have been called "the West Moss" in medieval times. At all events the place which Brother Adam tried to improve was described as very dangerous and the cause of many accidents for lack of a firm foundation. On 20th August, 1327, the King granted him a protection and safe conduct while travelling through the Kingdom to obtain carriage and alms for the repair of the road.[78] The protection was renewed on 15th September, 1330,[79] and 16th October, 1332.[80] On 12th August 1333, a similar protection was granted for the same purpose to Robert de Skitheby, hermit of the Chapel of St. Augustine, Huntington by York.[81] Whether the efforts of the hermits really improved the road is a matter which is open to doubt. If it was in fact the York-Easingwold road there seems to have been no great acceleration of traffic. Somewhat later in the century a much smaller amount of £200 on a pack horse, under the guard of two men-at-arms and four archers, took three days to go from York to Durham.[82]

Earl Henry of Lancaster, who had become lord of the manor of Easingwold and Huby in 1327, died in 1345. The lordship descended to his son Henry, created Duke of Lancaster in 1351. On Duke Henry's death in 1361 a moiety (and in 1362 the remaining moiety) of his estates descended to his daughter Blanche, who at the age of twelve married John of Gaunt, fourth son of Edward III. John of Gaunt was created Duke of Lancaster in 1362. On 13th February, 1397, he granted the manor to his daughter Joan de Ferrers and her husband Ralph Nevill, Earl of Westmoreland, for their joint lives.[83] Ralph Neville died in 1425 and Joan in 1440. On the accession of Henry IV, the son of John of Gaunt and Blanche of Lancaster, in 1399 the Duchy had merged in the Crown, so that when Joan died in 1440 the manor came back into the King's hands in the person of Henry VI. The latter did not take immediate possession, but on 30th January, 1440, granted it to Richard, Earl of Salisbury, the son of Ralph Nevill and Joan for twenty years in satisfaction of a debt of £666. 13s. 4d. A lease of the manor was made to Earl Richard on 13th February. 1452. The Earl, appointed Chief Steward in the North Parts of the Duchy of Lancaster on 15th February, 1456, for the term of his life, and re-appointed with his son Richard in 1460, was executed in Pontefract Castle on 30th December, 1460. This followed his participation in the Battle of Wakefield and subsequent capture.[84]

Two successive Archdeacons of Richmond, Thomas Dalby, Archdeacon from 1388 to 1400, and Stephen Le Scrope, Arch deacon from 1400 to 1418 (except for a two day break in 1401 when Nicolas Bubbewith held the office), were responsible for the complete rebuilding of the parish church. Only the old North door, known as "the Raskelf door" and, apparently, the old West window survived from the previous structure. The old West window is that at the west end of the nave, not the one in the West Wall of the tower. Basically the church as rebuilt by the two Archdeacons is the present parish church. The side windows with their straight heads and four arched lights are later insertions, probably from the late 15th century, and the tower is attributed to the early 1500's. Originally a large open arch was left in the West Wall of the tower, perhaps with the intention, never carried out, of inserting there the old West window and door. The arch was filled in, and a window inserted, in the 17th Century.[85]

The chancel roof was raised in 1858 to accommodate a larger East window and at the same time the interior furniture was lagely Victorianised. The North door has long since been built up. The vestry is probably old apart from its east window, which looks Victorian, and the extension for the present organ, which is 20th Century.

Archdeacon Dalby's arms, (gules) a chevron ermine and three round buckles (or) were carved on the stone sill of a window in the North aisle, where they were noted by Gill, the historian of Easingwold, in 1852.[86] An inventory of Dalby's estate made in 1400 lists a fee owing to John de Stanton for riding to the churches of Easingwold, Thornton, Bolton and Clapham with a carpenter and a stone-cutter to supervise repairs. It is possible that de Stanton was a master builder and had the work of rebuilding Easingwold church in hand.

Gill thought, probably correctly, that there was a chantry on the North side of the parish church. There was certainly a chantry guild in 1452 known as "the Fraternity of St. Mary in the High Church of Easingwold", Thomas Rawson, who died in that year being its Chaplain. He may have been a local man, a connection of the John Raufson, who was living at Easingwold in 1361. The chantry was dissolved in Edward Vi's reign, about 1547.

It also seems probable that the light of St. Katherine, to which Mrs. Paynot made a bequest in 1346, was in the parish church of Easingwold and that it was transferred to the new building.

A churchyard cross on a stone base stood near the South door of the church at least as early as 1446 and as late as 1549.[87]

Two men named Norton held the living in the later 14th and early 15th century. William de Norton, then a deacon, was instituted on 30th April, 1379, and was vicar for about forty-six years. John Norton succeeded him on 4th July, 1425. Torr, the York antiquary, thought that he held the living until his death in 1437. Another authority makes him resign in 1429 on his institution to the living of Wath.[88] There is very likely some confusion between members of the numerous family of Norton, hailing from the Richmondshire district, to which indeed the two vicars of Easingwold may well have belonged.

Far less is recorded of the people of Easingwold and their affairs in the fifteenth century than in the fourteenth. Whether the Scrope rebellion of 1405, with its culmination on Shipton Moor, where the crown forces faced the rebels for three days without a battle, or the battles of the Wars of the Roses from 1455 to 1485, much affected the life of Easingwold is not known. The town must have been assured of plenty of outside contacts, lying as it did on a main route from the North and not far from York and the important seats of the Nevilles at Sheriff Hutton and of the Percies at Topdiffe, as well as the Bishop of Durham's castle at Crayke. Its church was regarded as one of the principal churches in the deanery of Bulmer, a place for the holding of church meetings and courts and even for the hearing of civil cases and perhaps also for the sessions of the Justices of the Peace when they were held in the town.

There were a number of absentee landowners, including Richard Cause, Esquire, of Beverley who on 12th January, 1461, let to Sir Richard Aldburghe all his land at Easingwold and Huby;[89] and Sir Peter Ardern, Chief baron of the Exchequer who owned property in the same places and in the Forest of Galtres at his death in June, 1467.

A native of Easingwold, who like Dick Whittington, went to London and made his fortune was William Bayneton, citizen and brewer, who died in 1499, and left £10 to the parish church of his birthplace.[91]

The name of Cowper, long born by a family of Easingwold yeomen, is first found in 1451.[92]

In due course the Manor of Easingwold and Huby came into the hands of the first of the Tudor sovereigns, Henry VII. A letter from him dated 26th July, 1485, to the Receiver of the Honour of Pickering refers to the fact that various grants and leases made at Easingwold by his predecessors in the Duchy of Lancaster had recently been voided by Act of Parliament. The Receiver was instructed to levy and account strictly for all revenues of the Manor, which seems to mean that it was in the King's own hands and not let.[93]

1   A. H. Smith : Place Names of the North Riding of Yorkshire, 1928.
2   V.C. History of the North Riding, vol. II.
3   Pipe Roll Soc. vols. for the reign of John.
4   Surtees Soc. Vol. XIV.
5   Justice in Eyre Roll for 1218-9 ed. by D. M. Stenton, Selden Soc. 1937.
6   Pipe Roll Soc. New Series Vol. 14 p. 159.
7   Mentioned in Fletcher's "Picturesque History of Yorkshire" Vol. 1 p. 223 without giving the authority.
8   VCH NR Vol. II.
9   Cal Pat Rolls Henry III (1216-25) p. 221.
10   YAS Rec Ser vol. XII; Cal Close Rolls (1242-7) p. 522; ibid (1247-51) pp. 31 and 1267; ibid pp. 241-2.
11   Prof. H. L. Cannon "The Great Roll of the Pipe for 1241-2" Yale 1918.
12   YAS Rec Ser vol. XII p. 39.
13   Cal Close Rolls (1242-7) p. 529.
14   Surtees Soc Vol 109 p.2. This does not refer to a rectory house, but to the Archdeacons interest as rector.
15   Belmont : Simon de Montfort Oxford, 1930; Cal Pat Rolls Henry III (1258-66) p. 35.
16   Cal Pat Rolls Henry III (1258-66) p. 424.
17   Placita de quo warranto temp. Edw. I. II. and III 1818 p. 194.
18   Cal Charter Rolls Vol. II p. 162.
19   N.R. Rec. Ser N.S. Vol. II p. 48.
20   Cal. Close Rolls Edw. I (1279-88) p. 233.
21   YAS Rec Ser Vol. XXI p. 73.
22   ibid Vol. LXXIV p. 142.
23   N.R. Rec Ser Vol. IV N.S. p. 161.
24   YAS Rec Ser Vol XLII.
25   Cal Pat Rolls Edw III (1334-8).
26   YAS Rec Ser Vol XXI p. 73.
27   YAS Rec Ser Vol. LXXIV p. 142.
28   N.R. Rec. Ser. Vol. IV NS p. 161.
29   Cal Pat Rolls (1313-17) p. 630
30   Cal Pat Rolls (1330-4) pp. 516-7.
32   YAS Rec Ser Vol. XXIII p. 118.
33   Surtees Soc. Vol. 114.
34   YAS Rec. Ser Vol. XCIV p. 25.
35   ibid pp. 29-30.
36   Surtees Soc. Vol. 145 p. 197.
37   Emden; Biographical Register of the University of Oxford to 1500, p. 652.
38   Surtees Soc. Vol. IV No. CXXXIV; Emden op cit p. 625.
39   Gill : Vallis Eboracensis 1852.
40   Surtees Soc Vol. 57.
41   VCH City of York.
42   YAS Rec Ser Vol. VI.
43   ibid.
44   Surtees Soc Test Ebor Pt II No. XII.
45   Surtees Soc. Vol. 113 p. 147.
46   Purvis A Mediaeval Act Book; YAS Rec Ser Vol. XXXVIII.
47   Surtees Soc. Test Ebor pt. III p. 211.
48   Gill op. cit and Purvis : Notarial Signs from the York Archiepiscopal Records. 1957.

49   Surtees Soc. Vol. 128.
50   Gill op cit.
51   In some parts of the North of England the strike seems to have equalled two bushels,
52   N.R. Rec. Ser. N.S. Vol II & YAS Rec Ser Vol. XCIV for the above account ol manorial services.
53   Gill, op cit.
54   ibid
55   Cal Pat Rolls Edw II (1313-7) pp. 543-4.
56   Cal Close Rolls Edw II (1323-7) p. 43.
57   N.R. Rec. Ser. Vol. IV p. 239.
58   Cal. Close Rolls Edw. III (1327-30) p. 78.
59   YAJ Vol. XIV pp. 240-1.
60   YAS Rec Ser Vol. C.
61   Cal Pat Rolls (1327-30) p. 122.
62   Surtees Soc. Vol. IV p. 21.
63   Cal Close Rolls (1255) p. 140.
64   Gasquet : the Black Death, 1908. p. 176.
65   Torre's Mss.
66   YAS Rec Ser Vol. C.
67   ibid
68   ibid
69   Cal Pat Rolls Edw III (1364-7) p. 397.
70   YAS Rec Ser Vol C.
71   Cal Pat Rolls (1340-3) p. 593.
72   Cal Close Rolls, Ric II, Vol. 1, p. 167.
73   YAS Rec Ser Vol. C.
74   ibid
75   Cal Pat Rolls Ric II (1388-92) p 513.
76   Cal Pat Rolls Henry IV, Vol. Ill, p. 367.
77   Ingledew: History of Northallerton.
78   Cal Pat Rolls Edw III (1327-30) p. 146.
79   Cal Pat Rolls Edw III (1330-4) p. 1.
80   ibid p. 359.
81   ibid p. 464.
82   Ingledew, op. cit.
83   Cal Pat Rolls Ric II, Vol. VI, p. 548.
84   Somerville : History of the Duchy of Lancaster, 1953, Vol. 1, p. 421.
85   VCH NR Vol. II.
86   Gill op cit.
87   ibid
88   McCall: Richmondshire Churches, 1910, p. 152.
89   YAS Rec. Ser. Vol LXV p. 81.
90   Surtees Soc. Vol. 53.
91   Surtees Soc. Vol. 116 p. 265.
92   Surtees Soc. Vol. 53.
93   N.R. Rec. Ser. N.S. Vol. 1, p. 120.

II

TUDOR AND STUART EASINGWOLD

Great changes took place in the North in the reign of Henry VIII (1509-1547). The monasteries and religious houses were dissolved, the smaller ones in 1536 and the remainder in 1539. Although this did not directly affect Easingwold, it was well surrounded by religious houses — Rievaulx and Byland Abbeys, Newburgh Priory, the small houses of Marton Abbey and Moxby Nunnery, and of course the numerous religious houses of York, including the great abbey of St. Mary's. Some of these establishments held land in or near to the manor. St. Leonards Hospital at York occupied lands known as Lestemere and Hoppethwayt near to Easingwold in the Forest of Galtres at a rent of one mark per annum, under a grant originally made by Henry III, the income maintaining a priest at St. Edmund's altar in their church at York. These two places are probably the modern Lessimers and Hopwith Carr on the south side of the town. St. Leonards also held land at Kelsthwaite (Kelsit) and Greenthwaite further south in the Forest.[1] Newburgh Priory also held lands in the Forest.

There were thus several simultaneous upheavals going on in the district — social, economic and in the sphere of land ownership — and on top of this the breach with Rome overturned the long settled religious habits of the people. More conservative, more feudal, more removed from the mainstream than the South, and economically comparatively undeveloped, the North smouldered and burst into flame in the widespread rebellion of 1536 known as the "Pilgrimage of Grace". After its suppression the King's Council of the North. which had existed in one form or another since the time of Richard III, was given a new commission and reconstituted as the instrument of royal power, operating from the former house of the Abbot of St. Mary's at York, now known as the King's Manor.

There was no major outbreak in the North during the religious comings and goings ending in the middle-of-the-road Elizabethan Settlement embodied in the Act of Supremacy of 1559 and the Thirty-Nine Articles of 1563, but in many places there was either more or less secret performance of the old religion or a strong wish to return to it.

At Easingwold the old guild of St. Mary was wound up about 1547, the guild masters selling a chalice belonging to the guild for 53s. 4d. and transferring the guild's cash in hand of 20s. to the Earl of Westmorland. During at any rate the later part of the guild's history the annual salary of the guild priest was raised by holding a "metinge of the neighbours yearly after the facion of a someringe" — no doubt what would now be called a church fete.

The reformers in the reign of Edward VI caused considerable changes to be made in the parish church and its furniture. At that time it was a building with a leaded roof, glazed windows and some bells. Queen Mary's return to the old religion led to the setting up of the altar and a rood with the crucifix flanked by figures of Mary and John and the bringing back into use of the Easter Sepulchre, and it is not difficult to infer that these were furnishings removed in the previous reigns or replaced such furnishings. A quantity of iron candle prickets were taken out also and sold to John Walker for 16d. The Lenten cloth of linen, which measured approximately 5 by 2^1/2 yards, six tunicles and two vestments were also sold. The proceeds of these articles and of the sale of the guild chalice were used partly to pay for a bible, a communion book and a book of paraphrases and for having the interior of the church lime washed and painted with scriptural texts. The rest of the money was paid for putting the bells in order and mending the window glass and leads.

In the first three years of Queen Mary's reign the Church-wardens paid for a "Royd with Mary and John xvis. viiid", as mentioned above, the work being carried out by Alayn Gaytt, had the altar set up again by a Mr. Walshe and the sepulchre mended by Robert Sharpp. They purchased "a lytle Messe (mass) booke prynted" for 2s. 6d., "a holy watter cane" for 5d. and two surplices and a vestment, among other things. They provided "a covering to the Sacrament of the aulter", which cost 20d. and was perhaps a carved wooden cover, and again had the glass and leads mended and the bells seen to. In 1557 they paid 8s. 6d. for a paten to the chalice, 13s. 4d. for "a table to the hy aulter", perhaps meaning a communion table, and 12s. 0d. for "the Image of the head hallow". The last must be the statue of a saint. One dedication of the church is to St. John and he may be the saint concerned. Alternatively the church is also dedicated to All

Saints or All Hallows and there may have been a group of which the "head hallow" was the principal figure. The former seems more likely.

Future items of expenditure in 1557 were expected to include the purchase of vestments to the value of £8, two altar cloths, a pair of censers and six books. The parish was faced with these special expenses at a time when a new frame was needed for the bells, the roof timber and the walls required repairs and of course there was the perennial mending of the "glasse wyndoes" and the "leaddes of the body of the churche even nowe in decaye".

No doubt all this was done and most of it undone again in Queen Elizabeth's reign. The rood would be removed, with the sepulchre, and the vestments, censers, books and "holy watter cane" would disappear. There would be new service books to provide and very likely the walls were re-"wesshed" and adorned 'with "scriptures". All this is probably funnier to look at from a distance of four hundred years than to experience at first hand.[2]

The new service books were a target for the rebels in the outbreak known as the rebellion of the Northern Earls in 1569. Many people from the North Riding joined the rebels. There is no record of anyone from Easingwold doing so, but no less than nineteen did from Thirkleby, two of whom were eventually selected for hanging. Six came from Kilburn, two from Crayke and one from Raskelf. Perhaps one or two came from most of the villages on or near the southward march of the rebel army.[3] York was hurriedly garrisoned by the county levies, three hundred men from Bulmer Wapentake being quartered in Bootham.[4] The rebellion was put down with comparative ease by the Crown forces, one detachment of which camped on Thormanby Carr, while on its way to the rebel Earl of Northumberland's house at Topcliffe.[5] In 1570 the churchwardens of Easingwold, the losers whoever won, had to buy new service books to replace those destroyed by the rebels.[6]

Their attempt to make the chapelry of Raskelf contribute to the expenses of the mother church of Easingwold was strenuously re-sisted and the matter had to be settled by the arbitration of the Archbishop's Vicars General, John Rookebye and John Dakin, in 1557. The award gave the inhabitants of Easingwold a contribu-tion of 5s. 8d. in the pound from Raskelf towards charges agreed between the churchwardens of Easingwold and four inhabitants of Raskelf, after due notice given in the Chapel of Raskelf. Easing-wold had asked for 10/- in the pound, though perhaps this was a matter of tactics rather than conviction.

The second half of the sixteenth century is in fact marked by a series of disputes and lawsuits between Easingwold and Raskelf. They seem to have been concerned mainly with the respective rights of the townships over the Lund. In 1589 and 1590 proceedings were brought in the Court of the Duchy of Lancaster by William Driffield and other inhabitants of Easingwold and Huby, against various tenants of the Manor of Raskelf for intrusion into the pasture and turbary on Raskelf Lund, but it seems unlikely that the matter was then settled. A survey of the manor of Easingwold and Huby made by John Norden in 1617 for the Prince of Wales states that: ". . . the tenants of Raskall doe intrute upon this manor by unlawfullie depasturinge their Cattle, in takinge turf e wood and Brakes in a place called the launde, containing by estimation about three hundred acr. properlie belonginge to this Manor wherin they doe his highnes and his tenants great wronge" .[7] Exactly how and when the dispute ended I do not know, but the inhabitants of Raskelf in the 18th century certainly enjoyed common of pasture in the shape of cattle gates called "Lungates" or "Lundgates", though this may have been over the two hundred acres allotted to them by the Commissioners for the disafforestation of Galtres in 1630.

Thomas Penkithman or Pyngithman, vicar of Easingwold from 1506 to 1533, is recorded as having a stipend of £8 per annum in 1527.[8] His chaplain William Gooderike, no doubt a member of the old yeoman family settled at Easingwold since at least the early 14th century, had £4 per annum.[9] Another local priest was Richard Woodward of a well known Raskelf family, buried at Easingwold in 1511.[10] He too may have been a parish chaplain, or possibly the guild priest at Easingwold. Mr. Penkith man was buried in the "Quere" of his church of "All Hallows". His successor John Plomber, vicar from 1533 to 1549, was buried in the churchyard before the cross.[11]

A dispute arising out of conflicting leases of the rectory led to an incident on 6th April, 1534, when John Barton of Whenby and eighteen other persons forcibly entered the parsonage house at Easingwold armed with swords, bucklers and other weapons and ejected Richard Collynson, who was in occupation under a three year lease of 6th May, 1533, assaulting his servants in the process. Barton claimed that he held under a prior lease for nine years made on 20th August, 1531, to himself and two others. The parsonage house referred to is no doubt the Archdeacon's Manor house at Easingwold. The case came before the Star Chamber on

Collynson's petition but the record of the result seems to be missing.[12] Collynson died in 1539.[13] Among his assailants in 1534 were three Easingwold yeomen, Thomas Brandesby, who was born about 1474 and died in 1549, Thomas Gybson, born about 1470, and William Gybson. A William Gibson died in 1545. Other Easingwold yeomen families of the Tudor period included the Paynots, Goodricks, Raynalds and Frosts, who had been established for two hundred years and more, the very numerous clans of the Couplands or Cooplands (the spelling is variable), the Cundalls or Cundills, the Driffields and the Cowpers, and the almost as numerous Wilsons and Linsleys. The Leathleys and the Leadleys were probably the same family, though this is not absolutely clear. Other families met with at this time are the Weares, Chapmans, Prestons, Ibotsons, Tewes and Dobsons. The family of Burnett of Boscar Grange, strictly in Raskelf, were closely connected with Easingwold. Richard Collynson already mentioned, Richard Chayse, who died in 1534, and William Lakyn mentioned in 1533, are all described as gentlemen. Also gentry, or near gentry, were the Staveleys, who in the person of Henry Staveley (d. 1593) moved to Easingwold from Thormanby towards the end of the century.[14]

In 1541 Henry VIII founded the see of Chester and transferred to it the property, rights and jurisdiction of the Archdeaconry of Richmond. The first vicar to be presented to Easingwold by a Bishop of Chester was Ralph Stringer, instituted on 10th March, 1571. Mr. Stringer made an important charitable gift to the parish in 1599, when he gave a house at the North end of Long Street, known as Fossbridge House, as an almshouse for two poor people.

The men and tenants of the manor of Easingwold and Huby and of its soke lands described in Domesday Book, were entitled, as has been mentioned above, by custom to general exemption from tolls and the dues known as stallage, cheminage, pontage, pavage, picage, murage and passage. Whether persons claimed this exemption who were not entitled to it, or on the other hand officials became more exacting, is not clear, but from 1550 to 1558 and possibly during a longer period the right of Easingwold people to exemption was challenged from time to time. Thus when John Cowper of Easingwold went to Leeds the King's Bailiff of the Honour of Pontefract and Manor of Leeds claimed from him tolls and customs on wool, despite Cowper's plea of exemption.[15] On 24th June, 1558, Queen Mary confirmed to the men of Easingwold their ancient right.[16]

What part the people of Easingwold played in the great events of the Tudor period, the dissolution of the monasteries the Pilgrimage of Grace, the wars with Scotland, the rebellion of the Earls of Northumberland and Westmorland in 1569, can only be conjectured. There is no doubt, however, that they would see the Armada signalled in 1588 from the Sunciffe Beacon at Husthwaite. Suncliffe was part of the nationwide system of warning beacons manned throughout the 16th and 17th centuries in times of emergency and revived during the Napoleonic Wars. It comm-unicated with Ampleforth Beacon to the North and Whitwell to the South. Some of the men may have been mustered as part of the North Riding array. In 1585 Bulmer Wapentake was expected to provide 40 "corslets" (pikemen), 200 "calivers" (musketeers) and 40 archers.[17]

In 1616 James I granted the Manor of Easingwold and Huby to his son Charles, Prince of Wales. The Prince had a detailed survey made on 30th August, 1617, by John Norden (1548-c. 1625), his deputy surveyor, one of the most experienced surveyors in the country, having been appointed Surveyor of Crown Woods and Forests in 1600 and Surveyor to the Duchy of Cornwall in 1605. His survey gives many details of the manor and its adminis-tration at that time. The steward and Bailiff of the manor was Sir Richard Etherington, who had been steward of the Honour of Pickering since 1599 and was also Deputy Justice of the Forest of Galtres. This manorial court or "court leet, view of frankpledge and court baron" to give it its full title, was held twice a year. The tenants were obliged to attend both this court and the swanimote court of the Forest of Galtres. The Prince was entitled to waifs, estrays, felons fugitives, outlaws and deodantes goods, escheats and all other royalties within the town, its fields and acre garths, but all such matters within the demesne moors and wastes open to the forest belonged to the King in respect of the prerogative of the forest. (This briefly meant that ownerless property or animals, together with the goods of fugitive offenders and outlaws and property which had caused a death, for example a horse from which a man had been thrown, and property the owner of which had died intestate or had done something rendering his estate liable to forfeiture, fell to the King as lord of the manor, unless in the forest in which case the King took them as sovereign.).

Customary land (copyhold) in the manor might be let for up to three years without causing a surrender to the lord. On the death of a customary tenant his wife had dower of a third of his customary estate for life, even if she was subsequently remarried or "was incontinent". A man who married "a maid that is an inheritrix or hath an estate of inheritance within the said manor" might enjoy the land concerned during his life. It appears from another source of 1621 that a copyholder at Easingwold might dwell away from his copyhold without having to obtain the permission of the lord of the manor. The tenants were liable to pay a customary fine on death, exchange or alienation. They claimed that such fines were certain, but Norden reported that in his opinion this was not so and that the Prince could make the amount of the fine whatever he liked.

At this time William Simpson had an improving lease of 600 statute acres of land at the Howe on the North side of the town, abutting onto Crayke Park on the east, Thornton Park and Husthwaite Common on the north and the fields, wastes and commons of Easingwold on the West and South. at a rent of £6 per annum. This had been granted at Easter, 1614 or 1615. This lease became the subject of a violent local dispute because it involved the enclosure of land subject to common rights. Simpson, the original lessee, seems to have felt that it was costing him too much to develop the land. Sir Richard Etherington then apparently helped him by taking an assignment and subletting to Thomas Driffield, his brother Gregory, his son William and a number of other Easingwold people. When they started to enclose William Gooderike, together with the Vicar (Ralph Stringer), Thomas Copland, Robert Wilson and Robert Leadley, led a movement to have the land thrown open to the rest of the forest again. They raised £400 for expenses, of which Gooderike himself spent £200, so that there is no doubt that matter was taken seriously. They seem to have started by petitioning the Marquis (later the Duke) of Buckingham in his capacity as Justice of the Forests, to have the enclosure removed. Sir Edward Stanhope and others investigated on Buckingham's behalf and on 16th September, 1617, ordered that the enclosure should remain, subject to the deer in the forest being allowed to use it as winter pasture only. It took Buckingham until 22nd January, 1619, to confirm this order, and the King until 10th December, 1619. to confirm Buckingham's order. In the meantime Etherington had brought an action against the tenants of Easingwold, probably for trespass. The King's order required Etherington to discontinue his proceedings unless the tenants disturbed him further. At the same time the King granted another enclosing lease of 205 acres at the Howe to other Easingwold tenants, with a similar reservation for the deer in winter, at a rent of 40/- per annum.

At about this time the dispute came to involve an adjoining area of land at the Howe of 640 acres in extent let to Robert Theakston for 40 years at £6 per annum, "being a hill well wooded overtoppinge and viewinge the sd. forest". The forest officers claimed that this land should have remained open for His Majesty's deer and the preservation of his woods, but that Theakston and his undertenants had converted it to their own use "and committed greate spoyle on yr Mats woods by cutting and lopping great numbers of trees for stoopes" (posts), "rayles, gates and hedginge as appears on view of the verderers by wh. means yr. Mats deere are banished their usuall haunt and feeding and a thousand families of yr. Mats tents, abridged of their wonted comon".

The lessees also put their case to the King by petition. Thomas Driffield, speaking for himself and twenty other lessees asserted that six or seven thousand acres of waste were still left for the inhabitants and that the enclosures at the Howe had actually been beneficial to the deer. "There are more deere", he said, "there at this pnt. (present) tym than hath been seene there within the memorie of man". (This indeed, may well have been so. Enclosed grazing land, especially if reasonably well sheltered and free from disturbance by commoners and their stock, could well have attracted the deer during the winter).

The King referred the matter of the 600 acre lease to what in modern terms might be called a commission of inquiry. This consisted of Chief Justice Hobart of the Court of Common Pleas and Lionel Cranfield, Earl of Middlesex, who held a number of important government offices and rose to be Lord High Treasurer. They fixed a hearing for 9th October, 1622, and requested the attendance of the steward of the Forest and representatives of the commoners from Easingwold and Huby.

It is not clear from the surviving records whether the petitions submitted in respect of the leases of the 640 and 205 acres were dealt with separately or whether the whole matter was consolidated. Some of it, if not the whole, was referred to the Privy Council who sent it to the "Lod: Prest. of the North, Sir Henry Bellasis and five other worthy knights of ye contrey", or some four

A typical page from the Easingwold Court Leet Book (16th October, 1677)

17th century house in Spring Street traditionally built by John Donald, who fought at Marston Moor. The door beam was inscribed "God With Us". Demolished 1907

H. F. Smith, Esq.

of them to investigate and report. The knights seem to have done this but "the Lords" (of the Privy Council) "what wth the pliamt (parliament) "and other weighty affaires" were unable to find the time to hear and determine the case. The representatives of the foresters and commoners, waiting in London to appear before the Council, requested a speedy hearing, complaining that they lay there at great charge, "And for theire Adversaries by sinister meanes and practises endeavor to crosse theire proceedings", (probably an allegation of bribery). The King then asked "Mr. Attorney" for his advice, but the Attorney General, "having many other businesses that he could not dispatch this soe spedily", seems to have been unable to help personally. He probably advised a reference to the Council of the North. which finally decided that all the enclosures should again be thrown open to the forest. A draft in the Temple Newsam Papers suggests that Lord Dunbar, then Deputy Justice of the Forest, should use his influence to obtain contributions from the inhabitants of Easingwold and Huby "in the late expense: Lade out by them about the saving of the how almost taken from them wch if it had bin taken from them they would have bin pinched and straightened in their comon as well as Ea: and Hubye". A statement by William Gooderike implies that the decision came from the Council of the North and describes how "the Right ho. the Lord President and the other Councs." had come to Easingwold, when some of the people had "for joye and gladness of such good newes" prayed for the King and the Council. Sir Richard Etherington and his "favorets" the Driffields were not among these. The latter in fact sarcastically advised the people to cry "hurrah" and it would serve their turn.

This was probably a remark of William Driffield, "a most earnest agent in those inclosures". He refused to accept the decision and brought an action against James Elmer, described in one place as "an honest poore man" and in another as "a verie poore man and sore charged with many children", who had assisted in removing the fences and gates of the enclosures. Elmer who had been Deputy Bailiff of the forest in 1608, died in 1631.

Thomas Driffield also brought actions for trespass against other inhabitants of Easingwold, though not apparently directly connected with the enclosures at Howe, and in the end the King ordered him to be brought to York and given "condigne" punishment, which no doubt in practice meant a stiff lecture from the Council of the North.

There is other evidence which suggests that this branch of the Driffields were not too popular in the town. Though their pushing ways secured them a position in the ranks of the gentry at the Restoration, it seems likely that they trod on a number of toes in the process.

At some stage in the Howe dispute William Gooderike and others also maintained an action at law regarding the 600 acre lease, which came to trial.[18] This was probably fairly early in the proceedings. Gooderike does not seem to have been afraid of controversy since Norden's survey of 1617 states that he "spent much monie of his owne and other mens in a sute to prove Esingwalde and Hubie to be noe member of the Honor of Pickeringe". At that time, to Norden's indignation, he was detaining in his possession many of the records of the manor.

Among tenants of the manor in 1617 was Thomas Leadley who held by copy of court rolls of 3rd May, 1615, property including a mill called Calverleys.

It has already been noted that an oxgang at Easingwold was eight acres, whereas it was twelve at Huby. There was another measure in use in the manor, that of a "farthing land", which was equal to ten perches. One, three and four farthing lands are mentioned in Norden's survey and no doubt there were also two farthing lands.

Nordens survey does not mention a 99 year lease of the manor granted in 1617 to Sir Francis Bacon and others and this was presumably made afterwards.

The Prince of Wales came to the throne as Charles I in 1625. In 1628 he tried to sell the manor to Edward Ditchfield and others, trustees for the City of London, but this grant had to be repudiated in 1629, the King having already agreed to sell his land in the Forest of Galtres, amounting to 14,178 acres, to Sir Allen Apsley for £20,000. Sir Allen presumably pointed out that the manor was part of the King's land in the forest. At any rate the sale to the City of London trustees was declared void, as also was a conveyance made by them in the meantime to George Clay of London and William Driffield of Easingwold.

This situation could have led to as involved a conflict as that for the Howe, but the parties seem to have negotiated a settlement in 1630 under which Peter Apsley, the son and heir of Sir Allen, who had died in the meantime, conveyed the manor to Thomas Lord Fauconberg, subject to the unexpired residue of the 99 year lease. The latter seems to have been vested in 1630 in Lord Fauconberg, Jordan Metham, Esquire, of Wiganthorpe and William Frankland, Esquire, of Thirkleby as joint tenants. They agreed to assign the lease at apportioned rents to the tenants. (strictly sub-tenants) of the manor. The latter agreed to pay for their tenements at the rate of 54 years purchase, according to the ancient rents, and the money was to be paid to William Driffield in three instalments payable in the church porch of Easingwold. The agreement was embodied in Articles Tripartite dated 22nd November, 1630.[19] George Clay was a party and had presumably agreed to William Driffield receiving the purchase money from the tenants.

William Driffield was also in possession in 1620 and 1621 of the Archdeaconry Manor under a lease for lives. Previously Sir Thomas Dawney had been a lessee, with Garvis or Gervase Dracotes as his sub-lessee. The court roll of 1625 names Gregory Driffield, Thomas Burnett and John Driffield as the lessees of the Bishop of Chester, but in fact they must have been sublessees since William Driffield is described as lord in 1628, 1635 and 1642. William Driffield's son Francis was lord in 1645. The 1625 court roll contains a terrier of the property of this manor, mostly land in the open fields. The manor house is described as: "An antiant manse or rectory house with two Barnes a dovecote and an oxhouse wth a yeard and backside wth Tyth Come and Tyth hey and other Tyth rented in the occupation of Gregorie Driffield, Thomas Burnett, and John Driffield or their assignes wth all those landes within the Town feildes of Easingwold by estimacon five oxgangs as hereafter is pticularly ressited wth comon of pasture wood and other rightes wthin the Forest of Galteres to the same belongeing payinge yearlye at two feast in the yeare to the Bishop of Chester rent p. Ann XXVli xiijs iiijd". It is of interest to note cottage rents still paid in kind — William Wood paid yearly "A henn And ten Eges", Thomas Goodrick "A Coke and ten Eges" and William Storye "one henn". This roll is signed on behalf of the executors of R. (probably Richard) Staveley, the steward. Richard Staveley died in 1642, but in 1635 the steward was George Hall and in 1645 and 1648 George Pumie.[20]

Richard Staveley had a son Robert, born in 1604, who went to live at Millington, Yorks. From him are descended the Staveleys of Stainley Hall.

Yeoman families included the Weares, Raynolds, Frosts, Goodrickes, Cundalls, Couplands, Cowpers, Leathleys, Linsleys,

51

Pannets and Gibsons already mentioned. John Lynsley, mentioned in the parish registers in 1681, lived at "Upleby Ashes". This place name was still in use on 19th February, 1728, when John Linsley "of the Ash" was buried, though the trees had evidently decreased in number. Other Easingwold families of the first half of the century were the Fewsters, Berrymans, Merrymans, Wilkinsons and Nolsons, together with the curiously named Frackpitts or Frogpitts. The earliest mentions of the well-known Easingwold surname of Bland are to be found in Jacobean times. Richard Bland was a churchwarden in 1624.

Enough has been said already to show that Thomas Driffield and his son William were founding the principal family of the town. Thomas married the daughter of a London merchant named Cundall, probably a member, or at least a connection, of the Cundalls of Easingwold. William's son Francis (c. 1621- September 1675) married Frances the daughter of Nicholas Towers, merchant of York, became a Justice of the Peace, and was from 6th October 1646, to 15th January, 1657, one of the High Constables for Bulmer Wapentake.[21] His coat of arms, ermine, on a bend sable three boars heads erased argent, was recorded by Sir William Dugdale, Norroy King of arms, at York on 13th August, 1666. Francis had an only son Towers, born about 1656, who served as a Captain in the Bulmer Regiment of the North Riding Militia about 1688.[22] His early death in 1690 brought this line to a close.

Francis also had two brothers, Matthias, who served in the Royalist forces during the Civil war, and Christopher, who was called to the bar and practised in the West Riding at least as late as September, 1709[23]

Part of the secret of the family's success was no doubt prudent marriage. Mrs. Frances Driffield was co-heiress of her father Nicolas Towers. In 1676 she gave a house in Little Lane, Easingwold, for the residence of four poor single women, with an endowment for their maintenance, and for apprenticing a poor boy to a trade.

William Driffield was sufficiently wealthy to have to pay a composition of £14 to Charles I in the period 1630 to 1632 for not taking up the order of knighthood at the coronation. The King collected a good deal of money by this archaic device before it was abolished by the Long Parliament in 1640.[24]

There were other branches of the family living at Easingwold, not all upon good terms with their rich relatives if we are to judge by the following entry in the records of North Riding

Quarter Sessions from the strict days of the Commonwealth:

"Mr. Tho. Driffeild of Easingwold, Esq., did sweare by the God of Heaven prophanely in the church; proved upon the oath of Mrs. Mary Driffeild, the wife of Mr. Will. Driffeild of Easingwold". This was in 1652. Of course Mrs. William Driffield's father-in-law was called Thomas, but he is hardly likely to have been alive in 1652. Possibly the Thomas Driffield referred to is the man who had property at Easingwold and Haxby and whose will was proved on 7th July, 1655,[25] though he seems to have been living at Haxby in 1653.

There is little direct evidence of the impact made by the Civil War and other troubles of Charles I's reign on this part of Yorkshire. The justices sitting at Malton on 12th July, 1636, referred to "this daingerous tyme"[26] no doubt having in mind the rising tide of discontent. In the First Bishop's War between Charles and the Scots the King rendezvoused with the train bands of the counties at York. There was no fighting, the parties negotiated and the troops were disbanded on 24th June, 1639. One of the returning soldiers was buried at Easingwold. The entry in the parish registers reads: "Willm a soldier brought fro Raskall wth another, was buried. His fellow said he was a Suffolk man and served Captain Drurye".

Following the success of the Scots in the Second Bishops War in 1640, when they stampeded the English force at Newburn-on-Tyne on 28th August, many soldiers seem to have been billeted in the district, both in Helmsley and adjoining places (October, 1640) and at or near Easingwold (probably from September, 1640 to July 1641, to judge from entries in the parish registers). Two Corporals and a "gentleman soldier" were buried at Easingwold in the period February to April 1641. The births of illegitimate children of soldiers by three Easingwold girls are recorded in February and March, 1642, as additional proof that troops were quartered there in the summer of 1641. One of the soldiers, Pears Evans, married Katheran Weyre (Weare) in the parish church on 25th November, 1641, so that perhaps their stay extended over the autumn and part of the winter as well.

A survey of the manor of Crayke made in December, 1647, and January, 1648, refers to the buildings of Crayke Castle as "very much ruined by soldiers quartered there since these unhappy differences". In April, 1646, and again in February, 1647, the House of Commons ordered that the castle should be rendered untenable and no garrison maintained in it. A cannon ball

53

weighing about 5 lbs. was found, apparently about 1875, on a hill traditionally called "Oliver's Mount", a small mound on the south side of the road to Oulston opposite Manyard House. Another cannon ball was found prior to 1852 by the side of one of the roads leading out of Crayke and is believed to have been kept in the rectory garden for a period.[27] The present owner of Crayke Castle, T. M. Higham, Esq., has heard of what seems to be an account of the castle having been sacked by the Scottish Army in the Civil War period.

The Battle of Marston Moor was fought on 3rd July, 1644. Peter Ingham, a soldier "from about Bradford", buried at Easingwold in that year could have been a Marston Moor casualty or have died in some other way. Two Easingwold men actually known to have served were both Royalists. One was Matthias Driffield already mentioned and the other was Cornet John Watson, who held that rank at the beginning of November, 1643. During the Commonwealth he kept an alehouse, but was deprived of his licence by the Justices in July, 1652, when they discovered that he had been a King's officer.[28] There is a tradition that John Donald, a native of Easingwold, fought at Marston Moor on the parliamentary side and afterwards carved on the door beam of his house in Spring Street the Protestant slogan "God with Us". The old half timbered house was demolished and replaced by a new brick one in 1907, but the carving was preserved and set over the door of the new house.

Troops of both sides are known to have been billetted at Oldstead during the war and no doubt other places in the district received their share.[29] Some villages too seem to have had particularly strong Puritan groups and these include Alne and Crayke.

Requisitioning was no doubt carried out by both sides and this is the background of a case at Easingwold in 1643 when three Easingwold men told the wife of John Myers that unless she gave them 40/— they would bring a troop of soldiers and drive all her husband's goods away. It seems that they actually brought some soldiers to the house. Whether this was debt collection, requisitioning or blackmail there is no means of telling, but in the upshot the justices sentenced one of the three men, a miller, to a month "at least" in the House of Correction, until he should find sureties.

Richard Sandeman or Sandyman, vicar of Easingwold from 1620, died in April 1644 and from that time until the institution of George Wilson in 1648 no vicar is recorded. The parish registers indeed contain scarcely any entries for these years. In August,

1653, the recording of births, deaths and marriages was by a Commonwealth Ordinance entrusted to an official elected by the ratepayers called the Parish Register. In 1654 it was required that marriages should be celebrated before a justice of the peace, after public notice by the Register, for example "on the Lord's day at the close of the morning exercise" or in the market on three several market days. At Quarter Sessions on 9th January, 1654, the intended marriage between John Coates of Easingwold and Dorothy Dobson of Husthwaite was ordered to be suspended till the next sessions when the objections made by Mary Homer of Newburgh would be examined.[30] At Northallerton on 24th April, 1654, the justices decided to allow the marriage to take place.[31]

The keeping of parish registers by the incumbent was restored in 1659. The performance of marriage ceremonies by the justices had already ceased some time before. On 4th May, 1658, Mr. Carr, one of the Commonwealth vicars of Alne, married William Bland of Easingwold and Mary Crosby of Alne, probably at Easingwold with the approval of Mr. George Wilson.

Mr. Wilson had to vacate the living of Easingwold about the beginning of 1662 due to his non-conformity, but nevertheless continued to live there until his death on 22nd September, 1671. He left the rent of a field called North Moor Close for the poor and for the supply of fuel to Fossbridge House. His son Andrew born on 30th November. 1658, went to Pocklington School and St. John's College, Cambridge, taking his bachelor's degree in 1680 and master's in 1684. He was vicar of Easingwold from 1685 until his death in 1713.[32] George Wilson also had children named Joseph, Mary, John, Nathaneal and Deborah. Nathaneal, born in 1656, is probably the man who left by his will made in 1726 a bequest to the poor of Easingwold and for a sermon.

Three vicars followed George Wilson in quick succession — William Anderson (1662-4); John Bradley, MA., educated at Pocklington School and Peterhouse, Cambridge, (1664-8); and Lucas Smelt (1668-9). Probably none of these made very much impact on the parish. The next vicar, Jeremy or Jeremias Hay probably made more. Not only did he stay from his induction on 11th June, 1669, till his death at the end of July, 1685, but he also seems to have been something of a character. In 1673, or thereabouts, there was an incident which led to the report that he was "a conjurer and did conjure and raise the devil". It was said that he had had a door stolen and had used enchantments to recover it. Two Easingwold men were presented at Quarter Sessions at Thirsk on 8th April, 1673 for spreading this report.[33] Possibly Mr. Hay used some simple trickery to recover his lost property. The justices at Thirsk on 3rd October, 1682. had before them a charge of scandalous words uttered by "an Easingwold clerk" who could perhaps have been the vicar.[34] Hay was succeeded by Andrew Wilson, vicar till 1712.

The goods of the parish church in 1636 included a bible, two communion books, two books of homilies, "Bishop Jewell's works" and a copy of the canons. (Bishop Jewell's "Apology for the Church of England" was ordered to be placed in all churches in 1564). There were two table cloths, a pulpit cloth and a cushion, no doubt also for the pulpit. John Crosbie of Raskelf, blacksmith, agreed with the church wardens on 24th August, 1636, to maintain the ironwork of the church clock for seven years at 5/- per annum. This clock may then have been about sixty years old, if not more, since in 1574 the Vicar General of the diocese had awarded, as between Easingwold and Raskelf, that bells and a clock, but not organs, were necessary and decent ornaments for the parish church of Easingwold. The point of the award was that if these things were necessary ornaments, Raskelf had to contribute to their maintenance. They may all in fact have been in the parish church at the date of the award. The term "organs", by the way, usually means one organ only in the modern sense, being short for "a pair (i.e. a set) of organs", that is an instrument of several pipes. Both organs and clocks are said to have been common in churches prior to the Reformation, though the former fell into disrepute in the century following. On 26th November, 1679, the parish agreed with the vicar, Mr. Hay, that he would buy and maintain suitable vestments, in return for an annual payment of 2/6d. In 1639 William Oldfield of York cast and hung a new bell which on 11th December, 1639, he agreed to maintain for one year for the sum of £8. 7s. 0d. This bell is referred to as "the middle bell", which logically implies three bells.

A little is known of the strength of dissent at Easingwold in Stuart times from the presentments and lists of recusants made to or by Quarter Sessions. In 1591 there were two recusants and in 1595 three recusants and a non-communicant. In 1595 a labourer's wife was presented, and the same woman again in 1616, by which date she was a widow. In Jacobean times there seems to have been one recusant at Easingwold. In 1624 a married woman was presented and in 1625 a yeoman's wife.[35] Two married women and a yeoman were presented in 1641.[36] Alne seems to have been a Presbyterian centre, with encouragement from the Bethells, in the 1670's and probably earlier. Richard Malton, born at Easingwold in 1641, was at Cambridge University and subsequently became a private chaplain to various Presbyterian families. He died at Gilling in 1683.[37]

The local government of Tudor and Stuart times was carried out by the justices of the peace, to whom it fell to deal, not only with crime and the preservation of order, the government of the Crown and the established religion, but also with a great many matters of a more administrative nature. These included poor relief, employment, the maintenance of highways, the sale of goods, the control of brewing and the sale of intoxicating liquor, and the prevention of immorality.

The system of poor relief established by the Poor Law Act of 1598 was administered on a parochial basis by officers known as Overseers of the Poor. They consisted partly of the church wardens of the parish and partly of substantial landowners nominated annually in Easter week under the hand and seal of two or more justices. The justices in Quarter Sessions supervised and assisted them in the performance of their duties. There were many changes of detail, but basically the Elizabethan Poor Law continued in being until the Poor Law Amendment Act, 1834. Parish relief was given both in money and in kind. In later times monetary relief was the rule, but even in the nineteenth century the Overseers sometimes paid for the making or mending of clothing, the provision of bedding, the cost of house repairs and the expenses of ilness or funerals. One of the great defects of the system was that, since a parish was only responsible for maintaining its own poor, an immense body of law grew up and an enormous amount of time and money was wasted by all concerned in determining whether or not a parish was in fact doing or ought to do this. Only those who could be regarded as legally "settled" in the parish were its responsibility. All others had to be taken or sent to their correct "place of settlement". Parish officers often incurred considerable expense in proceedings at Quarter Session to determine the place of settlement, or in returning individuals or families to the parishes where they ought to be maintained. The justices at Helmsley in January, 1637, ordered the parish officers of Easingwold to pay 10d. a week to a poor man, having presumably decided that he was legally settled there. On the other hand the justices from time to time lent the weight of their authority to the overseers in collecting the poor rate, as in

1646, when the overseers of Easingwold were authorised to distrain for sums due.

Petty constables were appointed on a parochial basis, normally by the manorial court. In default the justices might make the appointment themselves. At Easingwold two parish constables were chosen each year by the Court Leet of the Manor of Easingwold and Huby. They had to submit the accounts for their year of office to Quarter Sessions for scrutiny and we find those of 1642 and 1645 being peremptorily ordered to do this on pain of forfeiting £10 each. The petty constables of each wapentake had over them two chief or head constables.

A very large part of the business of the justices consisted in enforcing the Statute of Highways, 1555, which expressly placed on parishes the responsibility (probably already theirs at common law) to keep in repair the public highways within their boundaries. Annually appointed officials known as "surveyors of highways" were supposed to see that whatever work was necessary was carried out either by the inh~bitants personally ("statute labour") or by contract. The latter method really only became practicable when the levying of highway rates was authorised in the later 17th century. The Act of 1555 obliged each occupier of a ploughland (subsequently defined as a holding of £50 annual value), and everyone keeping a team of horses or a plough, to provide a cart and team and two men. Other inhabitants had to come themselves, or send someone in their place, to work for eight hours on each of four days in the year appointed by the surveyor or surveyors. In 1563 this liability was increased to six days. A Commonwealth Ordinance of 1654 authorised parish meetings to levy a rate (often called a "lewn" or "lay") of not more than a shilling in the pound for highway maintenance. Though this was apparently repealed in 1660, an Act of 1670 (22 Chas. II, c. 12) did provide that anyone who failed to perform or provide statute labour was to pay a penalty of 1/6d. for a day's labour by one man, 3/- for a man and a horse and 10/- for a cart and two men, and such penalties were in effect highway rates. Moreover fines could be imposed by Quarter Sessions on parishes which failed to maintain their highways and the justices normally ordered such fines to be spent on the required repairs. Finally the Highway Act of 1691 authorised the raising of a sixpenny rate for highway repair. The surveyors were supposed to report to Quarter Sessions on the condition of their highways and on any default in carrying out statute labour, and to account for any money in their hands. In practice the part played by the more active justices by personal inspection of the condition of the country roads was probably equally important. The equipment and methods used for maintaining highways under the parochial system were of the most primitive kind and remained so down to the early 19th century. In 1794 the two surveyors of highways at Stillington had charge of three stone breakers hammers, a "how", a paving hammer, a "javlin", a shovel, a hack, a rake and two centres for bridges, the whole valued at one pound. Their material consisted of local stone from Yearsley, Ampleforth and Brandsby, bricks from Tollerton and Huby, with sand, coping stones for bridges, and timber. In 1678 the Easingwold surveyors of highways brought stone from Oulston and sand from Barker Hill in that township. The Stillington surveyors paid for materials and labour partly by accepting the payment of compositions for statute labour and partly by a "sess" or highway rate. The six "common day works" required by the Act of 1563 were still being worked in 1795 by or on behalf of those who had not compounded. At other times labour was paid for in the usual way.

The justices in Quarter Sessions were continually dealing with presentments of parishes for not repairing their highways. At Thirsk on 2nd October, 1639, for example, the inhabitants of Easingwold were presented for not repairing the highway "in a loaninge between Dawny bridge and a yatesteade called Turner yate"[38] At the Epiphany Sessions following, held at Helmsley on 7th January, 1640, one of the constables of Easingwold appeared on behalf of the inhabitants and asked for time to carry out the repairs. A suspended fine of £20 was imposed.[39] In 1654 Easingwold was in trouble for failure to repair the York road between Tollerton Lane End and Shipton Gate. The justices seem to have been still trying to enforce repair in July, 1657.[40] Again in January, 1638, the parish was given time to repair North Moor Lane.

Parishes were also liable to maintain bridges which were part of highways. In 1650 Easingwold was presented for failure to repair How Bridge.[41] New Bridge, which replaced the former ford of the Fleet beck on the main road to York on the dis-afforestation of Galtres in 1630, was a constant headache. There were presentments of the inhabitants of Easingwold for failure to repair the bridge in April, 1648, and October. 1654.[42]

As the countryside was still only partially enclosed, even main roads in the 17th century might be gated, and gates across by-roads were frequent. Parishes were often obliged to repair these gates as well as the roads themselves. From 1631 to 1638 the justices from time to time chased Easingwold to repair what was sometimes called the New Lane or New Loaning Yate and Yatestead and sometimes Lund Leys Yate. In July, 1637, the justices requested a local justice, William Frankland, Esq., to investigate and report. He reported the following January that it was convenient for traffic and in repair,[43] and the matter was not proceeded with. (The use of the word "loaning", now not generally found south of the Tees, will be noted. It or the alternative form "loan" was in common use in the Easingwold district in the 17th century).

Sometimes the repair of a highway was a private liability attached to particular land. This is nowadays rare but was a more frequent situation in the 17th century. Part of the Alne road was repairable in this way down to modern times. Liability in such cases was again enforced by Quarter Sessions, as in October, 1639, when an Esquire was presented for not repairing part of the highway between Easingwold and York.

The same gentleman was at the same time presented for actually obstructing the highway between Easingwold and "le Gunfitt Cross" with a hedge and ditch. The Gunfit or Gunthwaite Cross was one of the crosses erected in the Forest of Galtres as landmarks. It seems to have been somewhere near Fleet Bank Corner. The present landscape of the forest in all probability bears little relation to that of Jacobean times, before the land was disafforested and enclosed in the 1630's. Norden's description of the bounds of the Manor of Easingwold and Huby in 1617 refers to a number of crosses in the forest — a cross in the "moores or wastes of Easingwold and Huby" near a close called Wesbecke, a cross on the south side of the "Hasells" (hazels), a cross "in the ground on a bracken hill' and a new cross "in the ground over against Huby Sand Gate", as well as more primitive "bounders" such as an oak tree marked with a cross "standing upon Linthwayte", an "old cast dike", a stone near Blackwood "newke" (nook), a marked oak "near to the Claypitts", the stump of an old oak, a great stone which was an ancient "bounder" and a hole with stones in it. There is an overwhelming impression of rough heaths and woods with occasional enclosures. Enclosure in the 1630's must have made a complete change in this rough country.

It is clear that there were sometimes complaints that the new enclosures took in land which was actually part of the highway. In the days of unmetalled roads this may not have been mere wilfulness on the part of the improvers. At common law the public had & right to deviate from the normal course of the highway if it became impassable by. for example, ruts or potholes. Occasional deviation did not make land part of the highway, though habitual might. Clearly there was plenty of room for argument and misunderstanding. The justices were of, course bound to prevent the obstruction of highways, but it was not always easy to tell which was highway and which not.

Under the statute of Labourers and Apprentices of 1563 (or Statute of Artificers as it is sometimes called) a labourer or servant could not leave his or her service without giving a quarters warning, nor could the master dismiss the servant without similar notice. In addition the servant, if he wished to leave the parish and go to a new employment elsewhere, had to obtain a certificate or "ticket" from the constable, which in turn had to be presented to the proper authorities at the new place. A constable would not grant the ticket unless he knew the master was willing to set the servant at liberty. A contemporary in the East Riding describes the system at the Martinmas Hirings. The chief constable or constables would call on the petty constables in turn to produce lists of the masters and servants in their respective constableries. He then called the masters in turn and asked if they would set such and such a servant at liberty :- "if the master will, then he maketh the servant his tickett and the servant giveth him 2d. for his paines: if the master will not sette him att liberty, then the chiefe constable is to lette them knowe what wages the statute will allow and to sette downe a reasonable and indifferent wage betwixt them, and hee is to have one penny of the master for every servant that stayeth two yeares in a place, or is not sette at liberty, and this the pettie constables are to doe for him, viz: to sende in bills of the names of all such servants as stay with theire olde masters, and to gather the money, and sende it to him".[44]

It was an offence to employ a servant without a proper ticket, or for a servant to leave his employment without a quarters warning. On 8th January, 1607, Thomas Gibson of Easingwold was presented for accepting and retaining in his service William Thompson without showing to the Head Officer (constable), curate or churchwardens any lawful Testimonial. At the same sessions Elizabeth Spawnton was presented for leaving her master at Easingwold without a quarters warning.[45]

It was also an offence, punishable by twenty-one days imprisonment, to receive wages higher than those fixed from time to time by the county justices. In 1658 the North Riding justices ordered that a cook or dairy maid should have £2 per annum; an ordinary maid aged over 21 30/-; a maid between 14 and 21 £1; a man servant £3; and a man servant able to take charge of husbandry £4. (The Rev. J. C. Atkinson's note in Volume VI of the North Riding Quarter Sessions Records[46] printed in 1888, is that the rate of wages then corresponding to the last was £22-£25). Carpenters, masons, "theakers" (thatchers) and mowers got 6d. a day with food or 12d. without. Mowing was considered heavier than reaping (4d. a day with food, 8d. without) or "ordnarye labour" (3d. with food, 6d. without from 1st May to 29th September; otherwise 2d. with food, 5d. without). There were reduced rates for apprentices and young persons between 14 and 18.

The rates seem to have been basically the same in 1680. The justices then confirmed the rate of £4 per annum for servants in husbandry able to mow, and plough well. Both cooks and dairy maids were to have £2 and other maids 33/4d. Ordinary men servants were to have £2. 13. 4d.[47]

Section 9 of the Act of 1563 fixed the hours of work for artificers and labourers hired at daily or weekly wages. "Betwixt the myddest of the monethes of March and September" work had to begin at or before 5 a.m. and continue till "betwixt 7 & 8 of the Cloke at night" with breaks not exceeding two and a half hours for "breakefast, dynner and drincking". "One hower" was allowed for dinner and half an hour for the other meals, "and for his slepe when he is allowed to slepe, the which is from the myddest of May to the myddest of August, halfe an houre at the most". From mid-September to mid-March work was from "the springe of the day, untill the night", with the meal breaks. For every hour not so worked a penny had to be deducted from the servants wages."[48]

Other forms of control administered by the justices were of course the licensing of brewing and alehouses. Thomas Linsley of Easingwold was presented for illegal brewing in April, 1611,[49] while Robert Driffield was presented in October 1614 for allowing unlawful card playing in his alehouse at Easingwold. His wife was also complained of "for that she will not sell anie of her ale forth of doores except it be to those whom she likes on, and makes her ale of two or three sortes, nor will not let anie of her poore neighbours have any of her drincke called small ale, but saith she will rather give it to her swyne than play it for them".[50] If necessary the justices could "suppress" a man from keeping a common alehouse, as they did with an Easingwold man in 1652, in this instance for three years.[51]

A fairly common offence was the rating or watering of hemp or flax in a running stream, a practice liable to pollute the water and make it undrinkable by cattle and consequently forbidden by an Act of 1542 (33 Henry VIII, c. 17). In October, 1607, a number of Easingwold and Raskelf men were presented for watering their hemp in the Kyle Water between its source and the mill called Driffeldes Milne.[52] Watering hemp in a running stream was also an offence against the forest law, being harmful to the deer.

Strolling players were anathema to constituted authority. There was a special reason for this in the North Riding. Small companies of players from the Scarborough and Whitby district from such places as Egton, Allerston, Danby, Boulby and Hutton Bushel, were rightly suspected of disseminating Roman Catholic propaganda. One company from Egton performed regularly in the years 1595 to 1616, including in the latter year a boy named Nicholas Poskett or Postgate, later a priest martyr in the reign of Charles II. This company was prepared to offer at least on a special occasion, a choice of Shakespeare's "King Lear" or "Pericles", or plays called "The Three Shirleys" or "St. Christopher". The last seems to have been a morality play.[53] In 1616 a sister troop came to Easingwold. Their leader was Richard Hudson of Hutton Bushel, aged 49, a weaver by trade; William and George Hudson, 12 and 11 respectively; another boy from the same place aged 16; Edward Lister of Allerston, weaver, aged 46; Roger Lister aged "7 and upwards"; and Robert Skelton of Wilton near Pickering, "7 and upwards". All were described as "players of Enterludes, vagabundes and sturdy beggars". The justices ordered Richard Hudson to be whipped at Thirsk.[54]

The official attitude remained unjoyful throughout the seventeenth century. In 1676 the justices ordered all petty constables to tighten up the watch against vagabonds as well as the enforcement of the laws against recusants; swearing; tipling and drinking and the driving of cattle to markets, carrying of loads and burdens and use of unlawful pastimes on the Lords Day. "All tinkers, pedlars and petty chapmen, Bedlam Common players of enterludes, gypsies, fidlers and pipers wandering abroad" were to be apprehended.[55]

The justices regulated the marketing of goods and took action against unqualified sportsmen. They collected pensions for old soldiers ("lame soldier money") from townships. They attempted to deal with outbreaks of plague and the occasional witch came their way too. Plague (not of course necessarily always of the same kind) occurred at fairly frequent intervals. It was at Alne in 1604; Sowerby from January to April, 1625, if not longer; Huby in late 1625 or early 1626;[56] Ripon in August, 1625;[57] Leeming during the months of August, 1625, to February, 1626;[58] Pocklington from 29th September, 1631, to 26th July, 1632;[59] and Bedale in about October, 1636.[60] It was in Barton, in Aldbrough near Richmond and in Hull in April, 1638.[61] There were outbreaks in Yarm in July, 1645,[62] and at Hutton Conyers and Newby Wiske in January, 1646.[63] At Richmond on 8th August, 1665, the justices took official notice of the fact that for three months previously persons had been leaving London and other places infected with the plague and ordered a watch to be kept throughout the riding for such persons.[64]

More direct action was taken against persons wilfully spreading the disease, for example by selling goods from an infected area. In 1626 Robert Bossall, a yeoman of Huby, and his son-in-law brought from London a quantity of goods believed to be infected. By selling them throughout the Riding he was thought to have actually infected Huby, Malton, Linton, Aytons Ambo and Hutton Bushel. He refused to get rid of his stock and abused the justices. They fined him £40, committed him to York Castle and made him sit in the stocks at New Malton for three hours with a scroll of paper round his head "written in Romaine capital letters — For bringing downe, receivynge into his house, and utteringe goods infected with the plague: And for contempte of the authorities seekinge to suppress his insolences".[65]

Witchcraft was firmly believed in by many people in the district at this time and indeed would be believed in for two hundred years to come. In 1623 the justices committed a Northallerton woman to prison for a year, and ordered her to stand in the pillory once a quarter in that time, for enchanting a black cow, so that it lost its calf.[66] In 1670 Francis Driffield J.P. of Easingwold took depositions at Alne in connection with a charge of witchcraft against a widow of that place. The widow protested

EASINGWOLD.

W.H.SMITH YORK.

G. H. Smith, Esq.

17th century house in Long Street known as Shepherd's Garth, now
demolished

18th century houses on the west side of the Market Place

Kurt of Easingwold

that she was "sacklesse" (guiltless) and was probably acquitted at Assizes.[67]

Occasionally the justices made special grants from their funds to relieve the victims of accidents, usually sufferers by fire. In 1640 they gave £3 towards the relief of Mrs. Dorothy Wood of Easingwold, whose husband had lost his life in the fire which destroyed their house.[68] In 1673 they made a grant of £10 to an Easingwold gentleman, who had lost his house and property to the value of £500 by fire, and said that they would give him another £10 in six months time if he was unable to procure letters patent from the Crown authorising him to make a collection on a national basis.[69] Such letters patent were known as "briefs" and were the recognised method of collecting for major sufferers by accident in the later 17th century and during the 18th century. Applications for briefs were often supported by a certificate of Quarter Sessions that the case was genuine.

There is some information about the occupations of Easingwold people in the 17th century. The trade of glover is mentioned in 1607, plumber in 1638, barber chirurgeon in 1657, chandler in 1658 and grocer in 1675. The usual rural occupations of "husbandman", labourer, butcher, tailor, carpenter and alehouse keeper are of course to be expected. A "wollinge weaver" is mentioned in 1640 and this again is to be expected. A clothworker is mentioned in a deed of 1634, as also is a skinner. Another. deed of 1653 names a draper and one of 1664 a cordwainer. Leather workers are of course appropriate to a country town and the trades of glover, harness maker, cordwainer and shoemaker probably overlapped a good deal — certainly the two last named. Francis Easterbye, who died in 1641, Thomas Weare named in the Court roll in 1678 and 1697. and John Gibson in 1680, were parchment makers. James Martine, named in 1680, was a "firkin maker" or maker of small casks. (Martine seems to have moved to Husthwaite about 1686). Schoolmasters are named in 1682 and 1691, the former being William Bows, the parish clerk, and the latter Richard Sinclair, Sinkler or Saintclare, who was presented to Quarter Sessions for teaching boys without a licence.[70] Schoolmasters were supposed to be licensed by the bishop of the diocese, though in practice this was probably frequently disregarded.

Perhaps Easingwold's earliest tobacconist, or one of the earliest at all events, was Michael Woodward, who in 1668 issued a trade token bearing the figure of a Red Indian smoking a pipe, the usual sign of a tobacco seller. The token, which was one of many intended to serve as small change during the years 1645 to 1672 when no regal copper coinage was issued, was inscribed: "MICHAELL. WOODWARD. OF EASING-WOVLD. 1668. = HIS . HALFE . PENNY".[71] Thomas Wilson of Easingwold is also known to have issued a trade token, in the 17th century, presumably during the same period. Thomas Wilson is mentioned in the court leet book in 1677. The passage apparently refers to his "signe", so that he may have kept an Inn. There was an excise officer or "gauger" in the town in 1689. Alehouse keepers were Robert Driffield (in 1614) and Cornet John Watson (in 1652), both mentioned above, while "Nanny" Driffield is named in Giles Morrington's poem "Praise of Yorkshire Ale", written in 1697. Thomas Atkinson's trade of "butterman" in 1667 calls for comment. He was probably a dealer who forwarded butter in quantity to York and probably also by coaster to London. During the 17th century there was a windmill at the top of Church Hill on the east side of the Church which was apparently in working order at the beginning of the 18th century. It existed in 1625, when this part of the Church Field was called Windmylne Hill. There was also a water mill on the Kyle in Jacobean times, owned or occupied by the Driffield family.

Crime during Stuart times consisted mainly of larceny and assault, with an occasional forcible entry, unlawful assembly or riot. Poaching cases had not yet achieved their later importance. Several Easingwold people were presented for scandalous words — two in 1673, one in 1675 and one in 1682. In 1696 an Easingwold labourer was presented for harbouring a deserting sóldier.[72] Three Easingwold men were charged with taking unjust toll in 1649[73] and one in 1650.[74] In 1657 one of the constables of Easingwold was fined 10/- for neglecting to execute a warrant,[75] and in the same year an Easingwold man was charged with allowing the escape of a prisoner secured in his house.[76] More serious criminals were Robert Hall, hanged at York in 1620 for coining and paying bad money at Easingwold and Ralph Raynard of White House on the Thirsk road, hanged at York in 1623 with Mark Dunn of Huby and a Mrs. Fletcher of Raskelf for murdering the latter's husband by drowning him in the beck at Dawnay Bridge. The bodies of the three murderers were taken to Lund Moor to hang in chains at a place still known as Gallows Hill. In 1649 Grace Bland of Easingwold was hanged at York Tyburn for setting fire to the house of her mistress, The Maypole Inn at Clifton, on 5th November, 1648. The Inn was burnt to the ground. The present "Old Grey Mare" stands on the site.[77]

The place of the present petty sessions or magistrates court was taken at Easingwold at this period by the court leet which met twice a year, in May and October. The court book covering the years 1667 to 1718 at Newburgh Priory makes it clear that not only did the court deal with such specifically manorial matters as the regulation of communal agriculture, but also matters of public order as assaults, affrays, the use of abusive language and the prosecution of nightwalkers. At the spring court in 1667, held on 4th May, Thomas Skelton was fined 10/- "for beating of Edward Wood and drawing blood upon him" and another 10/- for doing the same to Mrs. Wood. Two Huby women were fined for assaults and for being nightwalkers. On 9th April, 1668 John Gibson was fined 1/- "for keeping an unlawfull dogge": Thomas Robinson 1/8d. "for making bread over light": and John Bayliffe 1/8d. "for his wife slaundering of John Flawith". The court leet dealt with obstruction of the highway, as on 4th May, 1669, when they fined "for suffering wood to ly in ye town gate", and enforced the payment of church rate. In 1677 the retiring churchwardens were fined 2/6d. each for not accounting within six weeks after vacating office. The court's jurisdiction included the non-payment of constable rates; failure by the constables to account; harbouring or receiving inmates (lodgers) or undersettles (sub-tenants) (by the Act 31 Eliz. c. 7 lodgers were forbidden in cottages on pain of the owner or occupier forfeiting 10/- a month to the lord of the manor); commencing suits out of the lord's court without his licence; non-repair of causeways, stiles and footbridges; breaking hemp by the fireside; laying manure in the street; lodging vagabonds without leave of the constable; having an insufficient chimney or making a fire in a building without a chimney; hunting the lord's game, not being a qualified person; harbouring a woman unlawfully with child for more than two days and two nights; underletting land without licence; failing to come to the common days work on the highways or coming too late; and failing to repair a house. In many ways the Easingwold court leet appears like a minor Quarter Sessions.

There was a highly detailed jurisdiction over agriculture and similar matters. A set of regulations or "pains" for the Easingwold leet does not appear to have survived, but they probably resembled fairly closely that made on 16th April, 1737, by the homage (that is the tenants attending) of a court leet on the Newburgh estates at a place not readily legible, but which appears to be Yearsley. These regulations fixed penalties for such offences as breaking hedges by taking "garcell" (dead wood) or going over them; leaving a gap in an outring fence for more than four days; rating hemp in running streams or cattle drinking places; having sheep unringed for more than seven days between Ascension Day and Michaelmas; failing to have one's corn ground at the lord's mill, unless the miller was unable to grind it within twenty-four hours; making new ways or stopping up existing ones; putting geese on other men's ground; having swine on the common without bow and ring for two or more days; lopping and topping trees not topped before; ploughing up fresh ground without licence; gathering casings or cow-dung for fuel; taking more than two corn-crops before fallowing; laying tillage down to grass on the first crop after the fallow without leave of the lord; paring or burning without leave of the lord; having hedges or ditches out of order; having scabbed sheep or horses, or farcy (glandered) horses, or infectious "goods" (livestock) on the common pasture; felling the lord's wood without leave; pound breach; unlawful commoning; putting more sheep on the common in summer than in winter; keeping "riggalls" (imperfectly 'castrated sheep) in an insecure enclosure between Holyrood and the 1st of December; unauthorised graving (digging) of turves; pulling others sheep; taking up the waste without licence; and failing to catch "mouls". In the particular set of regulations quoted it was also an offence to keep the village ladder (which was "based" on the Bailiff's house) above three days.

Both Easingwold and Huby had bailiffs or graves. These, according to the 1721 edition of "Les Termes de la Ley", had the duties of ordering the husbandry, felling trees, repairing houses, seeing to fences, payment of rents and so on and were therefore in fact successors to the medieval reeves. The Easingwold-cum Huby leet in the seventeenth century swore one of the homage for Easingwold and one for Huby as "prepositus", which is usually translated as "reeve". Probably, however, by the reign of Charles II the word meant no more than the foreman of the jury. Other officers appointed by the court leet varied from time to time, the aletasters for example not being appointed later than the court of 4th May, 1669, in the period covered by the court book at Newburgh Priory. The chief manorial official was the steward, who held the court on behalf of the lord. In 1667 Allan Chamber of Coxwold (c. 1615-1690), who was Clerk of the Peace of the North Riding from 1681 to 1689, was steward. He was succeeded between the courts of 20th April and 16th October, 1677, by

Christopher Goulton of Highthorne, Husthwaite, a local lawyer, and Goulton in turn was succeeded between the courts of 17th April and 16th October, 1716, by Francis Goulton. The October court in 1667 appointed, in addition to the graves, two constables, four byelaw men, two aletasters, two watersewer men and a pinder for Easingwold. For Huby there was one constable, two byelaw men and a pinder. The October court in 1668 chose for Easingwold two graves, two constables, four watersewer men and a pinder, while for Huby there was one constable, four byelawmen, four watersewer men and a pinder. At the court held on 4th May, 1669, there were chosen for Easingwold four "sheriff's turne men" and four aletasters. Four Sheriffs turn men were also appointed in 1682 and 1688 but not at any other time down to 1718. The Sheriff's turn or tourne was the old county court (not to be confused with the modern statutory County Court which is little more than a hundred years old) when it sat to deal with criminal matters and the preservation of the peace. In theory it was held twice a year within a month after Easter and Michaelmas in the various hundreds or wapentakes in turn, but it is probable that by Charles II's time it sat only very occasionally. The four appointees of the Easingwold court leet presumably attended sessions of the county court somewhere in Bulmer Wapentake in the years mentioned. In 1684 Easingwold had two graves, two constables, four byelaw men, three leather sealers and searchers, no less than six breadweighers, four "supvisors com. via." (surveyors of highways) and four "wattersuermen". In 1697 the list was as in 1684 with the exception of the breadweighers and with the addition of a pinder. In 1710 the list had been amended to two constables, four byelaw men, two breadweighers, four surveyors of highways and watersewermen (combined) and two leather sealers. Appointments were no doubt varied to meet particular situations — probably for example, the breadweighers were increased to six in 1684 because there had been complaints in the market of short weight and it was decided to pay particular attention to this problem.

The duties of the various special officers are reasonably clear. The pinder took charge of straying livestock until duly reclaimed by the owner and any fines of the court paid. The watersewer man saw that watercourses were properly scoured. The leather sealers presumably saw that any leather sold, by itself or as part of leather goods, was of proper quality. The surveyors of highways seem to duplicate the parochial officers with the same name, but they may well in practice have seen to the minor highways in the manor — the footpaths and the common ways and balks of the town fields. On the other hand they may have been appointed because the parochial officers were not doing their job. More evidence is necessary before a definite conclusion can be reached about this. The byelaw men's task was to ensure that the regulations of the court were observed. A town shepherd is mentioned in the mid-eighteenth century who may have been an officer of the court leet, though in that case it is surprising that no such officer is mentioned in the court book at Newburgh. The breadweighers were still being appointed in 1797, when one of the local joiners made a box for holding their scales and weights.

An idea of the usual business of the court may be obtained from a few of its decisions. On 4th May, 1667, the homage or jury of Easingwold presented John Bayliffe for letting his horses go onto the common land and on a similar charge in respect of his cows. He was fined 3s. 4d. in each case. This may have been a matter of taking pasturage to which he was not entitled or of stock trespassing on the arable fields. John Cundall at the same court was fined 1/- "for digging pitts at his garth side to ye hurt of his neighbours" and Christopher Talbot 2/- for encroachment on the King's highway. William Nightgell was fined "for taking up some of York Lane", which seems to be another highway encroachment. There were five cases of assault or battery, leading to fines. Richard Coopland was fined 2/- "for plowing of ye Uppleby Croft unto his headland yt adioyns upon it" and John Leathlay 1/- for the like. Richard Coates was fined 1/- "for suffering his waine gapp to ly downe" (which probably means leaving open a hurdle gate at a time when there was temporary fencing in one of the town fields). The Huby jury at this court made presentments relating to Huby, including several for not maintaining "gutters" (watercourses). They presented Robert Pecket for rating hemp in his watercourse and he was fined 2/-, another example of concurrent jurisdiction with Quarter Sessions.

At the court on 2nd October, 1667 there were fines for making a new way "to ye hurt of his neighbours" (1/-); "for not weeding thistles out of his corn" (2/- in one case and 4/- in three others); for lodging beggars (6/-); for "over stinting in ye fallow field" (grazing more than his entitlement there) (3s. 4d.); for "buying meat and selling it again" (presumably not having served an apprenticeship as a butcher) (1/-); and for a "causey" (causeway) out of repair (4/-). Other presentments included several "for his goods" (stock) "eating ye — field before it was broken" (thrown open to grazing); one for having unringed swine; and one "for carrying his neighbours flaughter turfes off Baskermoor" (Boscar Moor). "Flaughter" or "flowter" turves were sods of turf taken with a long shafted triangular spade, forced in from the surface, as distinct from peat taken from a peat hole. These "fire flowts" were regarded as inferior to peat. Turf was a common fuel in the district until at least the mid-18th Century. It was probably collected from the turbaries or turfgraves in large baskets carried on the back or on asses as in present day Ireland. At Quarter Sessions at Thirsk in April, 1656, an Easingwold woman was found not guilty of stealing a burden of turves worth 1d.[78] There were turbaries on Lund Moor, Raskelf Common and Boscar Moor.

The court on 9th April, 1668, fined William Burnet 3s. 4d. "for keeping one grabb'd mare in ye field contra pac." (i.e. where it might infect other stock); Mathew Driffield (probably Mathias the ex-Royalist Soldier) 3s. 4d. for a battery; and Francis Driffield the justice "for plowing his headland to ye Wandales over broad". Widow Hopkin had to pay 1/- because her children took wood from the neighbours fences. Other fines were 1/- "for keeping an unlawfull dogge"; 1s. 8d. "for making bread over light"; a like sum "for cutting a thorn out of his neighbours fence"; 1/- for abusing a man in his own house; and 3s. 4d. for abusing the jury. John Cundall was fined for a "rescous" (resume of impounded stock) from the pinder of Huby. At the court on 20th April, 1677, Towers and William Driffield were each fined 3s. 4d. for assaulting John Lynsley.

Presentments at other courts included one for "goods getting into ye winter cornfield"; for "plowing up the highways on the common balke leading to the Mill Stile and in the highway that leads to the upper side of the Mill field"; for keeping a horse in the common lanes after 8.00 p.m.; for suffering a fence to hang over the highway; for "plowing away the poor folk's land"; for "keeping misteched (badly broken) or unlawful goods to the hurt of his Neighbours"; for geese trespassing in the cornfield; for "Lodging of Bedgares without the licance of the Constable"; for "powling down the watergap"; for "overstinting the fallow"; for "not skowreing his watersewer"; for "his garth fence lying down to the pdigiss (prejudice) of his Neighbours"; and for "powling his Neighbours fences downe". The first of these was at the court on 4th May, 1669; the others at that of 16th October, 1667.

At the April Court in 1678 Thomas Williamson was fined 3s. 4d. for a pound breach Thomas Wood 10s. for "a blood and fray" upon the body of Richard Coates and John Dawson 1s. 6d. "for his wife's evel tongue". The officers seem to have had campaigns from time to time against certain offences (apparently without much success). Thus on 24th October, 1668, sixty-three persons from Easingwold were fined a pound each for rating hemp and line (flax) in the Kyle, a testimony to the prevalence of this offence. On 15th October, 1678, sixty persons from Easingwold were fined for failing to carry out "common day works" for the repair of the parochial highways. The Huby homage presented a great many unscoured water sewers or gutters. At the October Court in 1669 Brian Abbot of "Old Brough" (probably Aldborough) was fined 3s. 4d. for bringing unwholesome meat into Easingwold Market.

The amounts of the fines imposed by the court suggest that the table of penalties was drawn up in Elizabethan or even earlier times when the quarter-angel of 1/8d. and half-angel of 3s. 4d. were in use alongside the shilling, halfcrown and crown.

A certain civil jurisdiction apparently to the limit of forty shillings and thus similar to that of the county court was vested in the court leet. At the court held on 20th April, 1677, Robert Morley sued John Berryman and Thomas Lynsley for ploughing away his land. Verdicts were found for the defendants. This case seems to suggest that there was generally no physical division between the individual lands in the open fields, the boundaries being merely indicated by small boundary stones. This could lead to a man gradually "winning over" some of his neighbours land by extending his furrow over the boundary line. Actions of trespass, trespass on the case, debt and quare clausum fregit (close breaking) were usual and the parties were sometimes represented by Counsel. (Actions of trespass on the case were for what would now be termed negligence. A good example was that by Mrs. Elizabeth Hopkin on 3rd May, 1701, against an Easingwold bricklayer, Robert Sheppard. He built an oven for her so "inartificially" that it fell down the next day. She recovered 18s. damages).

Not every manor had a court leet and in fact the great majority probably merely had courts baron and customary, with far less extensive jurisdiction and powers. The court of the

Archdeaconry manor was of the latter type. During the Common-wealth this manor was conveyed to Christopher Driffield and George Potts by the Parliamentary Commissioners for the sale of church lands. In 1655 they also conveyed the manor house and two oxgangs of land to George Potts in fee simple. The manor reverted to the see of Chester in 1660 and was retained by it until 1860 when it vested in the Ecclesiastical (now the Church) Commissioners under the statute 23 & 24 Vict. c. 124.

Francis Driffield seems to have regained possession in 1660. He died in 1675 and was succeeded by his son Towers, who in 1688 assigned the lease to Thomas Raines. Raines is said to have sub-let for short periods, but was described as lord at the court held on 17th April, 1697. Thomas Fewster was steward from October, 1661, to November, 1668, and probably longer. He was dead by the spring court in 1697, John Todd being then steward.

While Easingwold had had the grant of an annual fair as far back as 1291, it had never had a regular market except for some six or seven years during the minority of Henry III. George Hall, a gentleman who lived at various times at Oswaldkirk, Sinning-ton and Easingwold, accordingly obtained from Charles I Letters Patent under the Privy Seal dated 16th August, 1639, for himself and his heirs and assigns for ever to hold a free market at Easing-wold every Friday, with two wakes or fairs on the Feasts of St. John the Baptist and Holyrood, and a cattle market every other week on Fridays, from the Friday after the feast of St. Matthew the Apostle, with a court of piepoudre at the fairs and to take all tolls and profits arising.

Having obtained his licence to hold these markets and fairs Mr. Hall then had to find a site for them. The obvious place must have been the central square of Easingwold now known as the Market Place, then a large open space traversed by tracks or "wain roads" and a stream, by which latter stood on a small mound or hill the cucking stool or ducking stool of the town. In the approximate centre of the open space was the bull ring, used for the baiting of bulls by dogs. In 1611 the bull is said to have broken his chain and gored to death a man and two women.[79] The traditional site is marked by a circle of cobbles between the butter market and the north end of the Town Hall. The butter market is a rebuilding of an old cross which may have been built in medieval times.

Several years of negotiations must have followed the grant of 1639 and it was not until 31st August, 1646 that Hall and the four byelawmen of that year acting on behalf of the inhabitants of the town executed a formal deed. This first of all conveyed to Hall part of the Market Place on which to hold a market. The boundaries of this market ground run along the north side of the two blocks of Tolbooth property on the north, along a line drawn from the westernmost Tolbooth block to the west end of the row of houses on the south side of the Market Place on the west (which line is the course of the former stream), along the fronts of the row of houses last mentioned on the south and back along the west side of the road from Chapel Street to Spring Street on the east. Hall agreed that he would build and maintain a tolbooth thirty feet long by eighteen broad, with stone steps, in which courts, byelaw and other meetings might be held. This was to replace the former Court House which was a little house in the Low Street of Easingwold (Long Street), which in return was conveyed to him. He covenanted to repair the pavement in the Market Place and that the inhabitants of the manor should be free of all market tolls. The present room known as the Tolbooth appears to date back only to the rebuilding of the property in the early 19th century, following a serious fire. Originally there was no doubt only the small rectangular building standing alone at the north end of the market ground. Some other buildings seem to have existed by the middle of the 18th century, including the butchers shambles, and these may with the Tolbooth have appeared during the second half of the seventeenth century.

It will be remembered that the manor of Easingwold and Huby had been conveyed to Thomas Belasyse, first Viscount Fauconberg, under the agreement of 1630. He was succeeded by his son Thomas the second Viscount, in 1652. The second Viscount was one of Charles II's Privy Councillors and married as his second wife, Mary the daughter of Oliver Cromwell. He died without male issue in 1700.

1   Cal Pat Rolls Edw. III (1334-8) p. 267 : Cal Charter Rolls (1327-41) p. 454.
2   Purvis : The Condition of Yorkshire Church Fabrics, 1300-1800 St. Anthonys Hall
    Publications No. 14 (1958).
3   YAJ Vol. XVIII, art, by H. B. McCall; Aveling : Catholic Recusants of the N. Riding. p. 81.
4   YAS Rec. Ser Vol CXII.
5   Gill op. cit.
6   Purvis. Tudor Parish Documents in the Diocese of York, Cambridge 1948.
7   N.R. Rec. Soc. N.S. Vol. 1.
8   YAJ Vol. 21. art. The Fallow Papers.
9   ibid
10 YAS Rec Ser Vol. VI.
11 Gill op cit.
12 YAS Rec Ser Vol. XLI.
13 YAS Rec Ser Vol XI p. 42.
14 YAS Rec Ser Vols. XIV and XXIV.

15 Cal. Pat. Rolls Edw. VI, Vol. III, p. 322; Ducatus Lancastriae, 1823-34.
16 Cal. Pat. Rolls, P. & Mary Vol. IV, p. 81.
17 Turton : History of the N. York Militia, 1907, p. 11.
18 Newburgh Priory Archives.
19 Newburgh Priory Archives.
20 Court Rolls in the possession of G.R. Drake, Esq., Easingwold.
21 N.R.Q.S.R. Vol. IV p. 260; NRQSR Vol. V. p. 231.
22 Turton: op cit, p. 173.
23 Surtees Soc. Vol. 77.
24 YAS Rec. Ser Vol. LX.
25 YAS Rec Ser Vol. IX p. 82
26 NRQSR Vol. IV p. 53.
27 Information given by Miss K. E. Knowles, Crayke.
28 NRQSR Vol. V. p. 110.
29 NRQSR Vol. IV pp. 253-4.
30 NRQSR Vol. V. p. 175.
31 ibid p. 184.
32 YAJ Vol. XXV.
33 NRQSR Vol. p. 193.
34 NRQSR Vol. VII p. 60.
35 Pubs, of the Catholic Record Society Vol. LIII p. 26. NRQSR Vol. 3 p. 207;
   Aveling: op. cit p. 412.
36 NRQSR Vol. IV p. 188.
37 YAJ Vol. XXXVI art, by Canon E. C. Hudson, M.A., F.S.A., — "A Yorkshire
   Country Parish 1676 — 1710."
38 NRQSR Vol. IV p. 124.
39 ibid p. 175.
40 NRQSR Vol. V, pp. 182, 189, 198 & 345.
41 ibid. p. 49.
42 ibid pp. 15 & 169.
43 NRQSR Vol IV p. 88.
44 Surtees Soc. Vol. XXXIII, pp. 134-5.
45 NRQSR Vol. 1, p. 60.
46 at p. 4.
47 NRQSR Vol. VII p. 45
48 Tawney & Power: Tudor Economic Documents Vol. I, p. 376.
49 NRQSR Vol. 1 p. 215.
50 NRQSR Vol. II p. 53.
51 NRQSR Vol. V. p. 119.
52 NRQSR Vol. 1 pp. 85-6.
53 Aveling op cit pp. 289-90.
54 NRQSR Vol. 2 p. 122.
55 NRQSR Vol. VI pp. 264-5.
56 NRQSR Vol. III p. 270.
57 Gent : History of Ripon, 1733, p. 149.
58 NRQSR Vol. III p. 28.
59 YAJ Vol. XIV, p. 115.
60 NRQSR Vol. IV p. 65.
61 Ibid pp. 89-90.
62 ibid p. 243.
63 ibid p. 25.
64 NRQSR
65 NRQSR Vol. III p. 275.
66 ibid pp. 177-8.
67 Surtees Soc Vol. 40.
68 NRQSR Vol. IV p. 182.
69 NRQSR Vol. VI p. 193.
70 NRQSR Vol. VII p. 117.
71 Boyne : Yorkshire Tokens, 1858.
72 NRQSR Vol. VII p. 157.
73 NRQSR Vol. V. p. 39.
74 ibid p. 59.
75 NRQSR Vol. V. p. 242.
76 ibid p. 241.
77 Criminal Chronology of York Castle, 1867, p. 28.
78 NRQSR Vol. V.
79 Gills Family Almanack, 1872.

III

EASINGWOLD IN THE 18th CENTURY

While an aerial view of the town in 1700 would show us more or less its present plan, without of course the twentieth century council estates or any of the development on Claypenny Hill, Crayke Road, Thirsk Road or Raskelf Road, the buildings, apart from the Parish Church, would probably be something of a surprise. Modern Easingwold is a pleasant town of mellowed brick, but very little of it dates back even to the mid-eighteenth century. The White House and some of the houses on the west side of the Market Place could be earlier and Allerton House in Uppleby is believed to be of similar, or even older, vintage, but the great majority of the streets were rebuilt in the nineteenth century. There is little evidence of the appearance of the previous houses. Old views or drawings seem to be non-existent. What little there is suggests that thatch was extensively used; that the structures were timber framed, the frame being filled with plaster or perhaps occasionally with brick and that the roofs were steeply pitched and not under drawn. The owner of a house at Easingwold sued her tenant in the Court Leet of 15th October, 1683, for removing the fir (deal) ceiling from "that pte betwixt the house & the parlor" as a tenant's fixture. Ceilings were not always found even in the 19th century. Gill in his "Vallis Eboracensis", published in 1852, states that "not a few" of these old thatched and timbered houses were then still in existence. Three examples survived into modern times - the "God with Us" house in Spring Street, pulled down in 1907; a house called Shepherd's Garth in Long Street, demolished in the 1940's; and a pair of houses on the south side of Uppleby, also demolished in the 1940's. In addition there appear to have been a number of brick built houses roofed with thatch, as for example' the "Blue Bell" Inn and the "Jolly Farmers" in Uppleby. Accounts of the expenses relating to the property of the Darleys of Aldby Park at Easingwold in the period 1748-1757 refer to bricks, timber, laths, plaster, thatch and tiles as building materials. Brick construction is very old in the district - Stocking House near Crayke, Huby Old Hall

and a dilapidated house at the rear of the "Black Bull" at Raskelf
seem to be seventeenth century examples. It is perhaps therefore
a fair inference that the town of Easingwold in 1700 was mainly
thatched and timbered, with a number of brick structures interspersed. The number of the latter would increase steadily as the
century progressed.

The Old Hall, or Archdeaconry Manor House, then let to
Thomas Raines, was very old, probably partly medieval, and
perhaps of mixed stone and brick construction. The house seems
to have been irregular with several wings, a parapet and a court
on the east or south-east side. The dining room was panelled in
painted black oak. The Driffields probably did a good deal to the
house in Elizabethan or Jacobean times and may have laid out
the walled garden known as "the Paradise". There was a curved
entrance drive of pine trees and a fish pond which in the 19th
century at any rate was L-shaped with the long arm running
from east to west and the short arm southwards from the west
end of the long arm. It appears to have been on the north side
of the Old Hall and was fed by a spring in the adjoining field.
The Old Hall itself was demolished in 1826, but the fish pond
survived till 1879, as probably did the remains of the garden.
Gill's account in "Vallis Eboracensis" (1852) is somewhat con-
fusing — he appears, for example, to refer to more than one fish
pond and to a moat. He also describes an island with a dovecot
and says that a double row of pines formed "a rich and shady
bower" round the fish pond which existed in his time. There may also
have been a bathing house belonging to the Old Hall since
Baines's Directory of 1823[1] states that Easingwold then possessed
several chalybeate springs of which the principal supplied the
reservoir of "a neat little bathing house". The spring which fed
the fish pond was in fact reputed to be medicinal and was said
to resemble the Cheltenham waters. Thomas Raines, the occupier of the
Old Hall, had taken an assignment of the lease of the Archdeaconry manor from Towers Driffield about 1688, the year of
his removal by James II from the office of Lord Mayor of York.
He was born about 1640 and seems to have lived at one time at
Appleton-le-Street[2] and to have practised as an attorney. His
removal in 1688 was for refusal to support the King's policy. He
became paralysed from about 1703 and in 1705 sub-let the manor
house to his niece Anne, daughter of his brother John Raines,
also of Easingwold, and her husband William Salvin (1662-1726).
The remainder of the manor, including the tithes of Raskelf and

Cold Kirby, had already been sub-let to Sir William Foulis, Bart. of Ingleby Manor, in 1704. A Protestant himself, Thomas Raines had a Roman Catholic wife.[3]

Three generations of the Salvin family lived at the Old Hall. William Salvin's family estate was at Newbiggin, near Whitby, and he was a Roman Catholic of an old Royalist family. He married Anne Raines in 1702 and died in 1726. His son Thomas (1703-65) succeeded him. In 1733-4 we find him taking the waters among the fashionables of Scarborough, presumably as an eligible bachelor.[4] It was not until 1740 that he married Mary the daughter and heiress of Edward Talbot of Hampstead.[5] Also a Roman Catholic, he allowed his friend Anne Harrison (c. 1665-1745), who kept the "Blue Bell" in Uppleby and was well known by the nickname of "Nanna Randan", to use his pew in the parish church, described as "the chief seat". She left him a silver tumbler and requested him to write her epitaph, which he did in such terms as to make her tombstone famous. Thomas Salvin sold the Newbiggin property of the family in 1736.[6]

His eldest daughter Mary married Sir John Webb of Odstock, Wilts, 5th Baronet, a Roman Catholic and one of the largest landowners in England. He was among other things, lord of the manor of Raskelf, which he left to an illegitimate son James Webb, in default of legitimate male issue.[7]

In 1765 the only son and heir, also called Thomas Salvin, succeeded to the Easingwold estate and in 1790 was one of the parties to an indenture relating to the Old Hall and the Archdeaconry Manor. He is described as an officer "in the Imperial Service", that is in the Austrian army. An English papist who wished to follow a military career seems to have had the choice of the French, Spanish or Austrian armies, the last being generally preferable for loyal subjects.[8] The history of the Archdeaconry manor during the 18th century is not fully clear, but the leasehold interest probably descended from Raines in 1713 to William Salvin, in 1726 to Thomas Salvin senior and in 1765 to Thomas Salvin junior. About 1734 there seems to have been a sublease of the manor to Edward Trotter of Skelton Castle, though this did not affect the occupation of the Old Hall by the Salvins. Francis Goulton of Highthorne was steward till his death in 1737 when his son Christopher took over. When Thomas Salvin senior died in 1765 the lordship vested jointly in Thomas Salvin junior and William Chapman, trustees of the elder Thomas's will. Chapman also acted as steward. They were still joint lords and Chapman was still steward in 1770, but by December, 1777, it appears that there had been a sublease to Allen Swainston and Thomas Swann, which subsisted until at least November, 1786. John Carter was steward in 1777 and William Lockwood from 1783. There were two William Lockwoods, father and son, both attorneys in the town, and the stewardship passed from father to son, probably about 1836, the date of the elder Lockwood's death. It rather looks as if the document executed by Thomas Salvin junior in 1790 may have been an assignment of the headlease from the Bishop of Chester since at the court of 9th November, 1791, the lords are named as William Lodge Rociffe, George Clarke, and Sir John Lawson Bart, and they remained lords until Sir John's death between 1811 and 1814.

The lease of the Old Hall appears to have become vested about the end of the century in Peter Bell, Esquire, who married Mary Salvin, daughter of Thomas Salvin junior. Mr. Bell sublet for a time to Sir William Vavasour, who seems to have occupied the Old Hall during his term.

The windmill at the top of Church Hill was still in working order at the beginning of the 18th century. It seems to have been part of the Archdeaconry Manor since Thomas Raines made an agreement with his son-in-law William Salvin, by which the latter undertook to keep in good repair the mill, millstones, sails and cloths.[9]

The parish church at this time had a much lower chancel, low pitched in the same manner as the nave. The walls were probably still plastered and lime washed internally as they had been in Tudor times. Some reconstruction of the chancel roof had been carried out in 1667 and one of the beams bears this date. It is not clear whether the nave and chancel were ceiled below the beams in the eighteenth century. There is a reference in the churchwardens accounts to the "quire" being underdrawn in 1827. Both nave and chancel appear to have been underdrawn at the time of the 1858 restoration. There was a south porch in 1630 and this, or another of similar construction, probably survived until the church was extensively restored in 1858. The porch removed in 1858 was smaller and lower than the present one and left room for a two light window in the wall above it. There would be a clock and bells in 1700. We know of the pew belonging to Thomas Salvin senior in the first half of the 18th century and since one would hardly expect a Roman Catholic family to go to the expense of making a pew in a Protestant church it seems probable that this had been made for Thomas Raines or even for one of the Driffields, the previous lessees of the Archdeaconry manor. There were no doubt other pews in the church, too, at the date of Anne Harrison's will (30th May, 1739), otherwise she would not have described Mr. Salvin's as "the Cheif Seat in the Church". The curate and churchwardens gave permission for a new pew on 1st December, 1746, and this was enlarged on 28th April, 1761, apparently by faculty. Some of the seating in the church in early Georgian times may have consisted of backless benches, since Gill writing in the mid-19th century referred to the "original open seats".[10]

There appears to have been more than one gallery in 1764, when a conveyance was made of a quarter share of a seat or pew in the gallery called the New Gallery. A faculty was granted for the building of a gallery in the parish church on 26th July, 1771.[11] One of the 18th century galleries seems to have been over the chancel arch, and we know that a north gallery was removed in 1858, when a west gallery was also rebuilt. There was certainly a west gallery in 1803, when the new organ was placed in it, no doubt because it was the gallery where the singers were seated.

There is no mention of stained glass prior to 1858 and it is unlikely that there was any. Box pews seem to have appeared in increasing numbers throughout the 18th century and were probably very similar to those still surviving in Sheriff Hutton church. Some wood from the old box pews seems to have been reused for partitioning underneath the new pews installed in 1858. If this was in fact the case some at least of the box pews were stained a rather hideous light umber.

An early seventeenth century communion table stood at the east end of the chancel.

So far as minor furniture is concerned the churchwardens paid twelve guineas in 1786 for two benefaction tables. A local joiner in 1803 varnished what he called "Moses and Aron and the 10 Commandments with a Mehogney Bord and Inscripton over the Poorbox". This probably refers to two things — a picture of Moses and Aaron holding tables on which are painted the Ten Commandments, and a board over the poorbox containing an inscription.

There do not appear to have been any wall monuments inside the church until that of Thomas Raines was put up following his death in 1713. This was described in the mid-19th century as on the north side of the communion table,[12] which ought to mean on the north wall of the chancel, though a photograph taken prior to 1902 shows it on the east wall of the chancel between the east window and the Yates monument. It may have been moved to that position in 1858. It is now in the north aisle at the west end. Raines's ledger stone was originally in the chancel floor, but was moved, probably in 1858. In 1737 an enclosure was made at the west end of the south aisle to contain the two altar tombs of the Rev. Thos. Prance, vicar, and Elizabeth his wife who both died in that year. These also appear to have been moved in 1858.

A vestry meeting of thirty parishioners on 15th January, 1788, decided by a majority of fourteen to purchase five new bells. These were made by Dalton of York and hung the same year.

The churchyard in 1700 was a fairly compact rough oval of ground round the church, less than half the size of the present churchyard. It would almost certainly present a much more open appearance than at present, since tombstones were still not particularly common. Instead graves might be marked by boards. Tombstones became commoner as the century progressed and there is a mid-18th century group on the south side of the church, including that of "Nanna Randan". There is evidence to suggest that some of the stones were painted or that at any rate that the letters were picked out in black.

The Market Place contained in addition to the Tolbooth and possibly some other buildings or structures near it, including the butchers shambles, what Gill in 1852 described as "the steps and base of a market cross of large dimensions". The old "cucking stool" still stood on the north side of the Market Place by a group of cottages roughly on the site of the present Midland Bank. These were known as "the Squad" and certainly existed in 1763. In that year Peggy Johnson, who lived in the Squad, was put in the stool and ducked in the beck, being the last person to undergo this punishment. Somewhere near to the stool was at one time the town pinfold and a lock up. Stocks existed in 1852, also on the north side of the Market Place, though they had apparently once been on the south-east side of the Market Cross, together with a whipping post.[13]

George Hall's grants of the market rights and the market ground had by 1728 become vested in the Darleys of Aldby Park and remained so vested in 1758. Their agent's accounts contain items from 1749 to 1751 for work done on the Shambles, but this was probably a rebuilding — indeed the last of these payments specifically refers to rebuilding. In 1755 work was done on the Tolbooth to put it in proper repair for the holding of Quarter Sessions. It seems probable that the Darleys sold their Easingwold property in 1758.

The present Old Vicarage in the north west corner of the Market Place replaces a previous vicarage on the same site. The latter was described in 1760 as "old built, but in good repair, with a barn, stable, garden & orchard on the west, a little garden or court in front and a little croft west of the orchard". It was destroyed by fire in 1770 and the foundation stone of the new house was laid on 5th June, 1771.

Inns and alehouses (certainly the latter) no doubt existed in the town before the 18th century — those kept by members of the Driffield family have been mentioned above — but the first one to which a name can be put seems to be the "Blue Bell" in Uppleby, which may have been so named because it was a house of call for Scottish drovers. This was kept by Anne Harrison who has been mentioned above. Her epitaph, composed by Thomas Salvin senior, implies that she had a temper, a tongue and a ready fist, but a kind heart:-

> S. M.
> Anne Harrison
> Well known by the name of
> Nana Ran Dan
> Who was chaste but no prude
> and tho' free yet no harlot
> by principle Virtuous
> by Education a protestant
> her freedom made her Lyable
> to censure whilst her extensive
> Charity made her esteemed.
> Her tongue and her hands were
> ungovernable, but the rest of her
> members she kept in subjection.
> After a life of 80 years thus
> Spent she died Novr. 15th 1745
> Passenger
> Weigh her virtues be charitable
> and speak well of her.

In 1753 there was an inn at Easingwold called "the Duke of Marlborough's Head", which may well have been the town's principal inn, since the first meeting of the trustees of the new turnpike road from York to Northallerton was to be held there. Twenty-six persons are named in the parish registers as innkeepers in the period 1739-65 and a directory of 1790 names thirteen.[14] Five of the thirteen are named as having another trade, and these probably kept the smaller alehouses. The principal inns in 1776 were the Rose and Crown and the New Inn.[15] The Rose and Crown, later the Old Rose and Crown, seems to have been the present Nos. 83-7, Long Street. The Angel appears to have been licensed at least as early as 1797, and the Old White House on the Thirsk road as early as 1786.

In 1700 there was no clear dividing line between a shop and a private house and while plenty of people in Easingwold practised a trade or bought and sold they probably did so in their own houses with merely a few minor adaptations. Many of the trades-people would sell in the weekly market, either from carts or stands or simply putting their wares on the ground.

The streets must have been largely unmetalled except possibly for some cobbled areas. There was a pavement of some kind in part of the Market Place in the mid-17th century.

The era of the modern highway in the district begins in 1753 with the Act for improving and maintaining the roads from Northallerton to York and from Topcliffe to Thirsk. The trustees appointed under the Act were empowered to charge tolls which were set out in detail, erect turnpike gates and milestones and to widen the road, for which latter purpose they might make com-pulsory purchases. There was exemption from toll for manures, hay, corn, farm implements, cattle moving to and from pasture, church-goers, funerals, soldiers' horses and baggage, post-horses, and horses, carts and wagons travelling with vagrants sent by passes to their place of settlement. There was a special exemption for voters travelling to York on county election days.

The York-Northallerton Trust was renewed in 1778 (18 Geo. III, c. 92), 1794 (34 Geo III, c. 118), 1808 (48 Geo III, c. 7) and 1830 (11 Geo IV, c. 4). It was subsequently kept in being by the successive annual Turnpike Acts Continuance Acts until 1875, when it was wound up (37 & 38 Vict. c. 95., sched. 7)[16]

A tollgate is shown across York Road on Jefferys map of Yorkshire of 1772 at about the entrance to the present Grammar and Modern School. The enclosure award map of 1812 does not show this bar, but instead one across the end of the Stillington road and not in the turnpike itself, what in fact was known as a side bar. In 1772 the next gates on either side were at Rawcliffe and at Stockhill or Stockwell Green, near Thirkieby, respectively. In 1824 the gates were Purgatory Bar, Stockhill Green Bar, Easingwold Town-end Bar, Shires Bar and Skelton Bar. At that date (28th February, 1824) they were let as follows:- Purgatory Bar £330; Stockhill Green Bar, with the weighing engine £584; Shires Bar and Easingwold Town-end Bar £519. 10s. 0d.; and Skelton Bar £650. The trustees gave notice that they would meet on 23rd March, 1824, at one of the Thirsk inns to let the tolls by auction for three years from 24th June, 1824, or for some other agreed term. Purgatory Bar takes its name from a close called Purgatory at Thornton-le-Beans. Shires Bar, mentioned in the Parish registers in 1799, was a later addition, probably made when Easingwold Town-end Bar was changed to a side bar, which could have been under the renewal Act of 1794. It was across York Road, half way between Shires Manor House and Low Shires, with a small gatehouse on the east side. It was perhaps designed to catch traffic by-passing Easingwold by way of Crankley and Knott Lanes.

Persons paying toll at turnpike gates often did so to pass not only the immediate gate, but several gates ahead. A small printed ticket, showing the gate of issue and the gate to which toll was paid, completed by hand with the date and initials of the gatekeeper, was generally used. Tolls were normally let by trustees on condition that the renters were not to take more than a specified number of tolls for the whole line. This might also be specified in the Act. Where a person hired a postchaise or travelled post in his own carriage using hired horses, the custom on many roads seems to have been for the postboy to pay the toll on the way back with the chaise or post horses, having recovered it from the hirer at their destination. This could place a postboy in difficulties if the hirer disputed the charge and refused to pay. Exactly this happened to a postboy on the Doncaster and Selby Turnpike in 1840 when Lady Feversham and the Honorable Mr. Duncombe, travelling post in Lady Feversham's carriage, refused to pay the toll for one of the bars, and the unfortunate postboy found himself served with a summons to appear before the Doncaster magistrates in consequence.[17]

The turnpike trusts in the district do seem to have produced reasonably good main roads, especially after Mr. MacAdam's method of construction, used by him on Leeming Lane, was applied. A writer of 1829[18] states that: "The turnpike roads in this

85

(the North) riding are generally good, but many of the parochial roads are in a very bad state, especially in that part of the Vale of York which lies between the Western-end of the Howardian Hills and the River Ouse; and still more in Ryedale where the soil is deep, the country wet, and good materials are at a considerable distance

Posting services were in operation in 1776 on the York-Northallerton road at rates of 3d. a mile for a post horse, 9d. a mile for a post chaise and 1/3d, a mile for a four horse chaise. The only stage coach through the town at that time was the Newcastle Fly, which left the George at York on Mondays, Wednesdays, and Fridays at 3.00 a.m. for the Cock at Newcastle. The full journey took a day and cost a guinea.[19] In 1784 a coach called the Newcastle and Edinburgh Diligence set out daily (Sundays excepted) from the George in Coney Street, York, at 4.00 a.m. The fare from York to Newcastle was 24/- and from Newcastle to Edinburgh 38/-. This could be the direct descendent of the Newcastle Fly of 1776.[20] It was still running in 1785, though the Newcastle to Edinbtirgh fare was down to 33/-.[21] This was possibly due to the commencement of the Edinburgh Mail Coach. The Mail started to run on the second Monday in November, 1785, at first through Leeds. After two or three months it was transferred to the York-Easingwold route to which it adhered till 1841, except for two years from 6th May, 1825, to 6th May, 1827, when it ran through Boroughbridge. Other coaches may have been more dashing or highly coloured and their "swell dragsmen" more spectacular, but nothing exceeded the sober magnificence of the Mails in their royal livery of black and maroon with the cipher of the sovereign in gold on the front boot and the stars of the four great orders of chivalry on the upper panels. The guards in their top hats and long red coats with blue collars and gold lace were perhaps the most eye-catching feature of the turn out.

In 1790 the north bound Mail passed through Easingwold about 2.00 am, and the south bound between 7.00 and 8.00 p.m. The inside fare from Easingwold to London at that date was £3. 7s. 0d., the outside £1. 13s. 6d. An independent London-Edinburgh coach, the Highflyer, came onto the road in 1788. This was considerably cheaper, the inside fare to London being £2. 14s. 0d. and the outside £1. 7s. 0d. It was forwarded to London alternately from the two principal inns, the excise office (i.e. the New Inn) and the Rose and Crown.

Although by this time coach travel was reasonably safe and speedy a journey of any length was still an adventure and a Husthwaite man who went to London on the Highflyer, probably in the early years of the nineteenth century, made his will at Easingwold before leaving.

The carriage of goods by road also increased considerably by the end of the century. In 1784 there were two carriers from Easingwold to York, one of them, Thomas Crawford, offering carriers services from the Black Bull in Thursday Market York, to Newcastle, Darlington, Durham and Edinburgh. In 1790 he met the London waggon on its arrival at York on Tuesdays and collected goods from it. He delivered goods to it on Thursdays prior to its return to London on Fridays.[22] He was still carrying to the Black Bull on three days a week in about 1802, at which time another Easingwold carrier was working to the White Swan in Goodramgate on two days a week.[23]

York was an important centre for water traffic, both coastal and inland and at any rate by 1784 large quantities of butter and bacon from Easingwold were carried to London by coaster. This traffic may well have started at a much earlier date. In 1784 there were three lines of coasters sailing to London every seven or eight days. Goods could be forwarded on the Gainsborough Sloop at about three weekly intervals, to Rotherham, Leeds, Halifax and Wakefield fortnightly, and to Boroughbridge, Ripon, Howden, Selby and Cawood every Saturday.[24]

The country outside Easingwold in 1700 was no doubt considerably more enclosed than a century earlier. In particular large tracts of the Forest of Galtres were enclosed in the 1640's and a number of farmhouses built in the formerly "empty quarter" between Easingwold, Huby, Alne, Tollerton and Shipton. The townships of Crayke, Oulston, Thornton-cum-Baxby and large parts of Thormanby and Raskelf seem to have been enclosed by 1700, apparently by agreement. A good deal of piecemeal enclosure of land formerly in the town fields at Easingwold had already been done and more would be done as the century progressed. Examples of such old enclosures are Dadman Ing in the Pease Lands and Kittlecount or Kittle Cant in the Toft Ings, which both existed in 1625. Closes existing at the end of the 18th century were numerous and included such picturesquely named fields as Button Wits, Vineyard, Dog Stiles, Purtenance Close, Nova Scotia, Chase Garth, Paradise, White Cakes, and Chancery Closes. Hopwith Carrs and Paulin Carrs were part of the old forest lands. Lady Carr and the Hurns were Jacobean enclosures and the Hall Reins and the Haverthwaites were probably also ancient. Acts of Parliament empowering large scale enclosure were obtained for Slingsby in 1755 (28 Geo II c. 25); Sutton-on Forest in 1756 (29 Geo II, c. 61); Newton Moor, Beningbrough, in 1758 (31 Geo II c. 26); Stillington in 1766 (6 Geo III c. 16); Sheriff Hutton in 1769 (9 Geo III c. 53); Terrington in 1772 (12 Geo III c. 102); Stonegrave and West Ness in 1776 (16 Geo III c. 66); Bulmer in 1777 (17 Geo III, c. 126); Thormanby Carr in 1782 (22 Geo III c. 20); Bagby Moor in 1788 (28 Geo III c. 40); Linton in 1790 (30 Geo III c. 2); and Thirsk in 1793 (33 Geo III c. 99). Agriculture was being gradually moderised.

The Easingwold court leet of course continued to regulate the open fields and common lands as long as these survived. At the Michaelmas Court in 1748 David Cass had to pay 1/- for "hens and cocks in ye field", John Foster 5/- for "his sheep going in ye Lanes all summer" and William Harrison junior 1/6d. for his "sew and piggs Dammiging his Neighbours". Several persons had to pay 2d. each for failing to scour their Rutland Sike ends (apparently a ditch maintenance obligation). At the October Court in 1749 there were fines for a man failing to ditch his Long Stone land (2d.); for not ringing swine and also for not mending a field hedge (1/6d.); for trespass on the field (i.e. one of the town fields) with swine (1/-); for a similar offence with cows (2/-); and with horses (6d.). A man turning a horse into the field was fined 6d. and another turning in sheep 2/6d. Thomas Salvin, Esquire, was fined 2/- for his horses trespassing in the fields. A man was fined 1/6d. for having his "Holscare" (Hows Carr) headland "over broad". Another had to pay 6d. for not ditching his Oxmoor Close. On 7th June, 1750, John Blades was fined 3d. for stopping the water (course) in "penicar" (Penny Carr). Fines at the court of 22nd November, 1750. included 1/8d. for breaking the common pound; and 6d. on Thomas Salvin for leading hay out of the corn field before St. James's Day.

In the early 19th century this was considered a district of small farms and a rating valuation of the township made in 1797 by George Stephenson, the Vestry Clerk, fully bears this out. Parcels referred to by him as farms include Moor Farm (50 acres); Crankley Farm (40 acres); Dawney Bridge Farm (60 acres); Rising Sun Farm (60 acres); Cock Farm (30 acres 3 roods); Haverwits Farm (63 acres); Hanover House (72 acres); Brier Banks (land and house) (22 acres 3 roods 20 perches); Blake

Stile Farm (40 acres); White House Farm (33 acres 2 roods); New White House Farm (31 acres 1 rood) and Lund Farm (58 acres). On the other hand the farms on the forest lands enclosed in the 1640's are four and five times as large as these — Shires (202.3.20); Hawkhills Farm (173.0.20); another Hawkhills Farm (280.3.0); Hollings Grove (236.3.20); Demains Farm (211.1.0); Moss Ends (236.1.20); Dodholme Woods (206.1.20); another farm at Dodholme Woods (256.3.0); and Fawdington Lodge (294.1.20).

The stock and equipment of a small farm were perhaps similar to that listed in a Bill of Sale given by a Brafferton farmer in 1785 to secure a loan of £50 and in return for a guarantee of the rent of the farm. The security consisted of the farm itself, the crops of corn, hay, "turneps", potatoes and "other grain" during the term, together with eight sheep, twenty-two pigs, four horses, eight cows, one bull, two stirks, four calves, eighteen geese, one cart, two pairs of harrows "with the gear", household furniture and utensils of husbandry. He probably borrowed or hired a plough since none is mentioned. This man could have farmed land scattered in common fields (the town fields of Brafferton were enclosed under an Act of 1809)[25] and not a consolidated holding, which would possibly make a difference.

Of the outlying farms of Easingwold, a Lund House is referred to as far back as 1639. This was probably not on the moor itself, since Jeffery's map of 1772 shows no house there. William Bland lived at "Lesmire house" in the period 1685-7. A William Bland who could be the same man, was living at "Haverthwaite" in 1697. "Haver-white-house" (Haverwits House) is mentioned in 1718. At that time and until the late 19th century there was no direct road from Easingwold to Crayke. A vehicle had to go along Binsley Lane or Stillington Road. There was a footpath through the Crayke Field which came out onto Daffy Lane on the south side of Halfway House. One of the common roads of the Crayke Field led from a gate at the top of Uppleby to Haverwits House, by a rather winding route. The name Haverwits is a corruption of Haverthwaites, meaning "oat clearings".

A house at "the How Hill" existed in 1722, perhaps near the present Hanover House. "The Shares House", mentioned in 1720, seems to be a house at the Shires. There was a house at White Houses in James I's reign. Blake Stiles is named in the parish registers in 1742. Jeffery's map of 1772 shows "Hawkwell's

Farm" at Hawkhills and "Shire House", and also apparently the house on Alne road, which was licensed in the 19th century as the "Travellers Rest"; Crankley House; Crown Hall (a house on or near the site of the present Briggfield); and Providence Cottage. The parish registers mention Baldrence in 1782 and Ox Moor House in 1788.

The district was and is primarily agricultural, though quarrying to the north and east and brickmaking to the south and west have a long tradition. There is some low grade coal, which was worked in Coxwold parish about 1815, though unsuccessfully. More serious working appears to have been carried on at Ampleforth in the reign of Henry VIII and colliers horses passing through the Forest of Galtres paid a fee of 2d. each to the Clerk of the Forest. A work of 1859 states: "Seams of coal which is heavy, sulphureous and burns entirely away to white ashes, are wrought in different parts of both the Eastern and Western Moorlands, at Gilling Moor on the Howardian Hills and in the Vale of York between Easingwold and Thirsk".[26] Working of coal between Easingwold and Thirsk is also referred to in 1829, but the quantity was small and the quality bad.[27] Ironstone with about 40% of metal is said to have been found at Coxwold, but it was not a commercial proposition.

In 1743 the Vicar of Easingwold estimated that he had 500 possible communicants. The census figure for 1801 was 1,467 so that at the beginning of the previous century there may have been between 900 and 1,000 people in the town. This gives an increase of 500 or so during the 18th century which seems conservative as there was an increase of very nearly that order between 1801 and 1821, to 1,912. It is fairly clear that from 1790 to 1830 or thereabouts, that is during the period of coach travel, the town enjoyed great prosperity and expanded rapidly and no doubt the population did the same. This was partly because of a rapidly increasing birth rate, partly because the town was attracting outsiders. In 1806 there were 272 houses, so that in 1700 there were perhaps 200 or less.[28]

In 1700 Thomas, second Viscount Fauconberg, died without male issue and was succeeded as third viscount by his nephew Thomas, who thus became lord of the manor of Easingwold and Huby. He was a Roman Catholic, but his son Thomas, fourth Viscount, conformed to the established church and in 1756 was created Earl Fauconberg. Earl Thomas's son Henry succeeded to the earldom and the estate. He was Lord Lieutenant and Custos

Rotulorum of the North Riding from 6th February. 1778, Lord of the Bedchamber to George III and Colonel of the North York Militia from about 1779. The lordship of the Manor thus descended through the first to the second Earl who held it during the remainder of the century.

Andrew Wilson, who had been inducted vicar in 1685, was succeeeded on 18th December, 1712 by Richard Musgrave. He seems to be the vicar of that name who was instituted to Stillington on 11th July, 1718. This fits in with the institution of the next vicar of Easingwold, Thomas Prance, on 22nd July, 1718. Mr. Prance and his wife both died in 1737 and were buried at the west end of the church.

George Thomson, appointed parish clerk about 1700, held the office for nearly thirty-three years. He was buried on 3rd August, 1733, and the vicar chose as his successor William Carter junior, who was clerk for sixty-one years, till his death in 1795.

Mr. Prance was succeeded by Radcliffe Russel, instituted on 4th April, 1738. The son of William Russel of Preston, Lancashire, Radcliffe Russel had been matriculated at Brasenose College, Oxford, on 8th March 1728 at the age of seventeen.[29] He was ordained deacon at Chester on 21st September, 1735, and priest at the same place on 15th January, 1737. He never seems to have resided at Easingwold, at any rate after the first six months. Archbishop Blackburn granted him a dispensation and in 1743 and probably earlier he was living at Manchester, where he was, as he put it, "entrusted with ye Education of a few Young Gentlemen". He married the daughter of the Rev. Jacob Scholes, Curate of Prestwich, on 3rd January, 1748.[30] He died at his house in Manchester in March, 1771, and is buried at Prestwich. His obituary in the "Manchester Mercury" of 28th March, 1771, describes him as "Chaplain to the late Duke of Buccleugh". His only daughter married the Rev. Samuel Hall, M.A., Curate of St. Ann's Church, Manchester, and then first rector of St. Peter's Church, Manchester.[31] Among Mr. Russel's pupils was Charles White, a founder of the Manchester Royal Infirmary.[32]

Parish records show other clergymen taking duties at Easingwold from 18th October, 1738. On 14th January, 1739, John Addison started to take duties and on 12th April, 1740, he was formally licensed to the cure, which he served for the next twenty years. He was a Bachelor of Arts and may have been the John

Addison of Queen's College, Oxford, who took his bachelor's degree on 7th March, 1731. At all events Mr. Addison was ordained deacon on 4th June, 1732, and priest on 12th August, 1733, in both cases at Chester. Mr. Russel in 1743 allowed him a stipend of £35 per annum, which was probably not unreasonable' for the period. In 1827 there were still apparently fifty-nine curates with annual incomes between £20 and £30, and six with incomes between £10 and £20. At any rate Mr. Addison was better off than Henry Bird, curate of Brandsby in 1743, who had only £25 per annum allowed him by the incumbent, the vicar of Terrington, and had to live in a house a mile from the church since the incumbent had let the parsonage house to Mr. Cholmeley, a Roman Catholic, who had sublet it to another Roman Catholic. He persuaded a number of the parishioners to sign a petition to the Archbishop that the latter should use his influence with the incumbent to raise Mr. Bird's stipend. Asked to comment, the incumbent wrote to the Archbishop, deprecating his curate's' "low proceeding in inveigling the Parishioners to sign a petition to yr. Grace to augment his sallary" and explaining that the value of the living of Brandsby had been over estimated and moreover he himself had a wife and six children!

John Armitstead (c. 1735-16.7.1812) was Mr. Russel's curate from September, 1760, the gap left by Mr. Addison having been temporarily filled by the Rev. John Nesfield, Rector of Thormanby. On 8th January, 1771, not long before Mr. Russel's death, Mr. Armitstead was inducted to the vicarage of Easingwold. He was licensed to the cure of Raskelf at about the same time, or perhaps a little before. Though a chapelry of Easingwold, Raskelf was served from 1730 to about 1761 by Mr. Nesfield, who in fact became its curate the day after he was ordained priest at York, some five years before his institution to Thormanby. The Rev. Isaac Wilson, later vicar of Brafferton, seems to have served Raskelf from about 1761 to 1771. After Mr. Armitstead's death in 1812 the Bishop of Chester presented to Raskelf as a separate benefice and it so remained until its reunion with Easingwold in 1951.

The Rev. James Wilson is described as curate of Easingwold in 1790 and 1791 and the Rev. Thos Hayes from the end of November 1805 to the end of December, 1812. In addition the Rev. Richard Barton. Master of the Westerman School at Easingwold, was taking duties at Raskelf in 1811 and 1812. All these may in fact have been assistant curates.

A glebe terrier of 10th September, 1760, lists the property at that time as consisting of the vicarage house; the glebe lands, one large close divided into four, containing about 11 acres; all the small tithes, with the tithes of wool and lamb in the chapelry of Raskelf; the statutory fees for mortuaries; Easter offerings being 2d. from each communicant; and fees as follows:- for publishing banns 1/-, for marriage by banns 3/-, for marriage by licence 10/-, for consulting the register 4d., for a certificate 1/-, for churching 8d., for burying, the office with a psalm, 2/6d., and for the office without a psalm 1/-.

Easingwold never seems to have been much of a Quaker centre, though in 1689 there were meeting houses at Crayke, Stillington, Huby, Sutton-on-Forest, Sheriff Hutton, Stittenham, another in Sheriff Hutton parish, one near Ampleforth and one at Wildon Grange.[33] It is true that in 15th July, 1707, the house of Joseph Shipheard at Easingwold was licensed for meetings of the Society, but in 1743 there was only one Quaker family in the town and on 6th September, 1768, Jonas the son, and Mary (aged 9) and Ann (aged 8), the daughters of James Shepherd, Quaker, were baptised into the Church of England.

The town's first sight of a Methodist seems to have been in 1744, when John Nelson was brought through under escort after being pressed for the army. He recorded that many people came to stare at him and that he was visited by "the head man of the town a professed Papist", of whom he nevertheless formed a good, opinion, despite his religion and gold lace. This would be Thomas Salvin senior. He seems to have treated Nelson with sympathy, giving him money for his immediate needs. Nelson is said to have preached outside the Old Rose and Crown Inn.

Methodism was first regularly preached in the town about 1763. Meetings were held for a year or so at Blayds House on the Stillington road and then at the house of John Skaife. There was much local opposition in the early years, most of it violent. Skaife had his doors and windows broken and had difficulty in getting redress from the local magistrates. Richard Birdsall, a local preacher, who was born in 1735 at Kirby Onslow, was attacked while riding through the town by men armed with 'pitchforks.[34] John Wesley himself is said to have been pelted with sods and other missiles at Easingwold. He first visited the town in 1770, when he preached at Mr. Skaife's house, and two or three years later, when he preached under an oak, or some say an apple tree, in a garden in Uppleby, traditionally a garden adjoining

"The Mount". He had the satisfaction of preaching on 8th May. 1786, in a new chapel completed earlier in the year on the site of the present Methodist Chapel in Chapel Street. Robert Spence, the son of a Stillington blacksmith, who became a leading trades-man in York, was an early Methodist local preacher in the district and John Foster of Easingwold, named in the parish registers in 1799 as a travelling preacher, may well have been another. He was a native of Weardale, Co. Durham, and married the daughter of a Pickering innkeeper.

As already mentioned the Salvins were an old Roman Catholic family. In 1735 there were eleven Roman Catholics in the town. There was then no priest or mass-house, but in 1741 Thomas Salvin senior had a chaplain, the Franciscan Fr. Yates, and from 1743 to 1754 Dom. William Hardesty, O.S.B. In 1745 Mr. Salvin had a Mr. Gordon, a Franciscan, living with him.[35]

There were quite a number of Roman Catholic centres in the district. The third viscount Fauconberg died a papist in 1718 in the guesthouse of the English Benedictine convent at Brussels. The fourth viscount was educated in the school of the English Benedictines at Dieulouard in Lorraine. He conformed to the established church in 1734, though his wife and daughter remained Catholics. In 1735 there were still a chaplain and a mass room at Newburgh Priory.[36] It was probably replaced by the Oulston chapel mentioned below. There were Roman Catholic chaplains at the same date at Brandsby Hall and Gilling Castle. The 9th Viscount Fairfax kept a Benedictine priest from about 1743 to 1750 and had his daughters educated at the English Bene-dictine convent at Courtrai. In 1741 there was a "Popish Chapel" at Oulston, served by a secular priest, who was chaplain to Lady Catherine Fauconberg, wife of the fourth viscount. This chapel was rebuilt or replaced by Lady Mary Fauconberg about 1760. From that date, if not earlier, it stood about midway along the south side of Oulston Green. The building was still in existence in 1857, but had been replaced by the Roman Catholic Church at Easingwold from the end of 1833. There was a Roman Catholic Chapel at Crayke in the latter part of the 18th century. In 1794 its priest was chaplain to F. Cholmley, Esquire, of Brandsby Hall.

The Jacobite movement, coming to a head in the rebellions of 1715 and 1745, kept alive the official repression of Roman Catholics, but with the decline of the movement in the 1760's concessions could be made and in 1778 and 1779 Catholic Relief

Acts were passed. An immediate result in most places in the district seems to have been a sharp rise in the number of declared papists. Whereas Easingwold in 1760 had only five, in 1780 there were twenty-four.[37] A further Relief Act of 1791 freed Roman Catholics, who took the oath of allegiance from disabilities relating to education, property holding and the practice of the law. One who quickly availed himself of this Act was William Smallpage of Easingwold, butcher, who took the oath at York Castle on 11th August, 1791. Complete equality for Roman Catholics eventually came in 1829.

In 1700 education at Easingwold was still a matter for private enterprise. Schoolmasters of the early years were Thomas Chester (died 1701) and Thomas Bowman (named in 1704). These men no doubt kept a school or schools where for small fees they taught the rudiments of an education. They were businessmen. The earliest charitable bequest for education was that of Thomas Raines, who died in 1713. He left money for teaching five poor children to be named by his niece Salvin or her heirs, or in default by the master. This must have been intended to pay the fees of an existing school. It was certainly not in itself the foundation of a school, there being, for example, no provision for a master's salary. Mr. Raines's gift and two later ones, those of William Kitchen in 1761 for teaching one poor boy and William Driffield's in 1778 for teaching four poor children to read, write and sew, together provided for the education of ten children. The school at which this was given appears to have been known by 1790 at any rate as "the Free School". In that year John Harrison was its usher. The master may have been the Rev. James Wilson, Curate of Easingwold, or John Skelton, the son of a cooper from Wrelton, near Pickering, who is known to have taught at Easingwold during the period 1776-1790.[38] The number of scholars was probably never confined to ten, since it would be quite normal for there to have been some fee paying pupils as well. This is probably the school which Gill refers to in the mid-nineteenth century as "the Town School" and if so it had then been for some thirty years at least on a site in the Market Place, perhaps in the north-east corner. The schoolroom in the Market Place was enlarged in 1822 to house the Sunday School. John Harrison, the usher, is known to have been teaching in 1799.

Mrs. Eleanor Westerman (c. 1726-24.2.1783), the wife of a local man who had been in business as an inkmaker in London, left by her will a fund of £2,500 to found a school for teaching thirty boys Latin, English Grammar, Reading, Writing, Arithmetic and Bookkeeping and thirty girls Reading, Writing and Arithmetic. The dividends of the fund were to pay an annual salary of £54. 12s. 0d. to a master, who was to be a member of the Church of England. He was to provide the premises for the school, but was allowed annual sums of £10 for rent, coals and candles and £8. 8s. 0d. for books, pens, ink and stationery. He was required to attend the parish church each Sunday, Wednesday and Friday with the scholars and Mrs. Westerman also allotted a sum of £2 per annum from the income of the fund for sermons for the school on 26th May and 1st September.

The first master was the Rev. Richard Barton, M.A. (c. 1759-12.5.1827), the son of the Rev. Girlington Butler Barton, Rector of Bowness-upon-Windermere. At the time of his appointment he was curate of Kilburn, which he had served from November, 1781. Though he must have moved to Easingwold in about 1784 to start the new school in a house at the Thirsk end of Long Street, on the south west side where the present Westerman House and Barton House now stand, he continued to act as curate of Kilburn until November, 1802. He seems indeed from time to time throughout his career to have supplemented his income by acting as curate or assistant curate of, or taking duties at, neighbouring villages. In 1811 and 1812 he assisted the Vicar of Easingwold at Raskelf and a glebe terrier of Raskelf made in 1825 contains his (very shaky) signature as Assistant Curate of that place. In 1823 he seems to have been officiating curate of Farlington for its incumbent the Rev. Major Dawson, vicar of Sheriff Hutton.[39] A christening carried out by him at Myton in September, 1802, was on the other hand probably an isolated occasion. When he died in 1827 he had been master of the school for some forty-three years.

A Sunday School was established in the town about 1791 and in 1798 John Raper left an annual sum of £1 for the teacher.

In contrast with earlier periods, we have abundant information about the occupations of Easingwold people during the 18th century. The town was becoming considerably more urban and increasingly more the centre of the district, not yet overshadowed, as it now is, by York. There were as before the usual utility trades of a small town, butcher, baker, blacksmith, tailor, breeches-maker, joiner, cordwainer, shoemaker, skinner, tanner and wheel-wright. Evidence of slightly more sophistication are a writing master (in 1727), a clockmaker (in 1743) a cabinet maker in the middle of the century and a dancing master named in 1754 and 1757. A "grosser" is mentioned in the mid-eighteenth century, though this was not new, since there had been at least one in Charles II's reign. John Gibson was still exercising his trade of parchment maker in 1712. In the 1740's and 1750's the town had two barbers and in the 1760's three, one of whom, George Metcalf. is described in the "Universal British Directory" of 1790 as a peruke maker. Weavers seem to be first mentioned in the parish registers in the latter part of the seventeenth century and a "lynning weaver" is named in the court leet book in 1713. It seems likely that the Easingwold weavers of the eighteenth century were mostly linen weavers. Examination of the parish registers between 1739 and 1765 reveals a large group of weavers, twenty-three being named. This was quite an important local trade in this century, but had declined by 1790, when there were only seven in business. Gill[40] in the middle of the next century described the trade as then extinct. He attributed its passing to "the late improvements in machinery". One of the last Easingwold weavers must have been Christopher Canby of Shires Bar, a stocking weaver in 1797. So far as "the late improvement in machinery" are concerned it is possible that George Amison of Easingwold, named as a "machine maker" in 1795, made some kind of weaving machinery. A millright, Thomas Nightingell, is named in 1716. No less than thirty-two cordwainers are named in the period 1739-65. One of them, William Farmary, served as a soldier in 1745, perhaps in a volunteer regiment. Other leather workers of the same period included a bucklemaker, three bridlers, a saddler, three saddle-tree makers, three curriers and nine glovers. The last named seems to have been disappearing as a separate trade and is not mentioned at all in 1790. Building tradesmen included a mason, a thatcher, three glaziers, four brickmakers and six bricklayers, perhaps indicative of the increasing victory of brick and tile. Indicative of greater shopping facilities are five grocers and two fishmongers. Other trades in the 1750's and 60's were those of cooper (3), fiaxman (4), heckler (1), roper (2), stapler (1), staymaker (1), tallow-chandler (5) and whitesmith (1).

Bushel Anningson or Annison, who died on Christmas Eve, 1750. practised as a lawyer in the town. There is evidence to suggest that he came from the Whitby district. His son James did not follow in his father's footsteps, but took up the trade of breeches maker and married the daughter of a labourer from Hutton Many Geese (Hutton Sessay). Robert Rocliffe, who died in

1760 and William Wales were also lawyers practising in the town, the latter in the period 1755-60. The latter is possibly William Wailes (1731-96) of Husthwaite, who practised at York for some time and from 1786-96 was Clerk of the Peace of the Riding. In 1790 William Lockwood, the son of a Leeds winemerchant of the same name, was in practice in the town as an attorney. John Close of Oulston and Christopher Goulton of Highthorne probably handled the town's legal business in competition with Mr. Anningson in the middle of the century. Christopher Goulton was steward of the manor of Easingwold and Huby from 1737 in succession to his father Francis Goulton (steward from 1716) and grandfather Christopher Goulton, and steward of the Archdeaconry Manor also from 1737 in succession to his father. He was also Deputy Clerk of the Peace from about 1743 to 1757. Mr. Close, an attorney, was certainly "stewart of Easingwold" (that is the manor of Easingwold and Huby) in September, 1744. He seems to have held the stewardship till at least 1750. He had been Deputy Clerk of the Peace from about 1723 to 1737 and was also in charge of a part time deeds registry at Thirsk in 1726, nine years before the justices decided to make Northallerton the place of registration.

Eighteenth century doctors were George Twhaite, surgeon, mentioned in 1756; Henry Yates (c. 1693-21.6.1781), surgeon and apothecary; his son Robert (c. 1728-18.4.1798), also surgeon and apothecary; William Watson, surgeon, son of a surgeon of the same name at Pickering, in practice in 1790 and probably as early as 1739; Jeremiah Wise, surgeon, son of Benjamin Wise, surgeon, of Maryport, who was also in practice in the town in 1790, but died in November 1793, at the early age of 28; and William Lodge Rocliffe M.D. (c. 1754-14.2.1839), surgeon and physician. The last named was the son of Robert Rocliffe the attorney and a well known sporting character in the district, particularly in the cock-fighting world. He is said to have been somewhat eccentric, wearing a powdered wig, light blue coat and knee breeches long after they had gone out of fashion. Stephen Featherstone, apothecary, is described as a "man midwife" in 1754 and a surgeon in 1779. William Watson, named as an apothecary in 1739 and 1740 could be the same man as the surgeon named above. Thomas Carter of Easingwold is named in the Court Leet Book in May 1717, as "farmacopol", which probably means apothecary. "Nurse Cooper", who was in receipt of parish charity from 1732 to 1737 may have been a midwife or sicknurse, perhaps both. She seems to have been Ann Cooper, a widow.

In 1790 the town boasted an auctioneer, a brewer, thirteen innkeepers, a liquor merchant, a peruke maker, five mercers and drapers, five tailors, two staymakers, nineteen shoemakers and two watchmakers. There was a basket maker, a turner, and a heelmaker. There was still work for a thatcher. From 1795 Thomas Moor or Moore worked as a potter at Easingwold. A native of Beverley, he had married the daughter of a Warwick potter, Andrew Wilson, and may well have learned his trade from his father-in-law. He sold his pottery in Easingwold market and survived to give evidence in the Toll Trials in 1839, being then 78. William Fisher, a joiner in the town in 1790, also made violins, acted as an auctioneer and painted houses. His father Anthony, a joiner from at least 1743, aspired to the title of cabinet maker. Easingwold is said to have been a clockmaking centre in the eighteenth century. William Todd was making clocks in the period 1740-2 and Joseph Barker had a business in the Market Place in the years 1807 to 1823 and probably longer, which is credited with many local grandfather clocks. Henry and Joseph Barker were still carrying on this business in 1857.

Examination of the trades of Easingwold during the century gives not only an impression of increasing diversity, but that the town was attracting new blood. In addition to Mr. Moor just mentioned Leonard Smith, who was the son of William Smith, a London cook, set up in the town as a ropemaker, which business he was carrying on in 1790. He married a farmer's daughter from Howsham, of the family which was to include the famous George Hudson, the "Railway King". Thomas Perrott, gardener, resident in 1777, came from Twickenham; Matthew Todd. cordwainer, also resident in 1777, was a native of Hurworth, Co. Durham, while Alexander Harper, in business as a staymaker in 1779, came from Aberdeen. Francis Little in 1784 was born in Londonderry, Northern Ireland, and James Thomburne, cordwainer in 1791, was a Carlisle man, while the brewer Daniel Cameron in 1797 was, of course, a Scot.

One source of new blood which may perhaps be described as involuntary was a group of girls placed into service by Ackworth Hospital or by the Foundling Hospital in London, in the latter part of the century. Some of these girls married local men, as for example "Jimarma" Bailey of the Foundling Hospital, who married Thomas Knowlson of Easingwold, cordwainer, and had a son on 6th January, 1791, but others in 1790, 1794 and 1796 had illegitimate children.

Resident in the town in 1794 was the curate of Stillington, the Rev. John Gilpin, who was a son of the well known sporting artist Sawrey Gilpin.

The first newspaper distributed in the district seems to have been the "York Mercury", from 23rd February, 1718. It was a weekly costing 1¹/₂d., measuring 7 x 5¹/₂ inches and consisted mainly of extracts from the London journals and a few advertisements taken in by the distributors at 2/- each. Among its distributors was "Mr. Wilson in Easingwold". In 1724 the paper was taken over and remodelled by Thomas Gent, under the name: "The Original York Journal, or Weekly Courant". It later became known simply as the "York Courant".⁴¹

At the County election in 1742 sixty-one "forty shilling freeholders" from Easingwold, including the vicar and his residing curate, voted for the Whig candidate and forty-four for the Tory candidate. Although some of the latter may have held Jacobite views it is noteworthy that when the Young Pretender invaded the country in 1745, thirteen of the Tories subscribed amounts, varying from 5/- to two guineas, to Archbishop Herring's fund for the payment of forces for the defence of the county. Forty-nine persons from Easingwold subscribed a total of £53. 0s. 6d. to the fund, the list being headed by the Roman Catholic, Thomas Salvin of the Old Hall, who should have supported the Jacobites if anyone did, with a donation of five guineas. As already mentioned William Farmary of Easingwold served as a soldier in 1745, perhaps in the Yorkshire Blues, a unit which was with Hawley at Falkirk the following year. The other local forces do not seem to have seen action, apart from General Oglethorpe's cavalry unit, the Royal Hunters, at Shap, but it seems unlikely that Farmary would be in this. The burial of a soldier at Easingwold on the last day of 1745 suggests the passage of troops, as do entries of the baptisms of children of a soldier in February, 1759, and of three militiamen in the months of March to June, 1760, during the Seven Years War. Militia may have been camped or billeted at Easingwold in the latter case. The Militia Act of 1757 which put the militia onto a modern and reasonably efficient basis, was violently objected to because a working man who was balloted might not have the means of hiring a substitute like his wealthier neighbours and might have to serve personally, probably losing his business in the process. This situation indeed gave rise to one of the earliest forms of voluntary insurance, when working men formed clubs to raise the cost of substitutes by weekly subscription.

There were riots in Yorkshire, one of the most serious being at York on 15th September, 1757, when a mob of persons from thirty parishes tried to prevent the constables of the Wapentake of Bulmer from presenting the lists of men subject to the ballot to the Deputy Lieutenants.[42] Eventually, however, a new North York Militia Regiment came into being, the Richmondshire Battalion on 2nd July, 1759, and the Cleveland and Bulmer Battalion on 20th July following. It remained embodied until 3rd December, 1762. This was not necessarily the unit at Easingwold in 1760 because the militia moved about the country a good deal. The famous Elliot's Light Dragoons (later the 15th Hussars) with their associations with Emsdorf and Sahagun, "the Old Cock of the Rock" (General Elliot), General Floyd and (unlikely as it may seem) the poet Coleridge, were raised and trained at Northallerton in 1758 and may have drawn some of their recruits from the Riding.[43]

The North Riding was seriously affected, together with many other parts of the country, by "the murrain" or 'distemper of horned cattle" (believed to have been rinderpest) during the years 1748-53. The movement of cattle was regulated by Quarter Sessions. This was done by watching bridges and markets; by requiring certificates that cattle had not come from a place within a prescribed distance of infection (five miles during most of the outbreak); by forbidding the sale of hides without a certificate of health; by forbidding sales outside markets or fairs; by suspending markets and fairs; and so on. There was widespread evasion.

Infected cattle were to be slaughtered and buried with the skin and horns left on, at least four feet deep, the hides having first been slashed to render them useless. The place of burial had to be carefully recorded. On due affidavit that all this had been done compensation would be paid pursuant to an Order in Council of 22nd March, 1748.

In 1750 one of the chief constables of Bulmer was in attendance at Easingwold market to prevent the sale of cattle without the proper certificate. Fairs were stopped throughout the Riding in the last quarter of 1751 and were not completely open again until July, 1753.[44s]

In 1741 there was an outbreak of smallpox at Easingwold which caused eighteen deaths, mostly of children. The register of burials from September, 1777, to April, 1780, gives what were believed to be the causes of the deaths. The "distempers" included smallpox in the case of sixteen children, whose ages ranged from infancy to eleven years. What smallpox was to children, consumption was to the old. Of twenty-one deaths from this cause, eleven were of people over sixty-five, though it is true that several children also died. Four children died of whooping cough, two each from two households. Other causes of death were four from dropsy, one from child bearing, one from palsy, one from apoplexy, one from asthma, one from marasmus, one from gravel, one from inflammation in the bladder, two from mortification of the bowels and two from fever. No doubt some of these deaths would have been differently diagnosed today.

An idea of the numbers of poor people in the town at various periods of the eighteenth century is given by the Charity book in the church vestry. In 1730 the bread distribution to the poor was 120 loaves each Sunday. On 2nd April, 1760, charity money was distributed to fifty-four poor people and on 22nd December in the same year to fifty-six. This number seems to have increased to about eighty at the end of the century. Money for the poor came either from poor rates, in which case the administering authority was the overseers, or from charity money in the hands of the vicar and churchwardens. In 1700, in addition to maintaining Fossbridge House and the almshouses in Little Lane for two poor people and four poor widows respectively, the latter had the Rev. George Wilson's gift of the rent of North Moor Close (1671) and two rentcharges respectively of 10/- (1640) and 40/- (1690). Further bequests for the poor during the century were Robert Driffield's (1712), Thomas Raines's (1713), Nathanael Wilson's (1726), Ann Cobb's (1728), Thomas Wray's (1739), William Coopland's (1759), George Westerman's (1783) and John Raper's (1798). Ann Cobb gave part of the rent of Tod's Close (later two closes called Whitebread Closes or the Whitebread Land) for a weekly bread distribution to twelve poor persons and George Westerman (c. 1709-13.12.1783), the husband of the foundress of Westerman's Endowed School, left £200 in Old South Sea Annuities for bread for the poor. Thomas Wray's gift was the interest of £20 to be divided among four poor widows and William Coopland's the interest of £10 for clothing two poor boys. John Raper gave £2 per annum to four poor housekeepers without trades and not in receipt of parish relief. In addition to these gifts, seven acres of land were bought in 1712 and 1713 and conveyed to the Vicar and churchwardens for the use of the poor.

There were two special bequests for the annual apprenticing of a poor child - Mrs. Frances Driffield's (1676) and Alice Smith's

(1698). William Farmery for example was bound for seven years to William Blake, shoemaker, with Alice Smith's legacy in about 1727. Mrs. Driffield's legacy was used to bind William Wetherel to George Rennard, tailor, for seven years in 1715. In one case, however, in about 1725 a general charity, John Foster's rentcharge for the half year amounting to 5/-, was paid to John Hall, glover, who had taken Hannah Craik as his apprentice. This was a special case since Hall was to return the money with interest when Hannah was out of her time. Some of the apprentices were put to masters well outside the parish, as in 1725, when one of the masters was at Helmsley, and in 1727, when one was at Kirk Hammerton. In a number of cases Mrs. Driffield's legacy was used to bind apprentices to their own fathers. This was done in 1716, 1722, 1723 and 1724.

A special subscription for the relief of the poor of Easing-wold, opened on 27th January, 1757, produced £15. 12s. 0d. It was also the custom to make gifts to the poor at funerals. Thirty shillings were given to the poor of Easingwold when Sir Bryan Stapylton, Bart, of Myton was buried in 1727. When Sir John Stapylton's wife was buried in 1731 he sent 40/- for the poor and when Sir John himself was buried in 1733, his son Sir Miles again sent 40/- for the Easingwold poor.

Almhouses were provided at the Spring Head in Spring Street under a deed of 1769 on the land now occupied by the Victoria Buildings.[45]

In adition to the almshouses, accommodation for the poor was also provided by the overseers. A poor house is mentioned in 1756. There seems in 1812 and perhaps earlier to have been a poor house or work house immediately outside the Easingwold Town-end tollbar in Stillington Road, though this is not definitely proved.

During the American Revolutionary War the North York Militia was again embodied under its Colonel, Earl Fauconberg, from 21st April, 1778, to 13th March 1783.[46] Earl Fauconberg, also raised the North Riding Volunteer Regiment of Foot, ten companies of 710 men in all, enlisted for three years or the duration. This unit, which seems to be the same as "Lord Fauconberg's North Riding Fencibles" was popular. It was raised in just over three months and the men were mostly under thirty. The regiment seems to have been in being during the years 1779-82. Private soldiers received 2d. a day.

From 1727, if not earlier, Quarter Sessions were held in the Tolbooth at Easingwold. These, except for one isolated court in September, 1746, were in mid-January and were known as the Epiphany Sessions. In 1747 they were ordered to be transferred from Easingwold to Malton, but in 1748, this was altered to provide alternate Epiphany Sessions at the two places.[47] The Epiphany Sessions were held at Easingwold on 12th January, 1801, but by 1809 Easingwold had ceased to be a venue for the court.[48]

A typical example of Georgian justice was done at the sessions held at Easingwold on 14th January, 1729, when William Wilson, being convicted of "several felonies and petty larcenies" was ordered to be transported for seven years "into some of his Majesty's plantations in America".[49] He probably ended up in one of the Carolinas. This could happen to women too, as at Thirsk in October, 1744, when the wife of the Rev. Benjamin Dawnay of Newton-on-Ouse was found guilty of picking a pocket and was given the alternatives of public whipping and seven years transportation to America. She chose the latter.[50]

In 1776, since they could no longer be sent to the American colonies, then in revolt, Parliament authorised the employment of convicts in improving the bed and foreshore of the Thames. One of the contractors, Duncan Campbell, undertook to house, feed and clothe the convicts in two hulks moored of Woolwich Dockyard. This was the beginning of the famous prison hulks of the Thames, which lasted until 1856, housing among others Magwich of "Great Expectations".[51] This explains the case of John Anderson, labourer, at the Easingwold Sessions of 14th January, 1777. Anderson, convicted of stealing two dozen printed linen handkerchiefs, value 10d., was sentenced "to be sent to some of His Majesty's ships of war to enter into the King's service and if he refuse to enter, then to be sent to the Thames for five years according to the Statute". He was thus given the happy choice of in all probability dying from gunshot, disease or drowning in a ship of war or from disease in a Thames hulk — although of course he may have ended up a hero after fighting De Grasse at the Saints.

The recreations of the gentry during this period consisted largely of field sports. Cock fighting was popular and in 1751 the gentlemen of Easingwold fought those of Thirsk, showing twenty cocks on each side, for four guineas a battle and forty the main (ten battles). Six battles were won by Easingwold and four by Thirsk.[52] There was the famous race meeting at Hambleton in the early part of the century, with the great cup displayed on the Dial Stone, and lesser meetings at, for example, Helperby, though the Forest of Galtres meeting was probably a thing of the past. Thomas Meynell of North Kilvington, a keen racing man, noted that one of his horses had won two bells at this meeting in 1621, as well as a silver cup at "Studfawde" (Studfold on Ampleforth Moor) and another at Bagby Moor in the same year.[53] The coursing of deer with greyhounds had long passed with the Forest of Galtres, and the district seems to have had no regular foxhounds until the Easingwold Hunt during the Napoleonic War. The average man's recreations would be informal. Hours of work were long and holidays confined to the great festivals and the free week at Martinmas for those who were not their own masters. The two annual fairs and the hirings with their accompanying stalls and travelling showmen must have represented the summit of entertainment for many people, apart from the bonfires on Guy Fawkes Day, the games on May Day and the bellringing on Royal Oak Day.

1   Baines : History, Directory & Gazetteer of the County of York, 1823.
2   Surtees Soc. Vol. LXII.
3   Aveling op cit p. 335.
4   ibid p. 395.
5   YAJ Vol. XXXIII, p. 103.
6   NRQSR Vol. IX p. 139.
7   VCHNR vol. ii.
8   Aveling op cit p. 401.
9   Gill. op. cit.
10 ibid.
11 Lawson : Collectio Rerum Ecclesiasticarum de Dioeces Eboracensi, Vol. II, 1840.
12 Gill op cit.
13 ibid and Gills' Family Almanack, 1872.
14 The Universal British Directory.
15 Armstrong : Actual Survey of the Great Post Roads between London and Edinburgh 1776.
16 VCH: City of York, 1961, p. 476.
17 Case papers with the Doncaster-Selby Turnpike Act, Leeds City Reference Library.
18 Allen : New and Complete History of the County of York, 1829 Vol. I p. 228.
19 Armstrong : op cit.
20 The Yorkshire Memorandum Book: or New Daily Journal for — 1784.
21 ibid for 1787.
22 Universal British Directory 1790.
23 The York Guide 3rd. ed. Printed by Geo. Peacock, Coney Street, for J. Wolstenholme, Bookseller, Minster-Yard.
24 The Yorkshire Memorandum Book for 1784.
25 49 Geo. III c. 112.
26 T. Whellan & Co. : History & Topography of the City of York & N.R. of Yorkshire Vol. II.
27 Allen op cit.
28 Hargrove : Yorkshire Gazetteer, Knaresborough, 1806.
29 Foster : Alumnus Oxoniensis.
30 Booker : Memorials of the Church in Prestwich.
31 Information given by the Rev. Canon Eric Saxon, Rector of St. Ann's Church, Manchester.
32 Brookbank : The Honorary Medical Staff of the Manchester Royal Infirmary, 1752-1830.
33 NRQSR Vol. III, pp. 102-3.
34 Memorials of Early Methodism in the Easingwold Circuit by A. Layman, 1872.
35 Aveling op cit p. 394.
36 ibid p. 396.

37 ibid p. 394.
38 Universal British Directory 1790.
39 Baines op cit.
40 Gill op cit.
41 Davies : Memoir of the York Press. 1868.
42 Allen op cit Vol. 1 p. 190.
43 Ingledew op. cit.
44 NRQSR Vol. IX p. 2.
45 Bulmer : N. Yorkshire, 1890.
46 Turton op. cit.
47 NRQSR Vol. III p. 226.
48 Langdale : "Topographical Dictionary of Yorkshire 1809.
49 NRQSR Vol. VIII p. 183.
5O ibid p. 248.
51 Capper. Moat Defensive 1963 pp. 182-4.
52 Fairfax Blakeborough : Northern Turf History 1948. Vol. 1. p. 51.
53 Aveling, op. cit. p. 287.

IV

1800 TO THE PRESENT DAY

In 1802 Earl Fauconberg, lord of the manor of Easingwold and Huby, died in London, leaving no male issue. He was succeeded by his son-in-law, Thomas Edward Wynn, who had married Lady Charlotte, the eldest of the Earl's four daughters. On succeeding to the estates Mr. Wynn took the additional surname of Belasyse. Mr. Wynn-Belasyse and Lady Charlotte were lord and lady of the manor in 1812. Lady Charlotte survived her husband and died in 1825, when she was succeeded by her sister Ann's eldest son George Wombwell, son of Sir George Wombwell of Wombwell in the West Riding. George Wombwell had served during the French Revolutionary War as an officer in the North York Militia, being Captain-Lieutenant in 1793 and Captain in 1794, at which period his home seems to have been at East Newton. Some years after succeeding to the Newburgh estates and the lordship of the manor he also succeeded to his father's baronetcy, though probably not before 1834. His son, Sir George Orby Wombwell, then a serving officer in the Crimea, succeeded to the baronetcy, Newburgh estates and lordship of the manor in 1855, all of which he held well into the twentieth century. Sir George was commissioned cornet in the 17th Lancers on 21st September, 1852. This was a fashionable regiment and he probably paid more than the official price of £400 for his commission. His second step to lieutenant on 26th October, 1854, was a casualty promotion to replace a Lieutenant Thompson killed in action. At the Battle of Balaclava as A.D.C. to the notorious Lord Cardigan, Major General commanding the Light Brigade, he took part in the famous charge "into the Valley of Death". He was actually captured for a time, but escaped in the confusion caused by a shell burst and seized a loose horse.

He was in danger again in the famous accident on 4th February, 1869, when the Newby ferry carrying members of the York and Ainsty Hunt and their horses upset, drowning the Master and five others. Sir George was one of the survivors.

The Archdeaconry manor lordship passed at some date between 1811 and 23rd May, 1814, from William Lodge Rocliffe,

George Clarke and Sir John Lawson to the first two gentlemen and the personal representatives of Sir John. These held it in July, 1822, but in May, 1827, Dr. Rocliffe was the sole survivor jointly with the personal representatives of both Mr. Clarke and Sir John. The enclosure award made in 1812 describes Edward Arrowsmith, Thomas Armstrong and John Wailes as then lessees for lives of this manor, the rectory and tithes, but they were probably sublessees in fact. At a date between 6th May, 1832, and 13th May, 1835, the lordship vested in Dr. Rocliffe, a trustee for William (later the Rev. William) Lockwood, and John Webb. John Haxby appears to have become steward about this time. Dr. Rocliffe died in 1839 and his interest passed eventually (in 1842 or 1843) to John Booth. Both John Webb and the Rev. William Lockwood seem to have died between May and November, 1851, and their respective interests passed to Wm. Frederick Webb and (by 1859) to Mrs. Elizabeth Lockwood, widow of the Rev. William. The last recorded court was held on 1st May, 1861, by which time the court had long been a mere device for recording copyhold conveyances and was probably even unnecessary for that purpose since the passing of the Copyhold Act of 1841.

Great Britain had made peace with Napoleon by the Treaty of Amiens on 27th May, 1802, ending the long French Revolutionary War which had begun in 1793. The North York Militia had been embodied from the end of 1792 to 1802. In October, 1794, articles of enrolment were drawn up at Northallerton for a proposed corps of North Riding Yeomanry to be equipped and paid as light dragoons, each troop to consist of not less than 54 men including officers. There is however no record of any troop so raised near Easingwold. Indeed information on troops in the district during the French Revolutionary War is extremely scanty. The 18th Light Dragoons may have been near Easingwold in April, 1801, a trooper of that regiment being hanged at York Tyburn on 29th August, 1801, for raping a Tollerton woman in a field in the parish of Easingwold on 20th April, 1801.[1]

War broke out again in May, 1803, the North York Militia being this time embodied from 18th March, 1803, to January, 1816. In 1809 William Fisher, son of the Easingwold joiner who varnished Moses and Aaron in the parish church, was serving as a private in this regiment, though it is not known whether he wore the red coat of a line company or the green jacket of one of the North York's two rifle or marksmen companies. The uniform of the latter is shown in Walker's "Costumes of Yorkshire", 1814. It closely resembled that of the 95th Foot, but had, it appears, black buttons. The regular Militia was also supplemented at this period by the Local Militia, a static force, somewhat resembling the Home Guard. The local battalion was probably the Fourth North Yorkshire Local Militia since E. S. Strangwayes of Alne was commissioned in it as major.[2] Many of the local men must have done a period of training in the local Militia. At Husthwaite for example they appear to have gone to Thirsk for three months, marching to Sutton-under-Whitestonecliffe for musketry training. No doubt some of the Easingwold men had similar training.

Mr. Wynn Belasyse of Newburgh had by 1804 raised a volunteer unit known as the Newburgh Rangers, which he commanded with the rank of Captain. It appears to have been a troop of Yeomanry Cavalry. It paraded at Easingwold in 1804, when the bellringers rang an appropriate peal. In 1806 its strength was 52 men and Mr. Wynn Belasyse's account book contains several references to "the Cavalry" between 1809 and 1817 so that it seems a reasonable inference that it was a troop of yeomanry. William Barker of Easingwold repaired the arms for "the Cavalry", being paid £2. 7s. 0d. on 16th October, 1809, and on 30th October, 1811, John Hornby, probably the tailor of that name at Easingwold, was paid £2. 10s. 0d. for making cavalry uniforms. Another volunteer unit, the Yorkshire Foresters, mustering 67 men in 1806, under the command of Capt. Charles Hoare Harland of Sutton-on-Forest Hall, may have been a foot or rifle corps. A trooper of the 18th Light Dragoons is mentioned in the parish registers at the end of January. 1803. Privates of the East Suffolk Militia, in mid July, 1805; of the 3rd West York Militia at the beginning of May 1806; and of the North York Militia in 1810 are similarly mentioned. Possibly these units were at or near the town at the dates mentioned.

A small memorial of the war is the pair of old gate piers in the west wall of "The Galtres", which formed the entrance to an earlier house on this site. They still bear the worn inscription: "To the ARMY of Great Britain and Ireland MDCCCIX". (This was the year of Talavera).

The tradition that "Lifeguardsman Shaw", one of the heroes of Waterloo, was a native of Easingwold and apprenticed at the "Horse Shoe" Inn, Long Street, is unfortunately false. Shaw was a Nottinghamshire man and his life before joining the army on 11th October, 1807, is well recorded.

The poll book of the 1807 county election shows an occupation structure very similar to that in 1790. The first printer in the town seems to have been James Todd, who started in 1805. Coach and carriage travel on the turnpike roads to York and Thirsk was heavy and increasing and the inns in Long Street were expanding accordingly. A work of 1809 gives the principal inns as the Rose and Crown and the Post Boy.[3] The 1822 edition of the same work names then as the Rose and Crown and the New Inn. The landlord of the New Inn, William Carver, who kept it from at least 1797, when he had a lease of it from William Knowles's heirs, till his death in 1820, may have changed its name for a short period to the Post Boy but if so he had changed it back by 4th May, 1809. A bill for a post chaise of that date is headed: "William Carver, The New Inn, Post & Excise Office Inn. N.B. From the Unicorn, Market Place". Carver had at one time been a butler, then, it appears from the bill head just quoted, he must have spent some time as landlord of the Unicorn (on the site of the Commercial) and then took a lease of the New Inn. He is said later to have purchased the freehold.

Carver died in 1820 and by May Thomas Hawkes had taken over the New Inn, which he held till at least 1823. He was succeeded by a Mr. Dodds, son-in-law of Benjamin Lacy, the landlord of the New Rose and Crown. Lacy died in September, 1824, and Dodds moved into the New Rose & Crown, being followed at the New Inn by a Mr. Stevenson and a Mr. Kempler.[4] In 1834 the New Inn was held by George Scaife.

Benjamin Lacy was at the New Rose & Crown in 1815, being succeeded there, as just mentioned, by Dodds about the end of 1824. In 1834 William Cartledge was landlord of the New Rose & Crown. This Inn is the large house in Long Street at the corner of Little Lane, later a convent. It had four or five postboys, one of whom, Tommy Hutchinson, was alive in 1889, aged 80. He rode five times to York and back in one day at assize time, a distance of 130 miles, four of the journeys, or 104 miles, being on the same mare. When coaches went off the road in the 1840's he returned to his previous trade of tailor.[5] Other Easingwold postboys were John Randill (in 1807), William Winn, who married a girl from Cleethorpes, mentioned in 1808. and William Elmer, the son of an Easingwold blacksmith, mentioned in 1811.

The Mail and the Highflyer had been joined in 1823 by the Wellington from York to Newcastle and by 1834 there was a fourth coach on the road, the Express, also from York to Newcastle. The Wellington lasted till after 1842, being the last coach on this road. It and the Express were horsed from York to Easingwold by Mr. Barber, landlord of the Black Swan at York during the years 1815-24. Barber had stables opposite the New Rose & Crown and adjoining them was a stable where the landlord of the George at York kept a spare chaise and some of his post horses. From Easingwold to Northallerton the Wellington was horsed by the landlord of the Golden Lion at Northallerton, who kept horses at the New Rose & Crown, Easingwold, for that purpose. Mr. Lacy of the New Rose & Crown horsed the Express to Thirsk. The Mail and Highflyer both continued to change at the New Inn. They were horsed from York by Messrs. Cattle & Maddocks, who had stables opposite where they kept up to two dozen horses.[6] (This partnership probably consisted of Robert Cattle, described in 1823 as a Coach proprietor, of St. Helens Square, and Samuel Maddock, of Blossom Street, in the same year an inspector of mail coaches).[7] A Mr. Scott of Northallerton horsed the Mail from Easingwold to Northallerton and Lacy the Highflyer as far as Thirsk.[8]

There was a coach called the Royal Times from York to Redcar and Sunderland which also changed horses at the New Inn, perhaps for a period prior to 1823 or between 1823 and 1834. For a time there seem to have been coaches through Easingwold called the Pledge and the Trafalgar. The latter was running in 1807. A coach called the Sunderland Mail, from York to Sunderland, was running in 1823, its north and south-bound coaches passing at the New Rose and Crown at 10.00 p.m. It was presumably one of the Royal Mails.

The evenings in Long Street at that date must have been fairly lively, with the southbound Wellington at 7.00 p.m., the southbound Highflyer at 8.00 p.m., the north and southbound Sunderland Mail and the north and southbound Edinburgh Mail all at 10.00 p.m., and the northbound Wellington at 11.30 p.m. The morning was comparatively dead, the only coach being the northbound Highflyer, which reached the New Rose and Crown at 8.45 am. and stopped twenty minutes for breakfast.

The Mail was timed from York to Edinburgh in 1823 in 25$\frac{1}{2}$ hours. In 1824 an advertisement for "The Public's Favourite Coach, The Old High Flyer" describes it as leaving St. Helen's Square, York, at 11.00 a.m. and reaching Newcastle at 10.00 p.m.

the same night. The following morning it left Newcastle at 6.00 a.m. and arrived at Edinburgh at 6.00 p.m.

The Post Office in 1823 was at the Fleece Inn, kept by the postmaster, Leonard Smith. The guards were in the habit of throwing the night mails through an open window, according to a family tradition.

In 1840 a coach called the Victoria from London to Newcastle and Edinburgh was running through the town, together with the Edinburgh Mail and the Wellington. All were off the road within two or three years. The Highflyer had already gone.

Goods carriers through the town in 1823 included the "old established and only North Waggons" of Pickersgill & Co.: of Leeming Lane, who claimed to run services to all parts of the North and to Scotland. The business was still in being in 1838, run by Richard Pickersgill.

Inns and taverns at the beginning of the 19th century seem to have included the New Inn, the Rose and Crown and the Unicorn as already mentioned. The George was in being in 1811, when it was held by John Preston. He was succeeded by Elizabeth Preston, no doubt his widow, and, by December 1835, by Robert Preston. A broadsheet called: "A Peep at the Publicans of Easingwold, sung by Mr. Smith at The Theatre" and probably printed between 1820 and 1823 refers to the Horse Shoe, kept by a blacksmith: the Green Tree "where the Scotchman may meet with his clan", perhaps a reference to Scots drovers: the New Rose & Crown; the New Inn, the Old Rose & Crown; the George; the Malt Shovel; the Jolly Farmers; The Blue Bell; the Unicorn; the Angel; the Punch Bowl; and the Sun and Punch Bowl. Of these the Horse Shoe, Green Tree, New Rose & Crown, Old Rose & Crown and the Sun and Punch Bowl are in Long Street. The last named seems to have been newly built in 1817. It is now No. 41, Long Street. The Old Rose & Crown is now Nos. 83-7 Long Street. The Malt Shovel was in Spring Street, the Jolly Farmers and the Blue Bell in Uppleby, and the George and the Punch Bowl in the Market Place. The Horse Shoe sold Messrs. John Rocliffe & Co.'s beer from the Easingwold brewery, Mr. Lacy at the New Rose and Crown sold Jackson's Strong Beer while Hawkes of the New Inn specialised in Hobson's Entire. John Britton of the Old Rose & Crown sold home brewed. The justices are referred to as sitting at the George at this date. William Calway of the Angel was an auctioneer and held frequent sales on the premises. In 1823 in addition to the above there were

112

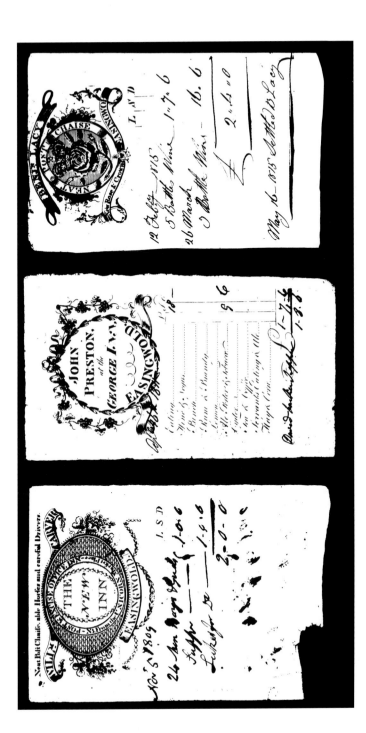

Bills from the "New Rose and Crown", "New Inn" and "George", early 19th century

Rev. A. C. A. Smith, M.A.

THE CONVENT — EASINGWOLD

The former "New Rose and Crown", about 1905

G. H. Smith, Esq.

the Bay Horse in Long Street, Red Lion and Waggon and Horses. There was a second Unicorn and the White House on Thirsk Road had a licence. The Royal Oak in Long Street certainly existed in 1825. By 1834 had appeared the Grey Horse and Nags Head also in Long Street, the latter of which could be the Red Lion renamed. Also open in 1834 was the Pig, in the Market Place, near to the Old Vicarage, kept by a pig dealer, John Cowling. By 1840 he had changed its name to the Wild Boar and it was licensed under this name till at least 1867. By 1834 there were two public houses at White Houses, known respectively as the Old and New White Houses. The Fleece in Long Street in 1823 survived until modern times. The Travellers Rest in Crankley is first mentioned in 1841.[9] Also mentioned in 1841 is the Black Swan in Long Street.

Some improvements were made to the parish church in 1803, an organ being placed in the West Gallery, in front of the West window which was boarded up. Mr. Fisher, the joiner, provided "A Large New Fraim to hold Donations for the Poor Yalla Ground" and lettered it at a total cost of 7 guineas. He also, as mentioned above refurbished the figures of Moses and Aaron with the Ten Commandments and the inscription of the poor box. He did some minor work including "Panting the Church Dour Oak Culler".

Before the organ was installed the Church music was presumably instrumental, provided, like that of Husthwaite at the same period, by violin flute, clarinet and oboe. In 1806 the wardens paid 2s. 4d. for two bass strings for "Hornby Fiddle". This was perhaps John Hornby the tailor.

In the years 1804 and 1805 the five bellringers were paid a guinea each per annum, with some fees for special rings, for example 1/6d. for a ring on 5th November, 1804, 6/3d. on the day in that year when the Newburgh Rangers came to Easingwold, or 15/- for a peal on Royal Oak Day, 29th May, 1809. An entry between 4th June and 22nd September, 1812, reads: "Alce. for Ringers on Ld. Wellington Victory 2. 6". This was probably Salamanca. No doubt the bells rang for other victories too at this period. They must certainly have done so for Waterloo, but the accounts for that year have not survived. In 1805 the Sexton was paid 10s. 6d. for ringing the Sermon bell. It was also the custom to "ring in" the new church wardens or warden, but this practice seems to have been discontinued in 1827. The ringers and singers (of both sexes) were given a supper on Guy Fawkes Night.

On 5th November, 1809, the wardens paid James Hirst and Mr. Rawling a guinea for conducting the boys and girls singing for half a year. In April, 1809, Thos. Jackson and David Barker received a guinea between them for playing the organ for half a year. There are references from 1806 to 1827 to keeping "the Engine", playing "the Engine", mending Engine pipes and so on. This may have been the organ, though it was perhaps more likely to have been a parish fire engine. In 1827 John Britton was paid £2 for keeping it and 2/6d. was paid on its removal to the church, so that a fire fighting appliance of some kind seems likely. Also rather mysterious throughout the period are frequent references to "rappers", sometimes three, sometimes five. This may have been some kind of knocking up service. In 1808 the wardens paid for "cutting snow twice to church 2/9d." and gave 6/6d. to the singers on Christmas Day (including a Christmas Box). They also paid l0d. for a "Bottle Screw". Maintenance and similar expenses included 1/6d. for mowing the churchyard, paid on 23rd June, 1806; 1/3d. in 1809 for removing the stile in the churchyard and 1/3d, in the same year for scraping and sweeping the roads. On 5th January, 1810, the wardens paid for clearing the road to church, presumably after a snowfall. In 1804 the wardens paid 7/- for two journeys to York "Disputing a Man Wanting for Army Reserve".

Among the more curious items in their accounts are the small bounties paid for the destruction of vermin under the Statute 39 Eliz. c. 18 (1597-8), which renewed earlier Acts of 1566 and 1572. The rate per head was 12d. for foxes, ld. for polecats, stoats and weasels, 2d. for hedgehogs and $^1/_2$d. for moles. In 1804 3/8d. was paid for fox and "fulmart" (polecat) heads and 3/6d. in 1806 for foxes, fulmarts and moles.

Enclosure of the town fields and waste grounds of Easingwold took place under an Act of Parliament of 1808 (48 Geo II, c. 27). The area to be dealt with was estimated in the preamble as 500 acres, but this was too short by about 65 acres. The commissioners appointed to allot the land were Thomas Scott of Oulston and John Tuke of York, with John Humphries of Ripon as the surveyor. Their award was made in 1812, though the allotment to the lord and lady of the manor of Easingwold and Huby in lieu of their interest in the waste seems from Mr. Wynn-Belasyse's account book to have been made by February, 1810. It was at any rate sold well before the date of the award to John Hutton of New-burgh and formed part of the small allotment of 2 roods 4 perches made to him in the award on the west side of York road, not far south of the grounds of the present Grammar and Modern School. Mr. Humphries' plan for the award is dated 12th November, 1812.

The award first allotted a number of public roads, then a number of private roads and foot roads, and two sandpits and the herbage of lanes for the surveyors of highways. Then came the tithe allotments, followed by the general allotments and finally certain partitions of old enclosures made by consent. The Commissioners allotted five foot strips on the north and south sides of Uppleby and on part of the north and along the east and west sides of the Market Place to the various frontagers for the protection of their houses. Many of the front gardens and bay windows on the north side of Uppleby are on this strip. The Commissioners were empowered to widen existing watercourses and set out new ones. Watercourses were to be inspected annually by the court leet within one week after Michaelmas, a duty still carried out at the end of the century by the jury of the court.

The most interesting feature of Humphries' map is Easingwold Town-end Bar across the end of Stillington Road with an island in the centre of the gate which may have contained the toll house. There was a small back lane or roadway leading down the backs of the gardens on the north side of Uppleby, from the east end to a point about half way down. This was split up among the owners of the gardens by the award and has now been fenced in for most part. The present field and farm pattern probably dates from the decade after the enclosure award. It certainly existed in 1843, as is shown by a map of the township prepared in that year for the use of the lessees of the Great Tithes. Very few farms have been added since then and the hedges were practically the same as they are now. A few farms have been since renamed. Cock Farm on Thirsk Road has become Prospect House and Ox Moor House has become Hollin Grove. The Ordnance Survey of 1858 shows Blayds House under the name of Lilac Grove; Shires Farm on the corner of Forest Lane, as Pigeon Cottage; and a building on the site of Nineveh called White Cock Hall. Huby Burn or Burn Hall was built in 1888.

Easingwold was lively enough to boast a theatre of some kind at the end of 1811. A playbill headed "Theatre - Easingwold" announces performances by "Their Majesties Servants" at 7.00 p.m. on Monday, 30th December, 1811 and on the following Wednesday, Friday and Saturday. This company of fourteen persons, at least three of whom were children, performed a play called "The Stranger, or, Misanthropy and Repentance", following which the principal of the company, Mr. Thompson, gave "Dolly Duggins", probably a song or recitation of some kind. There was then a musical farce, and finally a Novel Exhibition called "Phantasmagoria", evidently a series of tableaux, including such ill-assorted characters as Macbeth, Jane Shore, Lord Nelson and "Paswan Oglou" (Osman Pasvanoglu (1758- 1807), so-called Pasha of Widdin in Bulgaria). Mr. Thompson also took profiles with a machine of his own invention, ladies and gentlemen waited on in their own houses, time of sitting one minute. Their Majesties' Servants remained at the Theatre until at least the week beginning 3rd February, 1812, presenting among other attractions a Grand Tragic Play entitled "The Castle Spectre", a farce called "The Ghost, or, the Affrighted Farmer", two comic operas, a "Melo Dramatic Spectacle" and "By Desire of Messrs. Crawford, Cock & Win. Lockwood Esqrs.", a comedy called. "The Honey Moon, or How To Rule A Wife". The doyen of the company, Mr. Abbott, aged 83, regularly took parts in the plays and even sang a comic song. A broadsheet of a song called "A Peep at the Publicans of Easingwold", already referred to, seems from the details given to have been printed between 1820 and 1823. The song is described as "Sung by Mr. Smith, at the Theatre". It looks therefore as if this theatre was in being for at least the period 1811-20, though where is not known. The bills of 1811 have prices for pit and gallery so that it must have been a building of some size, though not necessarily a very grand one.

Another attraction of the town in the Napoleonic period was a hunt. That the Easingwold Hunt existed during the years 1810-14 is known from the subscription made by Mr. Wynn-Belasyse.[10] This was paid to Thomas Barker. The hounds were perhaps Thomas Crawford's, since he is said to have had a pack which went to form the nucleus of the York and Ainsty Pack.

Races, probably horse races, were held at Easingwold in 1818, when Mr. Belasyse gave a pound towards expenses.[11]

By 1823 there were two printers, James Todd from 1805 and Thomas Dalton of Windross Row (the row on the south side of the Market Place) from at least 1820. There were two druggists, a furniture broker, two hardware dealers, two spirit merchants and two straw hat makers among other tradespeople. There was a gunsmith, Thomas Clemenshaw or Clemetshaw, who was in business in 1807 and continued till at least 1840, five hat dealers and manufacturers, one of whom was also a furrier, and two

116

corn millers. one of the latter was William Beedom, who seems to have owned a small brick windmill of the tower type, probably built after 1817, on the north side of Mill Lane, or the Haverthwaites Road as it was called in the enclosure award of 1812, which now forms part of the Crayke road. In 1839 Beedom sold this windmill to William Gibson, miller, of the Abbey Mill, Marton-cum-Moxby, and from at least as early as 1841, it was worked by Thomas Gibson. George Gibson may have been operating it as a mustard mill in 1857. In 1878 Thomas Gibson sold it to John Smith who died in 1886. It was probably killed by competition from the steam powered Union Flour Mill in Long Street, opened in 1856. The windmill was ruinous in the 1920's and only foundations now remain. It can be picked out on the frontispiece to Gill's "Vallis Eboracensis", 1852, a view of Easingwold from the west.[12]

A famous Easingwold business was probably started by William Barker in the 1770's. Mentioned in the parish registers in 1777 as a whitesmith, by 1823 he specialised in the making of butcher's steels.[13] In the years 1834-41 George Barker was the proprietor.[14] At the Great Exhibition at the Crystal Palace in Hyde Park in 1851 Robert Barker obtained honourable mention for his exhibit of butcher's and house steels,[15] and he is named as the proprietor of the business in 1857.[16] It was no doubt the Great Exhibition which gave the business its wide and even international reputation. In 1867 it was being carried on under the style of "Robert Barker & Son" by John Barker[17] and in 1890 another Robert Barker was the proprietor. At the beginning of 1893 his widow, Mrs. Annie Barker, sold out to Mark Raynard. Robert Barker's eldest son George, who had been apprenticed as a printer to Thomas Gill, the Easingwold historian, and had worked for some time with the Queen's Printers, died in London in November, 1893.[18]

Early 19th century lawyers were William Lockwood senior who died in 1836, his son William Lockwood junior, Jonathan Foster, in practice from at least 1823 to 1834; Robert Gill (c. 1807-1893) in the Market Place in 1834; John Haxby, steward of the Manor of Easingwold and Huby in 1840; and John Robinson in the Market Place in 1834. John Haxby acted for the plaintiff in the toll trials of 1839-49 and John Robinson acted for one of the defendants. Both gentlemen were still in practice in 1867. Mr. Haxby died in 1873 and Mr. Robinson, who succeeded him as steward of the Manor, in 1888. Robert Gill above mentioned had a three year lease of a room in the Tolbooth every Friday from 10.00 am. to 4.00 p.m., starting in January, 1839.

Doctor Rocliffe, who died in 1839, has already been described. Other doctors were George Cock and John Scott, both named in 1823 and 1834, William Jones Hall, named in 1834, Robert Thomas Skaife, named in 1834 and 1867 and William Teasdale, named in 1857 and 1867. Edward Buller Hicks, practising in 1867, became the first Medical Officer of Health of the Rural District Council in 1894.

A new Wesleyan Methodist Chapel, replacing that opened in 1786, was completed in 1816 at a cost of £970. This is the present Methodist Chapel in Chapel Street. A school was built at the back of this chapel in 1836. The Primitive Methodists had a chapel at Easingwold in 1823 and probably earlier.[19] William White's directory of 1840 states that: "the Primitive Methodists worship in the Toll-booth", but this looks like a temporary arrangement while their new chapel in Spring Street was being built. The latter, completed in 1840 at a cost of £562, was built for 300 persons. It was later enlarged. The Independents, Calvinists or Congregationalists are said to have had a chapel at Easingwold from 1814.[20] In 1820 they built a chapel in a yard off Long Street at or near the backs of the "Bay Horse" and "Fleece" Inns to hold about 200 persons. There was a succession of Independent ministers at Easingwold until at least 1868.[21]

The Rev. Edmund Paley, MA., became Vicar of Easingwold on 7th August, 1812, and resigned in 1839. He was responsible for adding the two wings to the Old Vicarage in 1813.

A son of Archdeacon William Paley (1743-1805), author of the famous "View of the Evidences of Christianity," 1794, and other highly influential works, his own son Frederick Apthorp Paley (1815-1888), born at Easingwold, won fame as a classical scholar by way of Shrewsbury and St. John's Cambridge, though his conversion to the Roman Catholic Church in 1846 kept him from formal academic status. Frederick Apthorp Paley was also one of the publicisers of Gothic Architecture, publishing a Manual on it in 1846 and a work on "Gothic Mouldings", which went into its sixth edition in 1902.

In 1825 Tom Cowling died from the effects of excessive drinking at the Royal Oak and William White, a joiner, was the victim of a somewhat similar incident in the Unicorn in Long Street, when he drank a pint of rum in mistake for a pint of ale. The events of the year were not exhausted. In the words of

118

Thomas Gill: "Frank Sellers, groom at the "New Rose and Crown" Inn, Long Street, writhing under the anguish of disappointed love in his ardent attachement to Miss Fanny Thorpe, a pretty dressmaker in the town, hung himself in the coach house".[22]

The town had an Agricultural Association in 1827 under the Chairmanship of William Lockwood. A cricket club, known as the "Easingwold Independent Crickett Club", was formed in July, 1829, the rules being signed by twenty members. Thomas Crawford was its president and Charles Henry Holgate treasurer and secretary.[23]

The building of the Roman Catholic church in Long Street seems to have commenced in 1830, though it was not opened for worship until 21st November, 1833, with the Rev. Richard Tyrer as its priest. It is regarded as the successor to the old Roman Catholic chapels of Oulston and Crayke.

In 1823 Francis Rawling was conducting a private school in Uppleby under the name of "Easingwold Academy", in the present Allerton House. Mr. Rawling was the son of Richard Rawling of Easingwold, cordwainer, and was teaching in the town in 1810. He died in 1853 and is commemorated by a large Gothic tombstone near the east window of the parish church. The dormitory and schoolroom still exist, showing that the school took a limited number of boarders. The Rev. Edwin Webster, who in 1857 was an Independent Minister living in Uppleby[24], in 1859 advertised the Collegiate School, Easingwold, with up to eight boarders, which would be about right for Allerton House. The Collegiate School had a Professor of Modern Languages and Chemistry named the Count of St. Alban. This looks like a French title and a branch of the Berthelot family were seigneurs of St. Alban in Burgundy at about this time, but there does not appear to have been any Count of St. Alban in France during the 19th century. Perhaps this was a case of self-inflicted promotion. Mary Champney had a ladies boarding school in Long Street in 1834.

In 1828 the churchwardens and overseers of the poor drew up rules for the workhouse at Easingwold. These were printed and ordered to be made available to any "lay-payer" (rate payer) on application. The government of the poor of the township was to be vested in the churchwardens, overseers and select vestry. Although the paupers were closely and sometimes fussily supervised (all must go to bed on the ringing of the evening bell; no ale or spirits except by order of the surgeon; talking to be avoided at meals; men and women to sit apart; no smoking after 7.00 p.m.

in winter and 8.00 p.m. in summer; normal visiting hours restricted to 2.00 p.m. to 4.00 p.m. on Thursdays; and so on), the general impression is of dullness rather than inhumanity, though clearly much would depend on the personalities of the Master and Mistress.

The dietary was as follows

Breakfast   (7.00 a.m. in summer, 8.00 a.m. in winter). One imperial quart of milk porridge and 8 ozs. of bread. The porridge was made of salt, milk, water and oatmeal.

Dinner   (Noon on weekdays; 12.30 p.m. on Sundays).

Sunday   Half a pound of boiled beef with potatoes and other vegetables.

Monday   A quart of pease broth (oatmeal and peas) and 8 ozs. of bread.

Tuesday   14 ozs. of dumpling and milk and treacle sauce. (One lb. of treacle and two quarts of milk for 20 persons);

Wednesday   Half a pound of boiled meat with potatoes or other vegetables;

Thursday   A quart of rice milk. (for 20 or more persons, 4 lbs. of rice, 2 gallons of milk and three gallons of water. The five gallons of liquid were to be sweetened by not more than $1/2$ lb. of flour and 2 lbs. of treacle per gallon). If flour reduced to 2/- a stone, it was recommended that this dinner be changed to cake and milk;

Friday   Boiled beasts head with potatoes and other vegetables;

Saturday   Beasts heart or sheeps hearts roasted and potatoes;

Supper   (6.00 p.m. in winter, 7.00 p.m. in summer) — Milk porridge and 4 ozs. of bread on Sunday, Monday, Wednesday and Friday. On other days, broth and 8 ozs. of bread.

In case of sickness the diet was to be according to the doctor's orders.

Children in the workhouse were as a matter of policy separated from their parents. Paupers in the workhouse were expected to attend church twice on Sunday, returning immediately after the services.

Casual paupers might be admitted to a room in the yard for one night, being allowed in winter $1/2$ lb. of bread and a quart of broth or water gruel for both supper and breakfast and in summer $1/2$ lb. of bread only for each meal. No fire was allowed in summer, which was considered to run from 7th April to 4th November inclusive.

Exactly where the workhouse was at this time is not known — possibly on the north side of Stillington Road, at or near the peculiar flat topped house at one time a common lodging house. The enclosure award map of 1812 shows premises belonging to the Poor of Easingwold at this point, then just outside the toll-bar. One thing which can be said with certainty is that there were several cottages in the poorhouse yard, the occupiers of which were subject to some restriction with regard to the closing of the yard door. They may have constituted an intermediate form of relief. Their occupiers certainly went out to work, but they could have been let at nominal rents or something of that kind.

The rules also take the opportunity of defining the general duties of the "Vestry Clerk, Inspector, or Town's Husband", which not only related to the Poor Law, but included such matters as making the highway and constable rates, the collection of land tax and the operation of the militia laws. The authentic parochial note may be heard in such sentences as: "He shall keep an eye on all unmarried females, who are suspected to be with child, and are likely to become chargeable to the town; and remove all such as do not belong to the township, by a Magistrate's order, to their proper settlement. He shall in cases of removal to this Township, from others, carefully ascertain that the poor so brought are ours, that the order is in all points correct". After this it is comforting to read that: "He shall on all occasions, treat the poor with the greatest humanity and kindness, that the peculiarity of their situations will allow".

Street names in the early 19th century were somewhat variable. Uppleby and Spring Street together were known as "the High Street", in distinction from Long Street, which was "the Low Street". This was a very old usage, which still survives in the common practice of calling Uppleby "High Street". Chapel Street at this period was "Long Lane". being thus distinguished from Little Lane. (The practice of calling it Market Street appears to be a late 19th century usage). Smith's Lane is the road from

121

Little Lane to Long Street, through the New Inn Yard. "Windross Row" seems to mean the houses on the south side of the Market Place, in 1839 owned by John Windross, and "Windross Square" may be the square at the north end of Little Lane, opening into the Market Place. Paradise Place, named in 1857, may be somewhere in the Back Lane. Church Street, named in 1871, seems to be the short street from Long Street to the bottom of the Church Avenue. It was also known as Church Lane, as Chapel Street was (and still is) often called Chapel Lane.

In 1797 the proprietor of the market rights was William Whytehead, barrister-at-law, who had purchased them from the Rev. William Edmund. They were later owned by Robert Spence, after whose death his trustees sold to a group of thirteen joint owners, including the attorneys William Lockwood junior and John Haxby; the surgeon R. T. Skaife; Charles and John Johnson, hatters and banking agents; and Robert T. Wiley, a chemist. This was about 1837 and the joint proprietors paid £2,000. They were naturally anxious to make the most of their property and in September, 1837, decided not to let the tolls as had been done in the past, but to keep them in hand for twelve months to ascertain their value. Their moveable property, consisting of 351 boards, 165 poles, 70 trestles, weights and other equipment, with the copy of the market charter, was valued at £34. 10s. 3d. The owners decided that all stalls and planks should be branded "E.T.Ho." (Easingwold Town House?) and that they should provide two 18 foot planks to be set on the south side of the market cross for the butter stand. They decided to repair the Toll Booth and have a decayed poplar tree on its east side removed.

The toll collector seems to have been instructed to pursue a 'strict line. At any rate there was almost immediate trouble when he demanded tolls of 6d. per week per stall from two Easingwold butchers, who promptly refused to pay on the ground that all inhabitants of Easingwold were toll free. It was decided to take Counsel's opinion and Mr. Haxby accordingly laid a case before Sir Frederick Pollock.

To summarise this briefly, it was that the toll owners based their right to take tolls on George Hall's grant of 16th August, 1639. The inhabitants of Easingwold, Huby and other places claimed to be toll free under a charter of 28th April, 1662, 'which recited that the men and tenants of the ancient demesne of the Crown were entitled to be toll free and that the men of Easingwold had been declared to be of such Crown lands by a certificate in Chancery taken in the reign of Edward IV. On 13th January, 1838, Sir Frederick advised that the privilege for tenants of the ancient demesne only applied to tenants of the manor bringing to the market the produce of their own land. In addition parts of the town outside the market ground could not legally be used for sales from booths or stalls, nor could a toll free person come onto the paved part of the market (where the corn and meat markets were held) with a caravan and expose goods for sale there, provided there was room for him elsewhere on the market ground. He advised that the owners' rights should be established by action of debt.

In April following it was decided to proceed against two of the several persons who had been selling from caravans and refusing toll. The actions first came on for trial at York Spring Assizes in 1839, after an abortive preliminary canter at the Summer Assizes of 1838, which for some reason never proceeded to a hearing, but was abandoned on payment of the costs of the defence. The plaintiffs called witnesses to show that inhabitants of Easingwold had paid for stalls or stands. Mrs. Smith stated that from the time of her grandfather, who appears to have been the original Leonard Smith, in the 1790's or late 1780's her husband's family had paid 1d. every market day for a stall near the Tollbooth (apparently for the products of their ropemaking business). The defence pointed out that such payments may not have been actual toll payments, but for the hire of stalls from the toll collectors. They also contended that payments made by butchers for space in the shambles were not toll payments. They called John Charles Lambert of Easingwold, innkeeper and lessee of the tolls from October, 1832, to October, 1837, who had owned the market stalls. He bought them from Jonathan Todd, the preceding Collector, and sold them to the thirteen proprietors in 1837 for £35. A dish turner, John Banks, gave evidence of having successfully claimed exemption in the past. At a date prior to 1797 he refused to pay and the then toll proprietor, Mr. Edmund, had seized a cheesevat, but Mr. Lockwood senior had got it back for him. If the weather was fine he laid out his dishes on the pavement, but if it was wet he sold from his cart. He had seen butchers carts and caravans standing in the market for upwards of fifty years. Thomas Moore, the potter, gave evidence that he had also been asked for toll by Mr. Edmund and on his refusal several pots had been seized and broken. Again old Mr. Lockwood had upheld his rights.

The result of the first trial was in favour of the nominal plaintiff, the Rev. Wm. Lockwood, with 1/- damages and leave to appeal. The judgment was reversed at the summer assizes in 1841, restored in favour of the plaintiff by the Court of Exchequer in 1844 and again reversed at the July Assizes in 1844. There was a new trial at the York Summer Assizes in 1846 when a verdict was given for the defendant. In 1848 leave was given for a new trial, but by this time the parties had had enough. There had been talk of settlement from 1845 onwards and this came to fruition in 1849, the action being settled on terms that the defendants and inhabitants of Easingwold were in fact toll free, but that the parties should each pay their own costs.

Legally the actions brought by the toll proprietors appears to have been soundly based to this extent, that exemption was limited to actual tenants of the manor selling the produce of their own land, who were in any event only entitled to sell from the market ground. The settlement may therefore be regarded as something of a victory for the Anti-Toll party. It is perhaps worth noting that when the actions were first brought, eighty persons agreed to share the costs of the defence, but the defence attorneys never seem to have been paid anything like their full costs. Mr. John Robinson and his colleague Mr. R. H. Anderson of York eventually shared some £796, but this can hardly have been the full amount. The plaintiffs solicitors bill was £1,955. 11s. 10d. and there cannot have been so great a difference between this and the defence costs.

Part of the market ground was paved and part occupied by the permanent butchers shambles. The toll owners decided to lay gravel on the unpaved ground in 1844. As already mentioned the butter stand was on the south side of the Market Cross. The corn market seems to have been on the improved part of the market ground. Fish was sold on what is now the green on the south side of the Market Place.[25]

Townships had long been able to combine into unions to build workhouses and make other provision for their poor. In 1834 the Poor Law Amendment Act made such combination obligatory, the country being divided into some seven hundred unions. The Easingwold Union formed under the new Act comprised an area of 96 square miles and consisted of the twenty-nine townships of Aldwark, Alne, Angrain Grange, Brafferton, Brandsby-cum-Stearsby, Carlton Husthwaite, Coxwold, Crayke, Dalby-cum-Skewsby, Easingwold, Farlington, Flawith, Huby,

Husthwaite, Linton, Marton-cum-Moxby, Myton, Newburgh, Newton, Oulston, Raskeif, Stillington, Sutton-on-Forest, Tholthorpe, Thormanby, Thornton Hill, Whenby, Wildon Grange and Yearsley. The controlling body of the Union was a Board of Guardians consisting of representatives of each township. The Guardians built a new workhouse at Easingwold, capable of accommodating 130 persons. It was completed in 1837 at a cost of £2,000. An infirmary for infectious diseases was added in 1869 at a cost of about £700.

In 1836 died a well known Easingwold eccentric, Ned Mountain, of whom Gill wrote: "He has been known to start off with the Mail Coach on foot from Thirsk or Northallerton and beat it into York. He was commonly known by the name of '. . . Neddy-ma-nox; who fought the devil in a 'bacco box.'."[26]

In 1838, Gill records, "Mary Barker, a girl from Ripon, who lived servant with Mr. George Scaife at the "New Inn",, Long Street, hung herself in the back kitchen in consequence of a love disappointment. She was cut down by H. Elmer, and a verdict of Temporary Insanity was returned".[27]

On 7th January, 1839, a violent gale blew down many trees, including a number of the tall poplars in the Paradise, rolled up lead on the church roof and damaged many other buildings.[28] On 17th October in the same year John Gibson, the son of James Gibson, farmer, of Crankley, was injured by the upsetting of a coach and later died. On 14th December, 1839, Dr. Rocliffe died at the age of 85, removing a well known character from the Easingwold scene. Even today one hears how old Dr. Rocliffe shot a snipe on the beck running through the Market Place and similar stories.

On 8th July, 1839, a new vicar was instituted, Mr. Paley having resigned. He was the Rev. Samuel James Allen, born about 1798 near the old church of St. Katherine by the Tower of London and educated at Merchant Taylors' School and Pembroke College, Cambridge. He took his B.A. in 1820 and M.A. in 1824. After taking orders he was presented to the living of Salesbury, near Blackburn, and was for a time Master of the Free School at Burnley. Mr. Allen's tastes were architectural and historical. He was an accomplished pencil draughtsman and family tradition has it that he was at one time a sketching companion of Turner. It is likely that he provided Gill with much of the material for the latter's history of Easingwold. Very probably the engraving of Raskelf church in this is based on a drawing made by Mr. Allen in August, 1841. Three beautifully written manuscript volumes, illustrated by heraldic drawings, were the result of visits paid by him as a young man, starting in 1813, to churches in the South of England. At this period of his life he wrote pleasant poetry, heavily influenced by Chatterton's Rowley poems, Barbour's "Bruce" and the "Lay of the Last Minstrel". If at times this is also reminiscent of Dr. Johnson's "Hermit hoar in solemn cell", young Mr. Allen was not without a mild sense of humour, as for example his "Elegy on the Death of a Canary Bird written at the command of his disconsolate Mistress" ("Be every Face prolonged by Grief, To twice its usual Sise, And ye who have a handkerchief Oh! hold it to your eyes"). Even as a youth his taste ran to Gothic. In 1843 he was a member, apparently recently joined, of the Yorkshire Architectural Society, a body "in communion" with the ultra-Gothic Cambridge Camden Society, a highly important pressure group in establishing the Gothic styles as the only true Christian architecture for the Victorian period. He therefore probably agreed with Gill[29] in considering the box pews in the church disfiguring. Certainly the Camden Society was particularly down on box pews. (As one of its pamphlets published in 1842, puts it: "For What is the HISTORY OF PUES, but the history of the intrusion of human pride, and selfishness, and indolence into the Worship of GOD?") — Mr. Allen died on 29th April, 1856, after suffering a stroke while he was in the vicarage garden superintending the arrangement of some stones which had formed part of the old market cross of Easingwold.[30] At the time of his death he was assisted by a curate, the Rev. H. Croft, who read the burial service at the funeral on 6th May.

The Great North of England Railway Company had obtained an Act of Parliament in 1836 authorising it to build a railway from York to Darlington. On 4th January, 1841, this was opened for goods traffic and on 31st March, 1841, for passenger traffic. There were stations at Shipton, Tollerton, Alne, Raskelf and Sessay and five trains each way during the day. The mail trains ran from Darlington at 3.30 p.m. and York at 7.20 a.m., connecting with the London trains. They were allowed 2 hours 35 minutes for the journey and stopped only at Cowton, Northallerton, Thirsk and Alne.[31] Alne named two of its public houses the Railway Tavern and the Great North of England Inn respectively.

Easingwold had heard of the railway for over four years and at first efforts seem to have been made to have it brought through the town. Robert Gill the attorney was a protagonist of this movement. When it was seen that the line was going to run through Alne the agitation switched to a demand for a branch. This idea was mooted at least as early as 1838 and a guide book of 1843 refers to a branch to Alne as then in contemplation.[32] In 1845 Mr. Plummer of New Parks, Shipton, owner of the celebrated racing mare "Alice Hawthorne", is said to have offered her winnings for a year as a contribution to the cost of this branch. The "Railway Party" seem to have been active into the 1850's and Bradshaw's railway map of 1851 shows a highly improbable line projected from somewhere about Pilmoor Junction directly to Easingwold, regardless of topography. A public house called the Railway Tavern had appeared in Easingwold Market Place by October, 1843, no doubt as a piece of intelligent anticipation.

One result of the coming of the railway was that coal, formerly carted from Co. Durham, could now be brought from Alne Station, where there was already a coal agent in 1841. But on the whole the railway was more detrimental to the town than otherwise. A major source of the town's obvious prosperity in the early 1800's was its position on the important mailcoach road from London to Edinburgh. Now traffic was being diverted to the alternative rail route. Stagecoaches, posting services and inns declined rapidly. The Highflyer came off the road in 1840 and the Mail in 1842. The Wellington struggled longest, but it was not for very long. The big carrying firms went out of business or transferred it to the railways. A country town not directly served by a railway was in for a period of stagnation at best. In 1851 the population of Easingwold was 2,240. Eighty years later in 1931 it stood at 2,043.

The Tolbooth was heavily damaged by fire in 1842, but was rebuilt. In the same year James Carter was transported for stealing straw from one of the town's carriers.[33]

At the beginning of 1847 H.M. Treasury began negotiations with the toll proprietors for the use of the Toll Booth for the holding of a small debts court (that is a County Court), and there seem to have been lettings for this purpose from Lady Day, 1848, until the opening of the Town Hall in 1864.

An annual foal show was established at Easingwold in 1847 and was held at least as late as 1860.

Slater's Directory for 1848 lists public houses named the Blue Boar and the Talbot. The Talbot later became the York Hotel. These premises had first been licensed at dates between 1841 and 1848.

In 1849 there was a boarding school in Long Street kept by Mary Jane Thickness and a day school in Uppleby kept by Mary Sturdy, who had formerly been a governess in the family of the Bishop of Lincoln.[34] Mrs. Sturdy was still teaching at this school in 1857. A Miss Cordukes had a boarding school in Crankley in 1852[35] and may have been the Miss A. J. Cordukes who in July, 1860, was keeping a boarding school at 6, Lord Mayor's Walk, York.[36] Ralph Barker in Long Street, possibly the man who kept the "Green Tree" in 1841, was a veterinary surgeon in 1849. Also in 1849 may be mentioned Richard Moncaster, machine maker in the Market Place, and William Reacher, millwright, and Frederick Webster, pianoforte tuner, in Long Street.[37]

In 1852 Thomas Gill, in association with Simpkin Marshall & Co. of London and R. Sunter of Stonegate, York, published his history of Easingwold and district entitled "Vallis Eboracensis."

It bears the imprint of Gill himself, a printer in the Market Place. Gill's "Vallis Eboracensis" is quite a handsome work in black cloth boards, with the arms of the lord of the manor in gilt on the front cover and illustrated with lithographic views. There were at least seven hundred subscribers, including a number in Australia and the United States. Copies are found with additional subscribers added to the original list and it is known that in February, 1856, Gill was selling the work at 7/6d. to subscribers and 10/6d. to non-subscribers.

Gill, who was born on 2nd May, 1811, was the son of Christopher Gill, a farmer at Easingwold. His education was probably local. On 8th June, 1834, he married Elizabeth King, "also of this parish", by licence, the ceremony being carried out by the Rev. Edmund Paley. There is a tradition that "Miss Eliza King wore black at her wedding".[38] Be that as it may, twin daughters, Ann Mary and Caroline, born on 14th February, 1836, both died in their infancy. At this date Gill was a grocer. A piece of printing by him dated 20th February, 1837, is extant and he developed a many sided business consisting of printing: the publication of small works, some of which he wrote himself: bookselling, book binding and the sale of groceries, patent medicines, preparations for cattle, and stationery. There was a shop in the name of Thomas Gill in Uppleby in 1841, but his business later centred on the Market Place. At the beginning of 1854 he started to issue a newspaper, the "Easingwold Chronicle", at first a monthly, later a weekly, which appeared till 30th November, 1861.

Easingwold Spring Races.

These Races will commence

On MONDAY the 20th of February, 1837, at 12 o'Clock at Noon.

The following is a correct list of the Horses already entered to run for the Freeholders, and Ratepayers Stakes, with the names of the Riders:

Mr. Gill's Grey Colt   "*SIGSWORTH*"   rode by John Coverdale.

Mr. Claro's Bay Horse   "*BAINBRIDGE*" rode by the Attorney General.

Mr. J. Johnson's Black Filly   "*REVEREND*"   rode by Dr. Cockpit.

Mr. Robinson's Brown Horse   "*WATSON*"   rode by Sir John Brandy.

The BETS at present are TEN to ONE in favour of "SIGSWORTH" although the Ratepayers bet freely in favour of "BAINBRIDGE." It is thought "REVEREND" may perhaps win, unless Dr. Cockpit the Rider is bribed. After the Races, "REVEREND" will be removed to Fencote near Bedale, and will be withdrawn from the Turf.

George Barker,   } Clerks of the Course.
Thomas Kempley, }

GILL, PRINTER, EASINGWOLD

A "race card" for the vestry election, 1837, printed by Thomas Gill

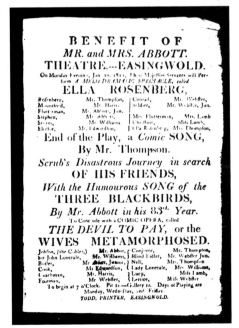

An Easingwold theatre bill, 1812

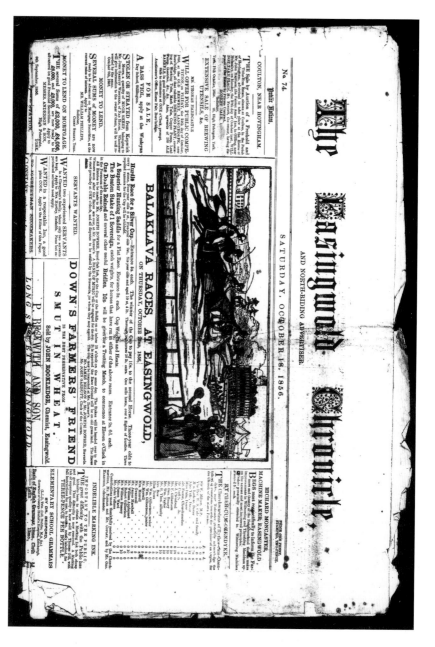

A copy of the "Easingwold Chronicle", 1856

Miss M. M. Smith

THE GRAND TERMINUS

OF THE

EASINGWOLD BRANCH RAILWAY.

In eighteen hundred and forty-two
A project there was made ;
To start a Branch to Easingwold,
To improve the Town and Trade.

But the Loggerheads could not agree
Which route the Line should take ;
One would have this, another that,
For his own party's sake.

So like the greedy dog, they lost
Their substance for a shade ;
Division weakened all their parts,
And the Line could not be made.

But the Shareholders had paid their brass
And the Treasurer held it fast ;
Though long and loud the call,—*Divide*,
Which has been done at last.

To C. T. B——, the credit's due,
T'was he that pushed the job ;
With Mr. R., and Dr. S——,
And their good friend little Bob.

When the division it was made
As near as it could be ;
A Balance small, there still remained,
In the hands of the Treasury.

So for the good of the "Old George,"
Where the Business had been done ;
A supper they would have, to close
The Traffic to the Town.

Thus ends the Great, Grand Terminus
Of the Easingwold Railway Branch ;
Nobly begun, and carried on,
And ended with a Lunch.

And here's the moral of my Song,
When you an effort make,
To improve the Town, or Public weal,
Let private interests break.

Had this been done when first begun,
The Easingwold Branch Railway,
Had now been running to the Town,
The holders well to pay.

The Town had been a thriving Place,
And Trade both brisk and good ;
Prosperity had stamped its name,
But now 'tis "Ichabod."

ANONYMOUS.

A broadside on the agitation for a branch railway to Easingwold, c.1845-50

The Town Hall, 1866, without the clock tower

Miss H. Sturdy

By this date he was involved in business difficulties and bankruptcy proceedings were started. He appears to have been for a time a debtor imprisoned in York Castle. He received his discharge from the Castle and adjudication in bankruptcy at the Leeds Court of Bankruptcy on 25th April, 1862, before Mr. Commissioner West, when his debts were found to amount to £912 and his assets to consist chiefly of doubtful or disputed debts. He stated that he no longer had any property in a paper which he had published and this seems to imply that he had sold the "Chronicle". A new paper, the "Easingwold Times" published by John and Joseph Smith, printers, from premises in the Market Place, seems to have first come out on 4th January, 1862, and the interval between this and the last issue of the "Chronicle" is so close as to suggest that it was the "Chronicle" renamed. The Smith's probably bought Gill's printing works, too. Further misfortunes followed. Mrs. Gill died at Thirsk on 7th March, 1865. His son T. W. Whitfield Gill, who seems to have been then Gill's only child, died on 13th April, 1868, at the early age of 25. (Whitfield Gill is named as a bookseller at Easingwold in 1867.[39]) Thomas Gill made a fresh start with a printing press in Chapel Street from which he published almanacks in the period 1870-2, but according to tradition, he started to drink more heavily, lost favour with his fellow Methodists, and finally ended his days in the York Union Workhouse, where he died on 11th March, 1882. His published work suggests a clever, self educated man, lacking in humour, who was frequently carried beyond the bounds of prudence by his enthusiasms or prejudices. One of the latter seems to have been against the legal profession and the "Chronicle" of 26th April, 1859, contains a public apology for libels in a previous issue on George Henry Smith, a York solicitor. His advertisement in July, 1860, for a new publication, "Gill's Monthly Register", is grandiose to the extent of absurdity. This was to commence on 1st August and consist of 48 pages, royal octavo, containing four times as much matter as a number of "Chamber's Journal", five times as much as a number of "The Leisure Hour", and three and a half times as much as a number of "Once a Week" or "All the Year Round". "In fact GILL'S MONTHLY REGISTER will thus embrace within its scope a greater uumber of subjects and topics than have ever hitherto been treated in one journal". No copy of the work, which was to sell at 2d. a number, seems to be extant.

As a historian Gill is not unworthy within the limits of the sources available to him, but his imagination could run wild, as in his Family Almanack of 1872, when he described a battle between the Romans and Brigantes in 57 A.D. On what appears to be the slenderest foundation, he stated that the Romans camped on the Lund at a spot in front of Mr. William Gill's house, and the Britons at Spring House Wood. On the other hand he is said to have been the first to appreciate the significance of the finds which led to the discovery of the Roman villa site on Oulston Moor in 1854, and he has preserved many useful facts in his writings. "Vallis Eboracensis" was undertaken, as he says, "not in the pursuit of pecuniary advantage, but in the gratification of a natural inclination", and it has had, it may be truly said, the affection of several generations of Easingwold people, including the writer.

Apart from publishing a number of small lives of John Wesley and other early Methodists, some small devotional works and an "Etiquette of Love, Courtship and Marriage", Gill edited a work entitled "The Life and Times of Louis Philippe",[40] and was a joint publisher of "Trade and Travels in the Gulph of Guinea", by J. Smith of Coxwold. about 1851. He wrote a novel entitled: "The Knight of Newbrough: or The Abbot of Byland: A Tale of the Fauconbergs" which he published in 1847. Part of this was printed, slightly re-hashed, in his Family Almanack for 1872 under the title: "Eliza Salvin, the Beautiful Heiress and Lovely Heroine of Easingwold Old Hall". Neither "the Knight" nor "Eliza" are very readable. He appears to much greater advantage as a newspaper editor, and clearly had a natural gift as a journalist. It is possible that Gill started the Easingwold custom of issuing "race cards" for local elections. This continued until the 1920s from at least 1837. In the example for the vestry election of 1837, the candidates became horses, the proposers their owners and seconders their jockeys. Nicknames were freely used — thus in 1837 Dr. Robert Skaife was "Dr. Cockpit" (No doubt like Dr. Rocliffe, he was a cockfighting man), while John Haxby, attorney, became "the Attorney General" and Mr. Garbutt, a wine and spirit merchant "Sir John Brandy". The Rev. William Lockwood, a candidate, was entered as "Reverend". As time went on a great deal of facetious rigmarole was inserted in the cards, much of which is now unintelligible.

Before Gill started the "Chronicle" Easingwold people had to rely on the "York Courant" (started in 1720), the "York Chronicle" (1772), the "York Herald" (1790) or the "Yorkshire Gazette" (1819). The "Courant" and "Herald" were Whig papers, the "Chronicle" and "Gazette" Tory. The fact that the Easingwold Inclosure Act, 1808, required as part of the procedure the publication of notices in the "York Courant" and the "Hull Advertiser" suggests that the latter then had some circulation in the district. At first monthly, the "Easingwold Chronicle" appears to have become a weekly, in a somewhat larger format, in 1855 or early 1856. Originally the full title was "The Easingwold Chronicle and North-Riding Advertiser". This was changed (by April, 1859) to "The Easingwold Chronicle and Thirsk Times and Advertiser".

In its earlier issues news of the Crimean War jostles such local "small beer" as the presentation on 23rd December, 1854, of a tea and coffee service to George Shepherd, stationmaster at Raskelf for upwards of ten years, on his transfer to Castleford station, the anniversary sermon of the Church Missionary Society in Easingwold Parish Church and a cricket match at Helmsley on 27th September, 1855. The issue of 1st January, 1855, contains a report of an accident to Mr. Shield's omnibus at Raskelf on the previous 22nd December, when the horses took fright at fireworks, together with a list of Crayke subscribers to the Patriotic Fund, a letter from William Britton, Private in the 7th Foot, from the Camp before Sebastpol, to his brother and sister at Crayke, an account of an address of sympathy made to Mrs Croft of Stillington Hall for the death of her son Harry in the great storm off Balaclava on 14th November, 1854, and the following advertisement:— "These are times when it is necessary for every Briton worthy of the name to do his utmost in order to furnish the means of humbling the grand enemy of civilization and to keep our soil from being polluted with his hordes of Cossacks and other barbarians. Every useless item of expenditure must be saved. The utmost economy must be used in all our dealings. One heavy item of expense may be saved in most families by keeping a constant supply of DR. TORREN'S HERBAL PILLS". (Though modern man is said to put his faith in tranquilisers to an inordinate degree he seems to have had nothing on his great grandparents who used all manner of weird preparations for man and beast — Croskell's Celebrated Female Pills, Dr. Coffins Celebrated Restorative and Indian Pills, Down's Farmers Friend, Luddingtons Róyal Driffield Remedy for Cattle, Dennis's Celebrated Family Pills "for bilious complaints, viscid concretions, disorders of the stomach and bowels, flatulency, giddiness, asthma, and sick headache occasioned by indigestion &c. &C." prepared principally from "the gums and other productions of the Eastern World" for Mr. Dennis, surgeon at Stillington, and Wiley's Chemical Essence for Lameness in Horses

131

first put up by Thos. W. Wiley, chemist of Easingwold, one of the market toll proprietors in 1855.

In 1854 Miss Rachael Whytehead offered to give to the toll owners £50 for a new Market Cross. The work was completed in 1856, to the design of Messrs. Atkinsons, architects.

A race meeting was held at Easingwold on 27th September, 1855, consisting of twelve races. Seven booths were erected for spectators and a band was in attendance. The Newburgh Stakes of £5 was run in two heats, there was a hurdle race for £3, a double reined bridle race and six bridle races for horses. The list was completed by a race for a new saddle and silver plated spurs, a donkey race and a foot race. The judge and starter was John Batty of Coxwold and the Clerk of the Course Ralph Barker, landlord of the Green Tree. James Nelson, grocer in Long Street, and Joseph Bowser of the "Royal Oak" were stewards.

The following year the races, run on 23rd October, were called the "Balaklava Races", no doubt in compliment to Sir George Wombwell, who had taken part in the charge of the Light Brigade. There was a silver cup for the hurdle race, a number of fiat races and a trotting match. The stewards were again Mr. Nelson and Mr. Bowser and the Clerk of the Course John Garbutt. (Mr. Nelson as the owner of a trotting horse named "Grey Charley of Easingwold" was no doubt specially interested in the trotting match).

These races may have been a continuation of the Easingwold Races which have been mentioned above in 1818.

The "Chronicle" for 1st March, 1856, contains an editorial on the peace conference, and reports that Sir George Wombwell had become president of the Easingwold Floral and Horticultural Society. There is an account of a case of supposed witchcraft at Sheriff Hutton, in which two "wise men" had been consulted, and a letter from William Smith of Oulston to his brother Richard Smith of Easingwold, describing the former's journey to the Great Salt Lake in Utah, with accounts of Sioux and Cheyenne encampments, Fort Laramie, Independence Rock and the Sweetwater Mountains.

A new police station in the north-west corner of the Market Place was completed in 1856, presumably for the establishment of the North Riding Constabulary under the compulsory County and Borough Police Act of that year. The superintendent of the Bulmer Division (an Easingwold man) seems to have been stationed there in 1857.

The Union Steam Flour Mill in Long Street was also opened in 1856, and a public meeting in the Toll Booth on 16th October decided to adopt the Lighting and Watching Act of William IV to enable the necessary mains to be laid for gas lighting. The Easingwold Gas and Coke Company Limited in fact opened its new gasworks in Long Street in 1857. In the last named year there was a library and reading room, recently established, in the Market Place.

A new vicar, the Rev. Henry Ainslie was instituted on 3rd June, 1856, following the death of the Rev. Samuel James Allen. (He had actually arrived on 9th May, three days after Mr. Allen's funeral.) Mr. Ainslie had an assistant curate, John Lomax, in 1857.

In 1857 the town had agencies of the Yorkshire Banking Company and of the Bank of London and National Provincial Bank, the latter held by John Rookledge, chemist in the Market Place (from Lady Day, 1856, prior to which he occupied a house in Chapel Lane). Agencies for the Knaresborough and Claro Banking Company had been held in the town in the years 1834-41 and for the York District Bank in 1841. Tradespeople included William Leadley, brewer, in Uppleby; George Robinson, brick-maker at Shires Bridge; Peter Beckwith & Son, drapers in Long Street; George Earnshaw in Chapel Street, one of Easingwold's five grocers; and Robert Rowntree, land agent in the Market Place. There were seventeen innkeepers, including John Charles Lambert of the Commercial Inn, and Leonard Smith, postmaster and ropemaker, at the Fleece. William Reacher in Long Street was in business as a millwright. Mrs. Ann Bradwell kept a girl's day school in Long Street, as did Misses Rhodes and Smith. Mrs. Frances and Miss Mary Caldwell kept a girl's day school in Uppleby, as did Mrs. Mary Sturdy already mentioned. Mrs. Ann Sigsworth and Gibson Gill kept day schools in Long Street and Mrs. Mary Steel and Miss Frances Ditchburn kept day schools in the Market Place. Mrs. Steel also kept a toy shop and was in business as a straw bonnet maker and milliner in Chapel Street. (Milliners and dressmakers in the town had increased fairly rapidly from 1823, when three were listed in a directory, to 1834, when six were listed and 1841, when there were no less than fourteen. The number had dropped to seven by 1857). A directory of 1857 lists the Westerman School as "Grammar School, William Barton, Springhead", which suggests that the master had moved his residence to the house in Spring Street but was still using the old schoolroom in Long Street. Mr. Barton at this time was supplementing his salary from the trustees by taking fee paying pupils, and by acting as vestry clerk and registrar of births, deaths and marriages for the Easingwold district. In 1850 we find him going to York to get the land held for the poor at Easingwold discharged from assessment for property tax.

It will be remembered that the broadsheet song on the publicans of Easingwold printed about 1820 referred to the justices as sitting at the George Inn. They were still sitting there in 1859. The court leet also met at the George. In 1857 a horse bus from the George met every train at Alne station. The 'bus running in 1870 seems to have been a four wheeler with a pair of horses, with two squareish windows on each side below which appeared the words ALNE STATION AND EASINGWOLD. The last horse bus on this route seems to have ended its days in the early 20th century in a field opposite Hanover House.

In 1858 the west gallery of the church was rebuilt and the north gallery removed. New flooring, new west doors in the tower, and a new west window in the tower were also provided, together with a new pulpit and reading desk. Broken tracery in the windows was restored and all windows were reglazed, three in the chancel of stained glass and three in the nave and six in the clerestory with coloured borders being special gifts. Gas fittings were installed and various repairs carried out. The cost of the whole restoration was £1,000.[41] The east window inserted in 1858 is a memorial to three vicars, John Armitstead (curate from 1761 and vicar from 1771 to 1812), Edmund Paley (1812-39) and Samuel James Allen (1839-56), as well as a relative of the first, George Armitstead, born at Easingwold and for many years in business at Riga, who died in 1848. The chancel roof was raised to accomodate the new east window and the former ceilings removed.

On 21st July, 1858, the Archbishop of York consecrated an addition to the churchyard. The original part of the churchyard contains few tombstones not of the 19th century and little of great interest. Perhaps the most interesting from a design point of view, is the handsome altar tomb of George Robson (1807-57), farmer, of Shires Manor House and members of his family. The side panels bear small figures copied from the famous statue known as the Vatican Ariadne. This figure was popular in the 18th century — there is one in the grotto at Stourhead — and it found its way onto tombstones, another example being on a headstone of 1848 at Little Ouseburn. Curiosities at Easingwold are an anony-

134

mous headstone to "A Professional Gentleman", who died in 1810, and a stone near the church porch with all the letters "S" reversed.

On 28th February, 1860, the market toll proprietors decided to hold a public meeting to invite subscriptions for a new shambles with a public room over. A special committee was formed and in June, 1860, the toll owners resolved to offer the Tollbooth property for £600. This was not taken up, but eventually in July, 1863 the owners agreed to sell the site of the old shambles for £400 and to give a donation of £120 and the materials of the old shambles The market rights and the Tolbooth property were retained, the latter being sold to Wm. Medd in 1903. The new Town Hall was opened on 31st March, 1864, with free beer and a large crowd, including the Easingwold Staghounds. The building had cost £1,423. It soon became the meeting place of the county court, petty sessions and other local bodies.

In the years 1860-67 there was a school in Easingwold called the "Easingwold Commercial and Grammar School for Boarders, Day Boarders and Day Scholars". Patron and visitor was the Archbishop of York, with the vicar as sub-visitor. The headmaster was James H. Dee, formerly of the Cheltenham Training College. This looks almost like a Church of England school. At any rate it does not seem to have survived into the 1870's.

An advertisement in the "Chronicle" for 28th July, 1860, by Win. Windross & Co. of the Emigrants Land Office, Cleveland, Ohio, suggests that one or more of the Windross family of Easingwold may have emigrated to the United States.

An Agricultural Society was formed at Easingwold in 1860, the Agricultural Association existing in 1827 having presumably dissolved. The first agricultural show of the new society was held in 1861. The second, on 9th September, 1862, was attended by the band of the 10th Hussars. A public dinner was provided at 5.00 p.m. and there was a ball in the evening. A grandstand was erected at this show. A photograph of the 1869 event shows an unroofed wooden grandstand on the west side of the Chasegarth with a marquee behind. In 1862 a silver cup was made for the show by Messrs. Joseph and Henry Barker, silversmiths.

The "Easingwold Times and Thirsk Advertiser" was issued against a background of the American Civil War and is full of news of General Grant and General Lee. In the issue of 20th June, 1863, Mr. Leonard Edson, of Crankley, showed where his sympathies lay by advertising his subscription bull. General Lee, to serve cows during the season at 10/- each. The same paper reported that Gunnett's Circus had visited Easingwold, but that there had been general dissatisfaction because Tom King, pugilistic champion of England, billed to appear, had not done so. There had been meetings on 10th June of the Easingwold Free Gift Benevolent Society and on 3rd July of the Female Interment Society (Annual Tea Meeting), both at the Royal Oak.

In 1862 the annual midsummer fair was attended by a conjuring establishment, a band, a tumbling clown in tights, an Aunt Sally on one of the greens, two or three bazaars and "the usual cake, toffy and nut stands".[42]

A hunt known as the Easingwold Staghounds existed during the years 1864-73 and no doubt longer. The master was John Coates of Peep o' Day and the hounds were kept at Woolpotts, Husthwaite. There was a stag pasture near Driffields Farm on the Alne road, surrounded by plum trees, the low branches of which prevented the stags from leaping out.[43] They had famous runs on 8th March, 1865, for 45-50 miles on the Wolds from Bossall Wood and in 1873 for 20 miles from Waplington Park to Osbaldwick On the former occasion the stag was taken alive and brought back to the stag pasture. Deer are still seen about the district from time to time.

A new organ was installed in the parish church in 1865, but in February, 1870, funds were still being raised to complete it. A photograph of the chancel taken prior to 1902 shows this organ at the east end of the north aisle. It was replaced by the present organ in 1903.

In 1867 the vicar had a curate, John Albert Kershaw, B.A. The new church organ had a regular organist, William Bensley of Long Street. There were a few changes among business and tradesmen. The commercial list in White's directory for 1867 shows four booksellers, five grocers, seven milliners, seven drapers, thirteen boot and shoemakers, seventeen public houses, three marine store dealers and four watchmakers. One of the grocers businesses had been started by John Bannister, who died at the early age of 40 in 1859. He had come from St. Andrewgate, York, and married the daughter of the landlord of the Angel, Annie Calway. She carried on the business for many years after her husband's death and it is still in the hands of the Bannister family. Another old established Easingwold business is that of Messrs. Chapman Medd & Sons, cabinet makers, antique dealers and undertakers in the Market Place, started in 1865.

136

Courtesy of aerofilms.com

An aerial view of the Market Place, early 1930's

G. H. Smith Esq.

The parish church from the Long Street cross roads, c.1905

G. H. Smith Esq.

Thatched and half timbered houses and the "Blue Bell Inn" (brick and thatch), Uppleby, c.1910

G. H. Smith Esq.

The "Malt Shovel" inn, Spring Street, c.1905

North-East corner of the Market Place, c.1905, showing the White House
in the background

Temporary building which housed Easingwold Grammar School from
1906 to 1911

Train on the Easingwold Railway with the first engine, 1891-1903

Long Street from the Thirsk end, c.1905. Note cobbled pavements

1867 was William Barton's last year at the Westerman Grammar School. The school had obviously declined. An account of a visit paid to it about 1866 is contained in Volume IX of the Report of the Schools Enquiry Commission. This reads: "At Easingwold I found a school along the middle of which was a partition, breast high, dividing the scholars into two groups. The master's desk was fixed in an elevated position and dominated both divisions of the school. He explained to me that the free scholars were on one side, and the paying scholars on the other. He had erected the partition, he said, in defence of his own interest, for unless he kept the two classes of pupils — the sheep and the goats as he familiarly called them — habitually apart, the more respectable parents would object to pay, and perhaps remove their children altogether. I learnt that while he was bound to admit a certain number of free scholars, it had been his custom to receive others on the footing of private pupils; and that even in the playground there was no intercourse between them. This marked and invidious distinction is not a common feature". At this time Latin was not taught, nor does it appear that the school received girls.

Local tradition has it that when a fee paying pupil required punishment it was given to one of the free scholars as his proxy! True or not, this tradition does not indicate a very high regard for the school in mid-Victorian times. Its history in the 1870's is obscure. It may even have closed for a period or periods. On 17th February, 1876, the Charity Commissioners approved a scheme converting it into a grammar school for boys with nine governors, including the vicar and the lord of the manor or the latter's nominee. Fees were not to exceed £6 per annum for Easingwold boys and £10 for others. In 1877 there is a reference to "the building formerly occupied by the Westerman Trustees", which seems to mean the schoolroom in Long Street. The Grammar School opened under its new scheme in October, 1881, in premises in the Back Lane behind a large house at the Spring Head. Mr. W. Williamson, M.A., was headmaster. He was followed by the Rev. Horace Townsend, M.A., in whose time the pupils wore mortar boards. Then came Mr. J. Davis, B.A., headmaster in 1890, succeeded in his turn by Mr. F. W. Long, BA., about 1893. In Mr. Long's time the school was housed in the former "New Rose and Crown", then called Longley House, and specialised in the principles of agriculture, chemistry, physiology, botany, mensuration and surveying. Longley House was sold in 1905 to the Sisters of Mercy and the school moved to a metal hut on Thirsk

137

Road. still standing on the south side of the present primary school.

The formidably titled National Society for Promoting the Education of the Poor in the Principles of the Established Church erected a school in the north-west corner of the Market Place in 1862, adjoining the police station. Now a branch library of the County Council, it bears the typically Victorian inscription: "Learn or Leave" with E.N.S. for "Easingwold National School, and HA. for "Henry Ainslie". An extension was built in 1877. Miss Elizabeth Ann Blyth also conducted a "seminary for young ladies" at Spring Head House, Spring Street, in 1867. In 1873 she was in partnership with Fraulein Koch, who seems to have come from Bavaria. In 1890 the school was in Long Street, apparently at Longley House under the direction of the Misses E. A. and F. K. Blyth. In 1867 a school conducted by Eleanor Rhodes took in boarders.

The Town Hall clock was presented in 1869 by Thomas Rociffe, Esquire, of Thirsk.

As a result of the passing of the Education Act, 1870, the Roman Catholic elementary day school was built next to the Roman Catholic Church and opened on 1st October, 1871. At first school boards had a discretion whether or not to impose compulsory education in their districts, but in 1876 this was removed and school attendance became compulsory everywhere. In 1891 education was made free of cost between the ages of three and fifteen to all who wished to send their children to a board school. The Act of 1902 abolished school boards and transferred the direction of the North Riding's education system to its county council.

At some date in the period 1870-2 the post office was transferred from Long Street to the north side of the Market Place. Before moving to its present position it was situated on the site of the present Midland Bank, in the same building as the then Yorkshire Banking Company's branch.

The last parish constables for Easingwold held office in 1872. The Parish Constables Act of that year provided that in future garish constables should not be appointed unless Quarter Sessions considered it necessary.

The Highway Act, 1862, had provided machinery for the setting up of highway boards to take over the functions of the parishes in the areas for which they were established. The Bulmer

West Highway Board must have been established under this Act. It consisted of waywardens elected by the thirty-three constituent parishes of its district, together with the justices of the peace resident there, and was in being in 1870. In that year John Robinson, attorney, of Easingwold was its clerk. In 1872 it met on the first Friday in the month at the Town Hall, the chairman being John Coates of Peep o' Day. The Board's accounts for 1871 show, out of a total expenditure of £3,136. 12s. Sd., £196. 13s. 5d. paid to local turnpike trusts. Of the latter sum £136. 19s. 0d. had gone to the Oswaldkirk Bank Top Turnpike Trust, mostly for work done in the parishes of Stillington and Sutton-on-Forest.[44] The Board was responsible for making a direct road connection between Easingwold and Crayke, by constructing a straight stretch of road linking the east end of Mill Lane, Easingwold, with Daffy Lane at Hallway House. The work seems to have been done during 1874[45] and on 5th February, 1875, the auditors of the Highway Board, passed the account for the work in the sum of £334. 3s. 4½d.[46]

"G. H. Smith's Family Almanack for 1873", printed by George Hudson Smith at the Post Office, has an interesting directory of Easingwold, which gives a number of addresses not otherwise met with. These include Hanover Place, which was part of the Market Place; Post Office Yard and Smith's Yard, also in the Market Place; Brown's Yard, Snowball's Yard, Britton's Yard and the suggestively named Wasps Nest off the west side of Long Street; and Eadingtons Yard and Feasby's Yard off the east side. The Wasps Nest seems to have been on the south east side of the Roman Catholic church. Resident in the Post Office Yard was George Cowling, Town Crier and impounder. The latter term must mean that he was the pinder of the court leet. A bellman is mentioned in 1838. At that date he rented a bell from the market toll proprietors for the sum of £1 a year, but just why they should be concerned with the matter is not clear. The court leet would have been a less surprising controlling authority. Bellmen or town criers exercised their function at Easingwold up to about the Second World War. In the years 1885-91 the bellman charged 6d. for crying once round the town, but this had gone up to 8d. a round by 1893.

Also mentioned in 1873 are Mary Wilkinson, who had a rag warehouse on the west side of Long Street, and Christopher Spence, also on the west side of Long Street, who was a goose dealer.

A new vicar, Frederic Brearley, was inducted on 13th September, 1873. He did not remain long and in December, 1877, was succeeded by Nathan Jackson, a graduate of Brasenose College, Oxford.

Old customs and beliefs were dying. The last case of the mock ceremony of "riding the stang" as a public protest against a wife beater took place at Easingwold about 1879.[47] Belief in witchcraft must have practically disappeared. A woman at Husthwaite was reputed to be a witch and to turn herself into a hare from time to time in the traditional manner. This must have been in the 1840's or 50's.[48] There was a case of supposed witchcraft at Sheriff Hutton in 1856, but by the 1870's it must have been hard to find anyone, among the younger generation at any rate, who seriously believed in witches and wise men. The old wedding customs, the practice of begging pigs feet and ears on Shrove Monday and wheat at Christmas for frumenty and much of the traditional horseplay of village life were also almost extinct.

A favourite form of help during the nineteenth century for "daytal men" and other working people who were liable to periods of temporary or seasonal unemployment, for example during prolonged snowfalls, was the soup kitchen. In 1877 at a public meeting in the Town Hall a soup kitchen committee was appointed to provide a soup kitchen during the winter months. The Committee's soup kitchen was at the back of the Malt Shovel Inn in Spring Street. When the committee felt that it was necessary to open it they sent the town crier round to make an announcement. In 1895 the soup kitchen was "cried" at least sixteen times in January and February and during the two months was open each Wednesday and Saturday. A charge, presumably a moderate one, was made for the soup. In suitable cases tickets were distributed entitling the holders to a free supply.

The committee's income came chiefly from collections and donations (£3 from Mr. Love of the Hawkhills, £2 or £1 from the Hon. Payan Dawnay of Beningbrough Hall, and so on) and from bank interest, but sometimes in special ways such as a penny reading in 1889, a "soldiers tea and concert" in 1893, a donation from the Wesleyan Institute in 1895 or a motor tour in 1921. Expenses included, besides the ingredients, payments to the crier and for making the soup, payments for the use of the kitchen and for repairs to the copper in which the soup was made and for coals.[49]

140

Another typically Victorian voluntary service was the Easing-wold Volunteer Fire Brigade, formed on 10th August, 1883.[50] The establishment consisted of a Superintendent, Deputy Superintendent, Foreman, Engineer and at least four active firemen. In February, 1884, it was decided to have eight uniformed active firemen and four reserves. Each member was equipped with helmet, tunic, belt, hatchet, life line and hose wrench. A bulls eye lantern was added for each fireman in 1889. There were to be drills at least once a month and the brigade was to attend all fires in the district. Members might be fined or dismissed for non-attendance. At fires extra men might be engaged on the spot and given counters, which they could later produce and be paid. 'The brigade's engine was a horse drawn Merryweather, manually operated, worked by long handles pulled up and down by men on each side.

Provision for fire fighting in the district had hitherto been 'somewhat scanty. A serious stackyard fire at the Old White House Inn on 3rd February, 1841, had been fought by the engine of the York and London Fire and Life Assurance Company, which had probably come all the way from York.[51] A fire at Robert Britton's lime dressing premises in December, 1859, was "quelled by the engine", again probably one from York.[52] Even when the Easingwold brigade got going in many cases there were long delays before it could be called out and reach the scene of the fire. It might be called by a farm servant on horseback in the middle of the night (who on at least one occasion lost his way) or it might be summoned by sending a telegram to the Easingwold police station. Members of the brigade would then be alerted by the police and in some cases apparently by the firing of a maroon.

In the first fifteen years of its career the brigade did much useful work on local fires, chiefly in stackyards, sometimes in co-operation with the York Police Brigade and on one occasion with Sir George Wombwell's fire engine from Newburgh. Fires attended included Flower of May Farm on 11th October, 1884 (stackyard); Tollerton on 15th August, 1886 (stackyard); Burton House, Yearsley, on 6th April, 1888 (farm buildings); Newton Grange on 7th October, 1888; Pilmoor Hall on 13th October, 1888 (stackyard); the Water Mill, Easingwold, on 26th March, 1889 (upper floors of house destroyed); Hollin Grove on 10th February 1894 (barn); the Lund on 29th May, 1896; Low Hawkhill, on 1st June, 1897; and the Bay Horse Inn on 22nd July, 1899.

141

In December, 1884, the titles of Superintendent and Deputy Superintendent were altered to Captain and Lieutenant. The first Superintendent and Captain was a local solicitor, Octavius Robinson, who resigned in 1893 on leaving the town. He was succeeded by Mr. J. C. Bannister, who was Captain till 1904, when he resigned after twenty-one years service in the brigade. In 1890 the word "Volunteer" was dropped from the brigades title since it was felt that this might cause difficulty in charging for services.

Inevitably in an amateur organisation of this kind, matters did not always go too smoothly. At the Flower of May fire, which was the brigade's second turn out in earnest, the call was received at 2.00 p.m. and the engine went off at five past two with five men, leaving the rest to follow on horseback and by dog cart. At a call out to a stackyard fire at Haverwits on 5th March, 1891 there was great delay in providing a horse and the farm staff and neighbours got the fire out by themselves. On 20th March, 1893, the brigade put out a haystack near the workhouse, set on fire by a disgruntled tramp who had just been discharged from the casual ward. The occasion seems to have been chiefly remarkable for the fact that one of the firemen could not attend and his brother came instead, in the uniform. On 3rd November, 1893, the Captain's own warehouse in the Back Lane was gutted. This is hardly surprising since the lower floor was used for tallow chandling and the upper floor for the storage of matches, but one can understand the Captain's feelings when it had to be recorded that there was "some delay in getting efficiently to work. The maxim "Make haste slowly" should be remembered on such occasions".

Reading between the lines, with Mr. Robinson, Mr. Bannister. Mr. F. E. Rookledge the secretary, and a number of other original members gone by 1904, much of the impetus probably departed. By 1905, when the equipment was transferred from the Town Hall to a special building at the Victoria Institute the apparatus was felt to require modernisation. The Parish Council did for a time consider providing a steam engine, but this came to nothing and in 1909 they merely bought a handcart and hose for the brigade. In 1914 the firemen resigned in a body as the result of a dispute with the Parish Council over the ownership of the equipment. This, it appears, was the end of the volunteer brigade, though in 1917 the Council appointed six firemen and bought them new hose and appliances. The Parish Council's brigade was, of course, superseded by the National Fire Service in the Second World War and later by the County Fire Brigade.

In 1884 the present Easingwold Vicarage adjoining the churchyard was built by the vicar with the assistance of the Ecclesiastical Commissioners, at a cost of over £2,000.[53]

In March, 1885, the Salvation Army commenced its work in Easingwold, services at first being held in the old Westerman Schoolroom at the top of Long Street.

The North Riding County Council was established under the Local Government Act, 1888. Easingwold's first County Councillor seems to have been Henry Hawking of the Hall, Raskelf, named as such in 1890.[54]

During the latter part of the century local government was in fact extensively reconstructed. The establishment of the Bulmer West Highway District has already been described. The Public Health Act, 1872, made the Easingwold poor law union also a rural sanitary district, with the Board of Guardians now exercising public health as well as poor law functions. The Local Government Act, 1894, renamed the rural sanitary districts rural districts and transferred to new authorities called rural district councils the health functions of the guardians and the highway functions of the highway boards. The Act of 1894 also created parish councils, transferring to them the now somewhat limited civil functions of the parish vestries.

In 1890 the largest landowner in the township was Joseph Horatio Love, Esq., J.P. He had purchased the Hawkhills estate in 1873 from Capt. J. W. M. Walker. In 1890 he was having the house altered and enlarged to the designs of London architects, at an estimated cost of £12,000 including electric lighting. Mr. Love owned the Cornsay Colliery in Co. Durham.

The firm of O. Robinson and Son, solicitors, seem to have held most of the public appointments. Octavius Robinson was Clerk to the Justices, Registrar of the County Court and Steward of the Manor of Easingwold and Huby. Francis John Haxby Robinson was Clerk to the guardians. About 1893 he succeeded Octavius Robinson as steward of the Manor. One of the two was clerk to the highway board.

In 1890 Miss Ruth Abel had a ladies school at Malham House, now No. 81, Long Street.

Agitation for a branch railway from Alne was renewed in 1880 and finally the Easingwold Railway Act, 1887, was obtained. The Easingwold Railway Company was formed on 23rd August, 1887, its first directors being Sir George Wombwell, Mr. Love,

143

George Hudson Smith and the Hon. F. H. Dawnay of Bening-brough Hall. A single track line to Alne Station was opened on 27th July, 1891, with a locomotive named "Easingwold". There is some doubt about "Easingwold's" colour, but she was a standard Hudswell Clarke contractors engine. She probably started off painted Midland red and was later green. The first coaches seem to have been dark red with first and second classes only.

"Easingwold" was sold in 1903 and No. 2 purchased, again a standard Hudswell Clarke contractors engine. No. 2 started off Midland red, but by 1908 was black. About 1935 she reverted to Midland red. For a period prior to 1915 the coaches were painted lake with cream upper panels, after which they were brown, except for one which was for some time bright green with cream upper works.[55]

A curious accident occurred on the Easingwold Railway in 1906. In August of that year the Easingwold magistrates had before them four boys who had managed to set off a truck in the goods yard at Easingwold, which gained enough momentum to crash through the level crossing gates at Crankley, coining to rest not far short of Alne Station.

The Easingwold Railway survived the Second World War and (technically) nationalisation, but by the late 1950s it was moribund and was closed towards the end of the decade, the track being removed by the Spring of 1960.

A new weekly newspaper, the "Easingwold Advertiser and Weekly News", was founded in 1892. In 1897 the proprietor was Reginald Ernest Smith in the Market Place and it has continued to be issued by members of the same family to the present day.

In 1893 St. Monicas Cottage Hospital was built at the expense of Mrs. Love. During the spring of that year the Easingwold Temperance Band was formed, with Mr. Love as its president. The great event of the summer was the royal wedding on 6th July, when the Duke of York (later George V) married Princess May of Teck (later Queen Mary). All the shops closed, there was a cricket match and sports and the band of the East Riding Artillery Volunteers played in the Chasegarth. At 3.30 p.m. the children sat on the grass in the Chasegarth and were each served with tea and "a good substantial bun". In the evening the band played round the town. Mr. Octavius Robinson caused all the children to be presented with a medal to mark the occasion. Trees were planted on the greens in Uppleby.

Mrs L. Foster

Lieut. General Baden Powell reviewing Yeomanry outside the "George",
1908

A parade of the Easingwold Volunteers, 1905

New Parks, Shipton, a former lodge of the Forest of Galtres

The streets of the town were still cobbled at this time. A photograph of Chapel Street in 1896 shows the carriageway formed of setts with the sides cobbled and no kerbs. The sides of streets, as many old photographs show, were all paved with neatly laid cobbles. Flagstones seem to have been almost unknown in Easingwold. Uppleby, Spring Street and Long Street had cobbled pavements without kerbs. In the early 1900's a few isolated stretches of flag pavement began to appear. Church Lane, carriageway and causeway, was entirely paved with rough cobbles.

The first meeting of the Easingwold Rural District Council was held on 28th December, 1894, when County Councillor Henry Hawking was elected chairman. He was at this time also Chairman of the Guardians. The early work of the District Council included the provision of sewers for the town and waterworks near Hanover House.

The Parish Council first met in the Church School on 13th December, 1894, when Albert Edward Hayden, solicitor, and Francis Eyre Rookledge, chemist, were elected chairman and vice chairman respectively, the latter being also treasurer.

In 1895 the Easingwold Volunteers, a detachment of "I" Company of the First Volunteer Battalion of the Green Howards were advertising for recruits. Instruction seems to have been given at the Royal Oak. Mr. W. Bensley had recently formed the Easingwold Philharmonic Society which practised in the Town Hall. A school called Easingwold High School and Ladies College, conducted by Mrs. Emma Newton Mangles and the Misses Mangles, was at Mowbray House in Long Street. This school seems to have ceased by 1906.

Mr. Long, headmaster of the Grammar School, left early in the year to become head of Dauntsey Agricultural School in Wiltshire. His successor Mr. J. E. Burton, BA. Cantab, BA. London, resigned after one term to become headmaster of Crediton Grammar School. He was followed by George Sandham BA. who retired in 1931. In 1895 there were about 25 boys at the school, a few of them boarders. They wore a black cap with a silver oak tree badge. The school played cricket and football and held an annual paper chase, as well as an annual prizegiving in the Town Hall.

It was in the period 1905-11 that girls were again admitted to the school. Mr. Sandham took a number of boarders in his own house nearby, including the late Lord Milner of Leeds.

145

The County Education Committee made the school a grant and later, on the representations of the governors, built a new set of buildings which was opened in 1911. It was a condition that the Westerman endowment should be transferred to the County Council. The buildings of 1911 became the Easingwold primary school on the erection of the new Grammar and Modern School in York Road.[56]

On 21st September, 1895, the 35th Easingwold Agricultural Show was attended by the Duke of Cambridge, then visiting Newburgh. The weather was fine, an excursion train brought two hundred visitors from York, the Temperance Band played selections and the distinguished visitor, who opened his speech by remarking that this was not the first time he had attended the show, said that, having been for 39 years at the head of Her Majesty's forces, he considered that our army was perfectly equal to the requirements of the Empire and the international situation.[57]

The Easingwold Hirings were still part of the accepted system of employment in 1895, though the "Advertiser" reported that the attendance at the first hirings in the Market Place on 8th November had been good, but not as great as in previous years. The second hirings took place on 29th November in the same place. Foremen obtained from £22 to £27 a year, strong men £17 to £18, youths from £13 to £15 and lads from £5 to £10. Head girls obtained from £18 to £20, second girls from £14 to £16 and young girls from £5 to £10. The hirings were accompanied by shows and amusements and on the day of the first hirings there was a grand dance in the Lower Room of the Town Hall with music by the Husthwaite String Band. Martinmas Week was the servants' annual holiday and a number of events were held including dances in the Town Hall on the Tuesday and Friday.[58] The Hirings seem to have gone on till 1923, if not a year or two later, but their importance by then must have been inconsiderable.

On 21st August, 1895, the third Annual Show of the Easingwold District Floral Horticultural and Industrial Society was held at the Cricket Field. An excursion train ran from York and entertainment was provided by the Harrogate Black Star Minstrels and the Easingwold Temperance Brass Band.[59] Fossett's London Circus visited the town on 5th September,[60] and Bostock and Wombwell's Royal Menagerie ("Brilliantly Illuminated by Electric Light") on 24th October.[60] The Easingwold Railway ran special trains to Alne at 6.40 a.m. and back at 9.45 p.m. for the church choir trip to Scarborough on 16th July,[61] and again on 16th

September to connect with the North Eastern Railway's excursion to see the Channel Fleet, then visiting Scarborough.[62] During the early months of the year the landlord of the new Station Hotel (opened in 1892) organised a series of pigeon shoots for prizes, giving for one a handsome marble and gold timepiece and for another a fat pig of about 20 stones weight. On 21st December the "Advertiser" reported that the waits had begun their Christmas rounds.

Queen Victoria's Diamond Jubilee in 1897 was commemorated by the building of the Victoria Institute and four almshouses in Spring Street on the site of the former Spring Head Almshouses. The Institute consists of a reading room, recreation room and caretaker's house. The Parish Council accepted trusteeship of the Almshouses and Institute under a Charity Commissioners' scheme in May, 1897. Their meetings, hitherto held in the Church School or the Tolbooth, were transferred to the Institute. At the same time the Council considered the repair of the Chapel Lane alms-houses, but were advised by the Local Government Board that they had no power to do this. These almshouses appear to have consisted of four small houses erected in the early 19th century on the site of the old Fossbridge House. This was on the north side of Long Street and on the west side of its junction with Chapel Street. The "Easingwold Advertiser" of 21st October, 1893, reported that a horse had entered one of them and tried to climb the stairs. They are now demolished. The cottages for widows in Little Lane were still in existence in 1868 but have also now gone.

The pace of traffic was leisurely by modern standards, some-times extremely so. On Wednesday, 1st March, 1899, Richard Coverdale of Easingwold was charged before the Easingwold magistrates with having on 17th February, 1899, driven a traction engine at a speed greater than 2 m.p.h., contrary to the Loco-motives Act, 1865. P.C. Lodge gave evidence that it was going down Tan-pit Lane and passed his house at a great speed. Cross-examined, he estimated this as between 5 and 6 m.p.h. Mr. W. Wilkinson for the defence called John Alderson, farmer, of the Lund, who had met the traction engine at the bottom of the Avenue as he was returning from the market in his trap. The driver could not have seen him until he was within a few yards, but the engine stopped almost at once and the flagman led his horse past the engine and he (Mr. Alderson) certainly had no cause to complain. Mr. Wilkinson also called Mr. E. J. Hodgson, owner of the engine, who said it was an old one and inca-pable of attaining a speed as great as 5 m.p.h. The case was dismissed.

147

Octavius Robinson, Esq., then of Redlynch House, Salisbury, accepted the Presidency of the Easingwold Agricultural Society for that year. The show was held on 16th September, the Newburgh house party including the Duke of Cambridge, the Duke of Marlborough, the Marquis of Londonderry and Viscount Castlereagh. The band of the Prince of Wales's Own Hussars came over from York.

The "Advertiser" at first made light of the situation in South Africa, but soon changed its tone. On 14th October, 1899, it noted that Sergeant Crosby, son of Mr. George Crosby of the Market Place, was serving with the Leicester Regiment at Glencoe. The first battle of the Boer War took place on 20th October at Talana Hill, about three miles from Glencoe. As is well known, within a few weeks there was a series of reverses which at the time appeared major disasters. The country rose to the occasion and volunteers poured in, among them Thomas Wilkinson of Cold Harbour, who had been a trooper in the Yorkshire Hussars. Other Easingwold men who served were Trooper (later Corporal) Sidney Smith of the Imperial Yeomanry, the son of Mr. T. Smith of Hanover House; Trooper Alfred Wilkinson, also of the Imperial Yeomanry; Gunner Albert Foster of H.M.S. "Monarch", who was wounded at Belmont, while serving with the Naval Brigade; and Trooper Thomas Walter Dale, who was killed on active service with the 9th Lancers. Some of the Easingwold Volunteers went to South Africa in 1900 and served in General Pole-Carew's Division They included Private Tom Cariss and Ted Webster, son of the landlord of the "Jolly Farmers".

In November, 1899, it was announced that Mr. Sydney Smith of the Post Office, Easingwold, had secured the contract for the conveyance of the mails between Easingwold and Huby, using a six horse power Benz motor car. In 1902, Edward VII's coronation year, the National Telephone was installed in the police station.

George V's coronation was celebrated in 1911 and on 2nd May the Parish Council, at the request of Thomas Cowling, Honorary Secretary to the Coronation Committee, agreed to contribute £50 from the rates. In the same year the parish room was built on land given by Mrs. Love, in memory of the Rev. Nathan Jackson, who died in 1910. His successor, Halsall Segar, was instituted and inducted on 1st February, 1911.

Since 1857 or thereabouts the town had been lit by gas provided by the Easingwold Gas Company. Owing to the scarcity of coal and an impending miner's strike, there was a breakdown of street lighting for a period at the end of February, 1912.

In that year, or soon afterwards, the Hanover House Water-works were replaced by those in Cockerdale, near Oldstead.

During the First World War the workhouse was used for housing German prisoners. A war memorial in the Market Place now commemorates the town's dead of two world wars.

In 1922 the Easingwold Branch of the British Legion of which Mr. Thomas Cowling and Mr. Walter Bannister were then respectively chairman and vice-chairman, purchased the market rights from the toll proprietors for £105, so that they might be conveyed to the Parish Council.

The gas lamps were replaced in 1925 when John C. Bannister & Co. Ltd. agreed to provide electric street lighting for the Parish Council at a cost of £100 per annum. This arrangement continued till the financial year 1931-2, when the North Eastern Electric Supply Co. took over the supply.

The services of the County Library were extended to the town in 1925 and further evidence of the transition to modern times was the permission given by the Parish Council in the same year to a London firm to publish an Illustrated Official Guide to the Town of Easingwold.

The vicar, Mr. Segar, was succeeded by Frederick Richardson, M.A. Cantab, instituted and inducted on 15th May, 1926.

A large extension to the churchyard was provided by sub-scription in 1929.

In 1931 the town had a cinema, operated in the lower floor of the Town Hall by Mr. Ernest Burton, three garage businesses and a golf club with a nine hole course on Ox Moor.

Under the Local Government Act, 1929, the poor law functions and premises of the Guardians were transferred to the County Council. It was decided to convert the Union Workhouse into a mental hospital by extensive rebuilding and the addition of new blocks. Now known as Claypenny Hospital, the establishment vested in the Minister of Health under the National Health Service Act, 1946.

The Act of 1929 also made the County Council the highway authority for main roads in the administrative county and for all public highways within its constituent rural districts. These (other than trunk roads) remain its responsibility

The Rural District Council in the 1930's occupied offices on the west side of the Market Place, but after the Second World War moved to buildings in Stillington Road originally erected for wartime services. The water supply undertakers for the district are now the Ryedale Joint Water Board.

The parishes of Easingwold and Raskelf were reunited by an Order in Council of 31st May, 1951.

Easingwold parish church has been furnished with a considerable amount of new woodwork from the workshop of the late Mr. Thompson of Kilburn, in particular the high altar, reredos and panelling in the chancel and a screen at the east end of the north aisle. There are side altars in the north and south aisles, and the ceilings of the nave and aisles were tactfully repaired in the 1930's. Electric lighting was installed under a faculty of 1934.

Recent vicars of Easingwold have been Sydney Morris Crow (from 1st October, 1936); Raeburn Simpson Hawkins (from October, 1950); and Anthony Cecil Addison Smith, MA. (from 28th March, 1966).

1   Criminal Chronology of York Castle, 1867, p. 139.
2   Bulner op cit.
3   Langdale, op. cit. 1809.
4   Bradley : Old Coaching Days in Yorkshire 1889.
5   ibid.
6   Bradley op cit.
7   Baines op cit.
8   Bradley op cit.
9   Baines on cit & Pigot & Co's Directories of 1834 & 1841 : Whites Directory of 1840.
10 General Account Book, York City Library.
11 ibid.
12 Deed : Directories; Gill op cit. A plan of the Crayke Field in 1797 shows a Mill Hill, but somewhat nearer to the hill top and without a building. This may refer to something much earlier.
13 Babes op. cit.
14 Pigot & Co's. Directorie. of 1834 and 1841.
15 Official Catalogue of the Great Exhibition.
16 Kelly & Co's. Post Office Directory of Yorkshire 1857.
17 Wm. White's Directory of 1867.
18 Easingwold Advertiser. 6.5.1893 and 11.11.1893.
19 Baines op. cit.
20 Miall : Congregationalism in Yorkshire 1868, p. 256.
21 Miall op cit.
22 Gill's Family Almanack 1872.
23 Holmes : History of Yorkshire County Cricket 1833-1903 pp. 17 & 18.
24 Kellys Directory.
25 Original papers in the office of G. R. Drake Esq., Solicitor, Easingwold.
26 Gill's Family Almanack 1872.
27 ibid
28 ibid
29 Gill op. cit.
30 Obituary in the Gentleman's Magazine, 1856, and material in the possession of the Rev. R. S. Hawkins.
31 Allen : The North Eastern Railway, p. 213.
32 Hargrove: A Brief Description of Places of Public Interest in the County of York within 26 Miles of the City, p. 113.
33 Gill : Family Almanack for 1872.
34 Per Miss H. Sturdy, Long Street, Easingwold.
35 Gill : Vallis Eboracensis 1852 and Easingwold Chronicle 28.7.1860.

37 Slater's Directory for 1849.
38 Per Miss M. Smith, Bank House, Market Place, Easingwold.
39 White's Directory of 1867.
40 T. Whellan & Co. op. cit.
41 Note by Miss M. Smith from a balance sheet of 1860.
42 Easingwold Times 12.7.1862.
43 Per W. Paragreen, Esq., Briggfield Farm, Easingwold.
44 Statement of Accounts in the possession of Miss K. Frank, Easingwold.
45 Note by G. R. Drake, Esq.
46 Accounts : Miss K. Frank.
47 Notes made by G. R. Drake, Esq., in 1934 of a conversation with County Alderman J. R. Sturdy, J.P.
48 Note by G. R. Drake, Esq.
49 Minutes and accounts furnished by Walter Bannister, Esq.
50 Minute Book in the possession of Miss Hazel Medd, Uppleby, Easingwold.
51 York Courant 11.2.1841.
52 Easingwold Chronicle 17.12.1859.
53 Bulmer op. cit.
54 ibid.
55 Kidner : Light Railway Handbook 1950.
56 Article by Miss M. Smith in the school magazine, "The Oak", for 1953.
57 Easingwold Adveritser 21.9.1895.
58 ibid 10.11.1895.
59 ibid 24.8.1895.
60 ibid 31.8.1895.
61 ibid 21.9.1895.
62 ibid 3.8.1895.
63 ibid 14.9.1895.

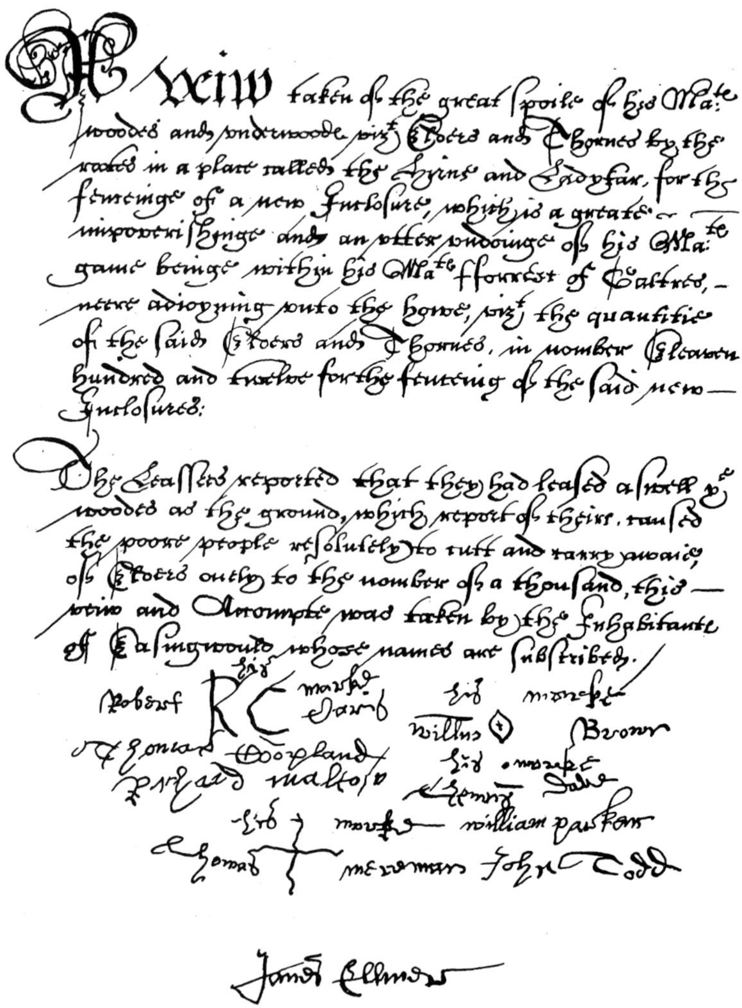

A View taken of the great spoile of his Ma[tie]: woodes and underwoode viz[t] Stoccs and Thornes by the wastes in a place called the Hyrne and Ladyfar, for the fencinge of a new Inclosure, which is a greate impoverishinge and an utter undoinge of his Ma[tie]: game beinge within his Ma[tie] fforrest of Galtres, neere adioyning unto the howe, viz[t] the quantitie of the said Stoccs and Thornes, in number Eleaven hundred and twelve for the fencing of the said new Inclosures:

The Leassees reported that they had leased a stock ye woodes as the ground, which report of theirs, caused the poore people resolutely to cutt and carry awaie of Stoccs onely to the number of a thousand, this view and Accompte was taken by the Inhabitants of Easingwould whose names are subscribed.

Robert his RC marke Davis

his marke William Browne

Edward Doopland

Richard Malton

his marke Henry Dale

his marke William Parker

Thomas Merriman

John Todd

James Ellmore

Leeds City Archives

A Forest of Galtres official document, from James I's time

V

THE FOREST OF GALTRES

The area which became the Forest of Galtres appears to have been in pre-Conquest times part of a belt of well wooded country extending up the east side of the Vale of York. Its name, of Scandinavian origin, means "boars' brushwood".

Exactly when it became a royal forest remains to be ascertained by further research. It was no doubt in the reign of one of the Norman Kings — William I or II or Henry I — that it became subject the law of the forest. Under this special code the game, timber and other products of the forests of England were protected for the benefit of the crown. While the interests of the King's hunting were always paramount, a forest was of great importance to the royal economy, a source of food, fuel, building material, and so on, no less than a means of rewarding service by gifts or offices.

Originally the law of the forest dealt harshly with offenders, but successive Charters of the Forest in 1217, 1225 and 1297 established the rule that: "nullus de cetero amittat vitam vel membra pro venatione nostra" ("None shall henceforth lose life or limb for our venison").

At its widest extent, that is when it first became a forest, Galtres seems to have covered most of the Wapentake of Bulmer. At a perambulation of 1316 evidence was given that prior to the reign of Henry II it included in the Bailiwick of Kyle Linton, Aldwark, Tholthorpe, Helperby, Brafferton, Flawith, Myton, Fawdington, Thormanby, Sessay, Raskelf, and Youlton; in the Bailiwick of Esingwald Baxby, Husthwaite, Thornton Hill and Oulston; and in the Bailiwick of Myrescough or Myreskew Brandsby, Whenby, Marton, Farlington, Cornborough, Sheriff Hutton, the Lillings, Stittenham, Thornton-le-Clay, Foston, Barton, Flaxton, Claxton, Harton, Bossall, Buttercrambe Strensall, Huntington, Earswick, Sand Hutton, Holtby, Warthill, Osbaldwick, Stockton and Heworth. In 1316 and later the bounds ran from the walls of York up the Ouse to the River Kyle, thence to the northern end of Crayke Park, along the northern boundary of the park to the River Foss and back down the Foss to York again.

The area was probably one of well wooded country, rather than continuous woodland. Originally natural, there may have been some deliberately planted and cultivated timber in medieval times, but of this the evidence has yet to be found. There was an important stock of oak trees. Part of the forest known as the "covert" or "great covert" was woodland devoted entirely to game and timber and uses compatible with them. The covert was regarded as the central sanctuary of the game, where the King was unlikely to permit any sort of enclosure or cultivation. Other parts of the forest were grassy clearings — lawns, or "launds" as they were called, which might be retained in the King's own hand as herbage for the deer, especially in winter. On the other hand there were an appreciable number of villages in the forest, with their cultivated lands. The inhabitants of these villages by custom or grant enjoyed many rights of pasturage and of gathering timber, turf and other material in the forest. The forest was not enclosed from the surrounding country.

Under the forest law the tillage of previously uncultivated land (known as the making of an "assart") required the King's licence. It was a standard condition of the grant of such a licence that the land should only be enclosed by a ditch and hedge low enough for the deer to jump in and out. Permission to assart was required whether the land involved was covert or open pasture surrounded by covert. An unlicensed assart was an encroachment on the forest and the maker might be punished by the forest courts. Encroachments on the forest other than assarts, as for example the erection of unlawful buildings, unlawful enclosure for purposes other than tillage or the unlawful working of minerals, were known as "purprestures". There was, of course, nothing to prevent the crown giving retrospective permission (on its own terms) for assarts and purprestures and this was in fact not uncommonly done.

Destruction or damage to the covert, for example by clearing it without tillage, was also not permitted. This meant that a landowner in the forest required the King's licence to fell his own woods.

As the Remembrances of the Forest of "Gaultresse", made on 1st May, 1566, put it: "And no man can inclose his grounds besides tofts and crofts without the like licence" (i.e. of the Justice of the Forest) "for els the Prince shall be letten and stopped of his disport in coursing and the deere of feading. And allso yt is to be doubted lest by gappes and gates in inclosures the deere may be distroyed divers wayes, for wh. cause noo man may inclose without licence of the Prince or of the Justice. And the pty. to be

154

bounden that the deere thereby shall not be hindred of the passage nor distroyed. And allso for the apparent knowledge of the same Lycence the pty. must pay a yearlly fyne in the nature of a rent to the Prince to be assessed by the Justice for a new assart and to be streated into the Exchequer to be collected by the Sheriffe. . .". "All inclosures to be presented that be noo pte. of the ancyent Tofts and Crofts. All ould assarts and inclosures approved" (i.e. proved) "by verdict to be inclosed above 40 years" . . . (to) "be fyned at a yearly rent. All new assarts at the pleasure of the Prynce or Justice to be fined by the Justice as he shall think good . . .". The savings for "tofts and crofts" refers to the existing buildings and garths of villages in the main.

Originally the Forest of Galtres was organised into three divisions (roughly the western, central and eastern divisions) known respectively as the Bailwicks of Kyle, Esingwald and Myrescough. These are referred to in the perambulation of 1316 quoted above as having existed in the 12th century prior to the reduction of the forest in area. These three bailwicks were later replaced, exactly when is not clear, but apparently by the early 15th century, by the re-division of the forest into North and South Bailiwicks. The South Baliwick contained such places as Tollerton, Newton, Shipton, Skelton, Sutton-on-Forest, Haxby, Wigginton and Rawcliffe. The area disafforested in Henry II's reign (1154-89) seems to have remained part of the "purlieus" of Galtres. The occupiers of land in the purlieus were termed "bounderers" and were subject to certain obligations, including one not to disturb deer found among their crops. In return they had grazing and other rights.

In Richard III's time Galtres had two riding and four walking foresters. Under the three bailwick organisation there may have been three and six respectively. A walking forester had charge of an area known as a walk. Walks were frequently called after their keeper, but in Jacobean times the North Bailwick or "bailey", was divided into the High Walk and the Lower North Walk, while the Southern consisted of the Knackenthwaite Walk and the Coper's (or possibly Ooper's) Lodge Walk.

There were other foresters in Galtres known as "woodwards". These were the keepers of private woods in the forest, who were sworn to keep the King's venison and had power to attach and present offenders.

Other forest officers were the regarders, the verderers and the agisters. The regarders were generally local gentry sworn to look after the forest boundaries and all questions relating to them and prevent encroachments. There were supposed to be at least twelve in each regard, which in Galtres seems to have been equivalent to a bailwick. The verderers were judical officers, who were sworn to preserve the vert (wood) and venison (game), keep the assizes (regulations of the forest) and to view, receive and enroll attachments (fines and small dues) and presentments of trespasses, their main concern being perhaps the vert. As John Manwood wrote in the 1598 edition of his "Treatise and Discourse of the Lawes of the Forrest" . . . "And thereof is framed this word Viridarius a Verderer, or one that doth take the charge of the Vert... ". The agisters controlled and took fees for the pasturage.

The chief officer was generally called the Justice (sometimes the keeper) of the forest. Very often, at any rate in Tudor and Stuart times, the office was a combined one not only for Galtres, but for all forests in the north of England, when the officer was known as Justice of the Forest beyond Trent. The actual chief officer was often the Deputy Justice. The business side of the forest administration was looked after by the Steward, an office combined in later years with that of Master of the Game. The regulations of 1566 refers to a Master Forester who had charge over the other foresters "to see them doo theire dutys for the preserving of the Game". It looks as if he was the same as the Master of the Game, particularly as the Ranger is described as his deputy. The Ranger was the officer responsible for the care of the purlieus or outskirts of the forest, his particular duty being to see that game was turned back into the forest.

The officer called the Bowbearer was probably originally a senior forester, who took his name from the fact that he had the right to carry a bow, while the ordinary foresters did not.[1] At an eyre held in Galtres on 17th June, 1528, it was said that the "Bowebearer and Receyvor" ought "dailie to walke throughe all the saide Forest as one keper ayther by hymselve or his deputie or deputies".[2] His duties by James I's reign seem to have been little more than to collect the attachment fines and attend forest courts.

Unauthorised taking of game or wood ("trespasses of venison and vert") was punishable by the forest courts. "Venison" included red, fallow and roe deer and the wild boar.[3] "Vert" included trees ("Over Vert"), underwood, bushes, thorns, gorse and the like ("Nether Vert") and fruit trees such as pears, crabs, hawthorns and blackthorns ("Special Vert").[4] There were three forest courts for Galtres in ascending order of importance. The attachment or "tachment" courts, theoretically held every forty days, dealt with minor trespasses, such as trespasses of vert by dwellers in the forest where the damage was not more than 4d. and breaches of the grazing regulations and other routine matters such as the receipt of payments for grazing. The forty day interval was certainly not rigidly adhered to in Jacobean times, nor were the amounts then collected very large. Attachment courts were to be attended by the verderers, ranger, bowbearer, foresters and woodwards. The swanimote court was held three times a year under the regulations of 1566, generally at Easingwold or Huby. In Edward II's time a court was held at a place called "Hillulidgate", which seems to have been in the open air at a gate somewhere in the forest. More frequent swanimotes may have been held in medieval times. The eyre or "justice seat" was supposed to be held at three yearly intervals by the Justice, according to the 1566 regulations. In medieval times the intervals between eyres seem to have been irregular and much longer. The forest of Pickering for example had an interval of over fifty years between the eyres of 1280 and 1334.[5] Sherwood seems to have had almost as great an interval between eyres in 1287 and 1334.[6] It has indeed been doubted whether the eyre in the fourteenth century was more then a confirmatory court. On the other hand the procedure supposed to be followed when offenders were found in the forest presupposed their ultimate appearance at the next eyre. Venison offenders taken in the act were thus normally imprisoned forthwith until they could find bail, when they were delivered by the King or the Justice to appear at the next eyre. Vert trespassers would be bailed to the next attachment court, which if the offence involved a value greater than 4d., or the offender lived outside the forest, would itself usually bail them to the next eyre.

All attachments and presentments by and proceedings of the attachment courts were supposed to be entered in the attachment rolls. These, duly engrossed by the clerk of the attachments, were subscribed by the verderers, sealed on the outside and committed to the custody of one of the verderers for production at the next swanimote following.

The jury of the swanimote court would consider the matters arising on the attachment rolls and direct presentments to the swanimote and pass verdicts on them, which had to be agreed by all the officers, duly sealed and committed to the custody of the verderers to be delivered to the Justice at his next "seat for causes".[7]

The forest prison, to which offenders were committed until bailed, appears to have been kept in the time of Henry II and Richard I by the hereditary King's lardeners, or larder keepers, at

York. In 1246 David the Lardener kept the prison in his house there. He died about 1271 and appears to have been succeeded, both as King's lardener and keeper of the forest prison, by his son David.[8] From one or other of these two Davids probably derives the traditional name of the Forest of Galtres prison, Davy Hall. or Davy's Hall. In 1284 the second David was succeeded by his son Philip the Lardener. In 1305 Philip died and his daughters and heiresses Margaret and Ellen became owners of the house called "the prison of the lardery" which Philip had held by the service of keeping trespassers taken in the forest.[9]

Many special fees were collected by the forest officers—for the grazing of pigs (pannage); for the passage of animals through the forest (cheminage or gatelaw); and for the "lawing" of dogs (that is the clipping of their forefeet to prevent them from hunting). Cheminage was not charged on persons living in the bailiwick in which they passed through the forest, nor was it supposed to be charged for the carriage of corn, underwood or charcoal, but in the early 14th century "les poures gentz (de) le Conte de Lancastre de Esingwold et de Hoby" are found complaining that the forest officers were making such charges. There was also a liability on townships to maintain foresters (puture) and they also complained that they were being charged more than their share. Later, by Richard III's time, this liability seems to have lapsed and we find the foresters being paid from the income of the King's Manor of Sheriff Hutton. There were special payments for movement through the forest in the "fence month", that is the fortnight before and the fortnight after Mid-summer Day, when the deer were fawning and needed special quiet; and in Henry VI's time (1422-60) a customary fee called "thistltak" of $1/2$d. a head from drovers for the taking of thistles by their beasts. In Edward II's reign the usual fee for lawing a dog was 3/-. Lawing consisted of removing three claws from each forefoot by cutting them off next to the skin. The charge to the swanimote jury in the early 1 600s (six pages of foolscap) included the admonition: "Item yf any of you doe knowe any unlawful dogs or bitches not having there clawes cutt off, you shall present the same". Pannage in Galtres in the mid-fourteenth century seems to have been at the yearly rate of $1/2$d. per pig under a year old and ld. per pig above that age. As an alternative the agisters might take, at their option, a tithe pig.

A curious regulation for the fence month was the prohibition of the milking of "kye" (cows) within three hundred feet of the covert.[10] Swine were not allowed to run free in the forest during the fence mouth, but were kept in enclosures. In James I's time

158

those belonging to Easingwold and Huby were kept in a two or three acre field called the Swines Close.

Townships or individuals enjoyed many rights in the forest. In King John's time (1199-1216) the men of Easingwold and Huby had common for oxen and cows, horses and mares and for their pigs in the forest for the whole year, except during the fence month, on payment of pannage as mentioned above. They were not entitled to common for sheep and goats in the forest, these animals being considered offensive to the deer.[11]

This right to take "estovers", that is wood for various specified purposes, from the forest was gradually extended after much dispute with the forest officers, until in 1538 the jury at what appears to have been an eyre at Easingwold found that the tenants had a customary right to take "rammell" wood between Michaelmas and the Annunciation of Our Lady at the rate of 4d. a load. Ramell appears to have meant thorns, hollies, hazels, sallows and other trees of small timber value. The tenants of Easingwold and Huby might also have yearly one load of "garsell" (dead hedge or underwood) for 6d. and one load of ordinary wood for 8d. They also claimed garsell for their "farmhoulds and layth (barn) walles" twice every seven years by delivery of the keepers or the verderers.

The Remembrances of 1566 also state that: "The freehoulders of woods within the forest preserving the Spring thereof" (i.e. leaving enough to grow again) "by the view of the foresters may take convenient howseboat plowboate wayneboate carteboate fyerboate and hedgeboate, prout boscus pati potest" (to the reasonable limit of the wood) "to be recorded in the attachment rolls". House-or husbote, plough-wain-and cartbote and hedge — or hayboate are rights of taking wood to repair respectively houses, ploughs, farm vehicles and hedges. Firebote means the taking of wood for fuel.

An inquisition at Sutton-on-Forest on 8th January, 1251, gave as its verdict that the men of Easingwold and Huby were not without special permission from the King or his justice entitled to vert from the forest for husbote, or even for building new houses when the towns of Easingwold and Huby were burnt, as many times happened, or for making or repairing their hedges.[12] Controversy as to the right of Easingwold and Huby in this respect was still going on in 1259. At some date during the years 1296-1322 Thomas, Earl of Lancaster, petitioned the King and Council to complain that the forest officers were preventing the men of Easingwold from having their accustomed housebote of thirty oaks

159

a year and the small underwood for hedge bote. The officers were instructed to allow these estovers. It is clear therefore that a certain right had been established.

The inhabitants of the various townships also enjoyed common of pasture in the forest. In 1538 those of Easingwold might pastured their beasts, including swine, in the forest between Michaelmas and St. Ellenmas, provided there was no destruction of the browse or of the herbage. Browse (the young twigs of trees and underwood) was not to be eaten by cattle between St. Nicholas Day (6th December) and Candlemas (2nd February). In medival times the various townships in Galtres intercommoned, enjoying, in the legal phrase, "common pur cause de vicinage", but by 1566 it seems that there had been so much enclosure by licence in the forest that this was to a great extent no longer the case.

Timber trees were not to be used for fuel and wood taken for this purpose was to be cut by the four foresters by lopping and topping after being marked out by the verderers so that the tree would grow again within fourteen to sixteen years. Each forester was entitled under the regulations of 1566 to two loads of wood "to be spent in his lodging". No freeholder of woodland in the forest might sell, give away or part with any such woods in the forest without leave of the King or the justice. The regulations of 1566 required a written licence from the justice, to be enrolled in the attachment rolls and confirmed by the swanimote.

In mast time the Justice, on the application of the foresters, verderers and agisters, was to regulate the agistment of the forest "as well in the demayne inclosures and woodds as in the foreyne" (i.e. on both the King's lands and those of others). The towns of Easingwold and Huby were entitled, according to the regulations of 1566, to have "conveynyent Pannage freely for their Larder Swyne without anything paying therefore as tyme out of mind of man hath been".

In 1538 the tenants of Easingwold and Huby claimed turfgrave (the right to dig turf) of the outmoor and "within the most necessary places where the King's highnes game may least have there Releiffe". In 1566 it was stated that the lord of every lordship in the forest was entitled within the bounds of his lordship to grave a reasonable amount of turves and to pasture cattle there "with a safeguard" (which may mean someone to look after them or perhaps a tether of some kind) provided their grazing did not do damage. Turf was not to be graved in the Prince's demesnes without licence of the Justice. The lord of every lordship in the forest also seems to have been entitled to a reasonable amount of fern there, to be cut within eight days after Michaelmas.

The "Justice deputy", the foresters and the Queen's tenants of Easingwold and Huby were to hold drives or "drifts" of cattle in the forest to check whether the grazing was being abused. Notice of such drifts, the Remembrances specifically provided, was not to be given" "lest by knowledge given men will take out there cattle of the forest". All unauthorised cattle were to be kept in pound and presented at the attachment court. By a statute of 1514 all forests and chases had to be driven at least once a year at the feast of St. Michael the Archangel or within fifteen days thereafter. A custom of the tenants of Easingwold and Huby was recorded in 1538 to ride twice every seven years and drive all horses and mares off the King's ground and impound them.

Originally the deer in Galtres seem to have been red deer, but by the reign of Edward I these had been replaced by fallow deer. A record of 1301 refers to roe deer. It was one of the larger forests of the north and a return made of the deer in the royal forests, chases and parks north of Trent in 1538-9 shows that it then had 800 fallow deer as compared with about 1,000 red deer in Sherwood, 700 red in Hatfield Chase, 435 fallow in Topcliffe Great Park, 247 fallow in Topcliffe Little Park and 400 fallow in Sheriff Hutton Park. Licences by the king to hunt in the forest in the late 13th century refer to the fox, hare, badger and cat. No medieval record seems to be extant of the wild boar in Galtres, but there may have been one or two. Certainly the name of the forest indicates that at one time the wild boar was the distinctive game.

Keepers of the forest in the 13th century were Richard Malebisse (1204), William of Cornborough (1209)[13] and Geoffrey de Nevill, Chamberlain of England (1217-23)[14]. The first and second of these were found to have misappropriated timber and allowed the forest to deteriorate generally. Malebisse took some 250 oaks for the building of his castle at Wheldrake and sold other trees to the value of 140 marks and William admitted to taking 426 oaks, of which only 65 could be traced. Steward in 1227 was Hugh Nevill.[15] On 30th May, 1234, John son of Geoffrey de Nevill was appointed keeper of Galtres, which office he still held in 1236.[16] In 1250-1 Sir Geoffrey de Langele was Justice of the forest.[17] John of York, King's sergeant, was rewarded for good service by a grant of the custody of Galtres and its lands in 1267, but he was removed at least five times for very substantial periods for "trespass of hunting and other misconduct" and was finally ordered to give up his charter in 1291.[18] At an inquisition at York on 20th July, 1291, relating to John of York's removal, there were present William Paytefin, William Gryvel (d. 1295) and Adam Pacocke, foresters (who all incidentally sound like Easingwold men); Robert Haget, John Maunsel, Baudewyn de Scipton (d.1293) and Simon de Gunnays, verderers; and Robert de Yolton, Simon de Roueclyve, William de Touthorpe, Walter Isahacke and Richard de Stoketon, regarders.[19] John de Hustwayt seems to have been clerk of the forest at the end of the thirteenth century, contemporary with the William Gryvel just mentioned.[20] Robert Faderles, probably of Easingwold, was a forester in Galtres in 1284.[21] Foresters of Galtres in October, 1304, were Robert de Burgo, Roger de Raskelfe and John de Hoby. John Maunsel was still a verderer, and other verderers were Robert de Schupton (Shipton) and Theobald de Tollerton. David de Routheclif', William de Crachale, Thomas Blaunkfrount, Thomas de Aldewerk' and John le Stabeler were regarders in 1304, with Walter Isacke', who had been a regarder in 1291 [22] Robert de Schupton's son John also became a verderer in Galtres, but was replaced in July, 1319, for insufficient qualification.[23] It appears that verderers were required to reside in the county and hold land in the forest. They could be removed for incapacity through age or infirmity (as was William de Ros of Youlton in 1320[24]), or, apparently, if unable to devote sufficient time to the office. Thus on 23rd May, 1320, the election of a verderer was ordered to replace John de Thornton, who was unable to act as he was performing the duties of steward of the forest.[25]

Normally the holders of offices in the forest could and did perform their duties by deputy. Sometimes leave to do this is expressly given in the grant, as in 1325 when Alan de Tesdale, appointed steward, was given leave to appoint a substitute.[26]

The King indeed seems to have come more and more to regard the grant of forest offices simply as a means of paying or rewarding his servants. Thus on 19th November, 1339, Roger Vynour was granted for his good service in Scotland and beyond the seas the forestership in the wood of Esyngwald.[27] On 20th June, 1343, the King made a grant for life of the bailwick of Esyngwolde. formerly held by John Page, to John Tesedale, one of his archers, for his good service in the King's wars.[28] In 1407 the King's servant Thomas Smyth of Easingwold was appointed a foot forester in Galtres.[29]

Forest officers, or those who actually carried out the duties for them, seem sometimes to have had a perilous time. They might be resisted by persons they found hunting without leave, or by "woodbearers" (persons taking wood without leave), or be involved in affrays with commoners, or be set upon by robbers or other criminals. There seem to have been dark doings at times in the forest. Poor John le Wodeward of Raskelf, one of the King's foresters in Galtres fell in with malefactors while on duty, and had his eyes put out and his tongue and fingers cut off. The King granted him a pension of 3d. a day from 1351. He was still living in 1378[30] It was no wonder if the foot forester out on a stormy night sometimes fancied that he saw "le Gros Veneur" (the Big Hunter), the resident ghost of Galtres, riding under the trees. In 1315 the keeper of the forest beyond Trent was directed to enquire into the circumstances in which certain men had proclaimed in the City of York that no forester should enter the forest on pain of losing his head. This particular incident looks like a dispute as to the bounds of the forest, since the offenders are said to have made a perambulation on their own account.[31] These men may have imagined that they were asserting legal rights, but the same cannot be said of the persons who in 1342 forcibly entered the forest, took deer there, killed some of the King's officers and maimed others.[32]

The officers themselves were not always above reproach and in 1331 inquiry was ordered to be made into trespasses and excesses committed in Galtres by (among others) John de Crumbwell, keeper of the forest; William de Ayet, steward; Richard Breredyk, John Messenger, William son of Peter de Alne, Henry Fossegrayne and John son of Adam de Overton, foresters; Philip the Forester of Myrescough; and Gervase de Rouclif, regarder. Offices held by them were ordered to be seized into the King's hands.[33] William de Ayet was in fact pardoned in 1332,[34] Thomas atte Gate, deputy or lieutenant of the steward, Walter de Whithors, seems to have been a man with a somewhat eventful past. On 1st February, 1352, he was granted a general pardon of all felonies, robberies and trespasses committed by him — except for the deaths of Sir John de Eland and Thomas de Sibthorpe, clerk.

Six foresters were named in connection with the 1331 inquiry just mentioned which seems to mean that there were then two for each of the three bailiwicks, Kyle, Easingwold and Myrescough. In addition certain special officers were appointed to look after the King's lawn of Ingolthwayt. It is not known exactly where this was. It is certainly tempting to say that it must in fact have been the King's Laund of Jacobean times near to the present New Parks, the memory of which is preserved by the two farms named Laund House. In November, 1334, John de Padebury, Kings Yeoman, was granted the bailiwick of the lawn of Ingolthwayt in

163

place of Thomas de Ousethrope.[35] an office which he was allowed to transfer in April, 1340, to Ralph de Nevill.[36] On 26th December, 1359, Walter de Whithors the steward was granted custody of the King's lawn of Ingolthwayt, with the right to make hay there, provided he did no harm to the deer, and on condition that he kept in repair its fence and lodge and paid the wages of a lander (keeper of a laund) and palisser (man who looked after its paling) and on condition of making no agistment in the lawn (i.e. of not grazing it, but 'leaving the herbage for the deer). The purpose of the Ingolthwayt lawn in fact was as a deer pasture, particularly in winter. Livestock, and pigs in particular, destroyed the pasture for the deer and were consequently supposed to be kept out of places to which the deer habitually resorted.

The other launds in Galtres were ancient clearings or sometimes no doubt natural open areas, among the woods. They might belong to the King, as did the the the "herbage called Gresselee" (or "Grysseleyes"). This seems to have been meadow land. In 1389 or thereabouts John Vausour, one of the King's archers had a grant for life of £4. 10s. 0d. per annum from its profits.[37] In 1438 Thomas Carre, King's sergeant, had a grant for life of its custody, to be exercised by himself or his deputy, at a wage of £4 4s. 8¹/₂d. per annum, plus fees.[39]

Other lawns in the forest were those of Hoppethwaite near Easingwold, (now called Hopwith), Greenthwaite on the road from Sutton-on-Forest to York, Kelthwaite or Kelsthwaite (now marked by Kelsit Grange), Linthwaite, Ulveswaite near Stillington, Knackenthwaite, Sandburn, Carlton, Cortburn, Gunthwaite or Gunfit (somewhere near Fleet Bank Corner), Langthwaite and Myrescough (near Strensall). A name ending in "-thwaite" or one of its corruptions "-wit" or "fit" in the Forest of Galtres signals the probable presence of a former laund. They do not seem to have been specially reserved for the deer, except in winter, though this is not to say that the deer did not share their herbage. Hoppethwaite was let to St. Leonard's Hospital, York, its title being confirmed in 1338.[39] Myrescough in James I's reign was described as "one of the three agistments for the forest". It was then three miles from the woodland of the forest and contained no timber trees or underwood. Though part of the Manor of Easingwold and Huby, it was pastured by the King's tenants of Sheriff Hutton and Lilling and the freeholders of Farlington, Cornborough and Strensall.[40] It appears to have been somewhere near Anchor Plain and is perhaps the area now known as High Roans. In 1315 reference is made to two launds in the forest called Hariterwayte and

Ercedekneclos ("Archdeacon's Close"). The Greenthwaite and Kelsthwaite launds were occupied by St. Leonard's Hospital in 1338.[41] The Kelsthwaite laund after the Dissolution seems to have been let to Henry Wildon. A lease to him of Kelthwayte Grange and three closes of land in Galtres dated 8th March, 1542, is recorded in the books of the Court of Augmentations. On 15th November, 1269, a grant was made to Thomas de Boulton of the lawns of Karleton and Sandeburn, with leave to enclose them with a low hedge and ditch.[42] In 1339 Thomas Gra of York was licensed to enclose his lawn of Cortburn within the metes of the forest.[43]

Reference is made in 1403 to "the North baillie",[44] in 1413 to "la North baillie" of the forest of Galtres[45] and in 1419 to "Ia North baillif' of Easingwold.[46] By the 15th century therefore the later division of the forest into the North and South Bailiwicks had come into force and at about the same period the division of the foresters into riding and walking foresters or foot foresters seems to have been made. A riding forester is referred to in 1392 when the King's Clerk, Laurence de Baylay, received a life grant of the office in place of Guy de Rouclif deceased, with power to execute by deputy.[47] This suggests that the later arrangement of one riding and two foot foresters in each of the two bailiwicks came into being in about the last quarter of the 14th century.

In 1367 we find John de Pulford referred to as forester of the Ingolthwayt ward.[48] There is a reference in 1328 to the Forestry of Ingolthwayt, when Queen Isabella, the regent, requested a pardon for Peter de Watford, who had been its bailiff, for giving certain men of the neighbourhood a doe, found by him in the forest slain with an arrow.[49] In the same year Henry de Acom (Acomb), who was an official of the King's Chancery known as "chaufcyre" or "chafewax" (literally, wax heater), had a grant of the bailiwick of of the forestry of Ingolthwayt in Galtres Forest.[50] Henry had had a grant of the bailwick of the forestry of Myrescough in 1325[51], which suggests that in the 1 320s the three bailiwicks or wards may have been known as Kyle, Ingolthwaite and Myrescough, the Ingolthwaite ward being simply a new name for the central or Easingwold ward. If this is correct it would render the theory that the Ingolthwaite laund is the laund near New Parks more plausible.

Foresters in 1367 were paid 4d. a day. In that year John de Pulford was given a special rate of 6d. a day for his long service.[52] By Richard III's time all the walking foresters received 4d. a day, paid from the issues of the Manor of Sheriff Hutton. Henry VII continued this practice, though William Wyman, whose grant was dated 9th March, 1494,[53] was only given 2d. a day presumably because he was also given one of the riding foresterships.

Offices in Galtres had by the 15th century in fact come to be regarded simply as property. They were not expected to be performed by the grantees personally and there was no doubt a tendency to make them as profitable as possible by appointing deputies as cheaply as possible. In turn the deputies would be tempted to make their own profits to the detriment of the forest. While this is surmise and must not be exaggerated, we find in 1538 that Robert Cowp, one of the deputy foresters, had for the past twenty years "by colour of dearfall and gatherin" sold wood to the tenants of Tollerton and Alne and this may not have been an isolated example.

Later grants of foresterships seem to have been made invariably to persons who were not going to perform the duties personally. Holders of foot foresterships granted by Henry VIII include William Hoggeson, yeoman of the King's' buttery (1510);[54] William Horsseley, yeoman of the guard (1523),[55] who later shared with Thomas Horsley, yeoman of the buttery[56]; and John Wyghell, groom of the chamber (1510),[57] with reversion of the office to Richard Agmonderham, page of the wardrobe of robes (1536),[58] and on Agmonderham's death to Ralph Eyre, groom of the chamber (1540)[59], which latter reversion passed to Christopher Boothe, one of the King's footmen on 27th June, 1544.[60] This last grant suggests that as an office of profit a foot forestership in Galtres was of some value, even in reversion, which meant waiting for the death or surrender of the present holder. One of the foot foresterships in Galtres was valued by the agent for the disafforestation commissioners in the 1630s at £35 10s. 10d. per annum, the holder having purchased it for £120.

Another foot forestership was granted by Henry VIII to an usher of the King's Chamber in 1509, together with a riding forestership to the same man.[61] It seems quite obvious that these various grantees were King's servants or bodyguards, who were required to remain with his person, and were not only expected, but obliged, to perform their office by deputy.

In Henry VIII's time the four foot foresters had come to be known as "pateners", perhaps a coruption of "patenters" that is persons holding under letters patent.

Of the higher officers in later medieval and Tudor times, Adam de Walton, one of the King's sergeants at arms, was granted the stewardship in 1343.[62] On his death in 1348 Thomas de Colevill replaced him, but did not hold the office very long, since on 16th August, 1349, a fresh grant was made to Walter de Whithors.[63] His deputy Thomas atte Gate has already been mentioned. A later deputy of Withors, Richard Godbarn, named in 1366, does not appear to have been entirely satisfactory, since we find him charged with trespasses of vert and venison.[64] Whithor's successor, Thomas de Maulay steward in the years 1367-71 and probably till about 1377, had a number of complaints of misdeeds and damage made against him and eventually the King took the stewardship away from him and granted it to one of his esquires, Richard Pontifreit or Poumfreit, in September, 1377[65] Thomas Fairfax was steward in 1382-9 and Henry de Percy, Earl of Northumberland, and Ralph de Neville justices of Galtres in 1389.[66] Sir John Colvill, who died about 1405,[67] held the stewardship at his death and was succeeded by Sir John de Etton, who from 1412 held jointly with his son Miles. In 1437 Richard Babthorpe, King's esquire, had a life grant of the offices of steward and master forester, converted on 31st December 1439 to a grant in tail.[68] Henry VII granted the stewardship to Richard Bourgh in 1485 and the master forestership to Ralph Lord Graystock in 1486[69] Justice of Galtres in 1502 was Henry Prince of Wales. In November, 1507, the office of Justice of the Forest was granted to Thomas Dalby, Archdeacon of Richmond.[70] John, Earl of Oxford, had a patent for the offices of steward and master of the hunt in 1509, with reversion to Sir Henry Marney.[71] A further reversion on the death of Sir Henry or surrender of his patent, was granted to Sir Anthony Ughtred in 1514 and took effect in July, 1523.[72] On Sir Anthony's death in 1534 the stewardship was granted to Sir Arthur Darcy, who surrendered it in October, 1537, to receive a new grant in survivorship to himself and William Maunsfelde or Maunsell, gentleman usher of the chamber. Both parties later surrendered and a grant was made to John Nevyll, Lord Latimer, on 5th June, 1542.[73] He held the stewardship only briefly and was succeeded by John, Lord Conyers, on 23rd March, 1543.[74]

Sir Thomas Cromwell seems to have been Justice of the Forest at least as early as 1533. A catalogue of documents belonging to him or in his custody in that year includes a bill for Hugh Braban, sergeant-at-arms, for the offices of bailiff and woodward of Galtresse forest.[75] Cromwell ordered a "warden court" (which seems to mean an eyre) to be held on 13th June, 1537.[76] A list of "remembrances" made by him in 1537 includes the note; "To speak to Thawytes to be my deputy in Gawteres forest".[77] This was probably William Thwaites, who was one of Cromwell's deputies

167

in 1539 for viewing the forests North of Trent. (The view of Galtres was held at a court at Easingwold on 18th June, 1539, by Thwaites and his colleague Matthew Boynton).[78]

Riding foresterships were granted in 1439 to Thomas Gower; in 1460 to the King's esquire Henry Langton "for good service against the rebels", the office being forfeit by the rebellion[79]; in 1461 to Thomas Gower, son of the grantee in 1439[80]; and in 1471 to John Nesfeld.[81] On 25th November, 1486, John Chambre was granted the office of ranger, together with a foot forestership. The offices of bowbearer and collector of the attachment money were held together by Richard Clarvys, who died in 1512, and were probably ever afterwards combined.[82]

Offices were of course liable to be forfeited if the holder failed in his service to the King. as in 1497, when Henry VII declared John Bawdewyn's forestership forfeit because he had not served the King in the last campaign,[83] perhaps the invasion of James III of Scotland in 1496 on behalf of Perkin Warbeck; or for high treason, as in 1554 in Queen Mary's time, when the foot forestership of Christopher Boothe deceased, who had been one of Henry VIII's footmen, was forfeited for this reason.

As has been mentioned above, the officers known as regarders had the duty of protecting the forest from encroachments. They were expected to see that its boundaries were duly preserved and to review from time to time the position with respect to assarts and purprestures. Thus in 1286 a regard was ordered to be taken in Galtres, prior to a forest eyre. The regarders were to make a record of all assarts made since the second year of the reign of Henry III (28th October, 1217 — 27th October, 1218) and of all purprestures both old and new. Instructions were given on 24th May, 1305, for the holding of a regard.[85] Regards do not seem to have been held at set intervals, at any rate in the 14th century. The next order for a regard is dated 28th October 1307,[86] and the next after that 10th April, 1311.[87] Another regard order followed on 30th January, 1313.[88] The order for the 1307 regard required the election of new regarders to replace those who were dead or infirm, so that there were twelve in each regard. The foresters were to lead the twelve knights through their bailiwicks to view all trespasses which were to be expressed in the written "capitula" sent to the Sheriff. As in 1286 all assarts made since the second year of Henry III and all purprestures were to be recorded.[89] Regards were ordered on 20th November, 1319,[90] 12th December, 1323,[91] 14th December, 1325,[92] 15th February, 1329,[93] and 1st July, 1332.[94]

The Hundred Rolls contain a record from about 1273 of purprestures in Galtres. The lord of the manor of Stivelligton (Stillington) had a purpresture called "Pratum Paulini" ("the Meadow of Paulinus") made in King John's time and worth 2/-. Its vernacular name in 1295 was Paulineng. The men of Easingwold held a purpresture of 14½ acres made in the time of Robert de Ros (in the 1230s or thereabouts) for which they paid a rent of 7/3 per annum. William Peitevin or Paytfyn held a new purpresture of 10 acres near to the Cross of Paulinus and called "Paytfinclos" (Paytfyn's Close). This enclosure descended from William to Richard Paytfyn and was then conveyed to Hugh Gryvel. It later passed to Thomas de Berewyk, who in 1345 obtained licence from the King to convey it to Sir Thomas Ughtred. In 1365 it passed, together with a close "behind le Lund in Hoby" to Sir Thomas's son Thomas. Its rent at that time was 6/8 per annum.[95] The Meadow and Cross of Paulinus were on or near the boundary of Easingwold and Stillington, where by tradition Paulinus preached to the heathen Angles at the beginning of the 7th century. It looks at least as if the tradition was mediaeval, whatever its truthfulness. The field named Pouland Carr by the Ordnance Survey, just south of Easingwold golf course, may be about the place.

Other purprestures listed in the same record are one of four acres at Easingwold made in the time of Geoffrey de Langele (justice of the forest in 1251-2); one of eight acres at Huby made at the same time; an old purpresture of 50 acres at Easingwold held by the master of St. Leonard's Hospital, worth 32/4 per annum; and a purpresture at "Raskelve" held by Robert de Nevil.[96]

As explained above licence was required to enclose or assart land in the forest and enclosure or assarting without such licence was contrary to the law of the forest. In July, 1238, orders were given for the seizure of all assarts made by William de Ros in the Manor of Linton in the forest of Gauteris and for his attachment to appear before the King a fortnight before Michaelmas to explain why he made them without leave.[97] Mention has already been made of the permission given in 1269 to enclose the lawns of Karleton and Sandeburn.[98] In 1284 St. Leonard's Hospital was given licence to enclose Beningburgh Wood, 56½ acres in extent, and distant a bowshot from the covert of the forest. (The King's highway ran between the two).[99] The prior of Marton was licensed to assart 40 acres of his wood in the forest in 1291.[100] In 1304 licence was granted for Giles of Merksden to enclose with a small dike and low hedge an assart called "Baystan" within the forest, containing 15 acres by the forest perch, which he had purchased from Moxby nunnery and which was an eighth of a league from the great covert. He was also given leave to build houses on it, although it was a repair of the deer.[101] In 1314 licence was given to Thomas son of Thomas de Tolthrope (Tholthrope) and Alice his wife to enclose with a little dike and low hedge 24 acres by the forest perch at Westwod and Wullecote Wra in the forest.[102] (It will be noted that when leave was given to enclose land in the forest it was normally given on condition that the dike was small and the hedge low, the reason being that if this was the case the deer might still enter and leave the enclosure). In 1315 licence was given to John de Thornton of Scowesby (probably Skewsby) to enclose and assart the Lund at Sutton in Galtres. In 1316 licence was given to the treasurer of York Minster to enclose with a little dike and low hedge and reduce to cultivation 40 acres by the forest perch of his own soil in his manor of Alne and Tollerton at places called Foxholme, Fulwyth, Mikelbusk and Tollerton Moor.[103]

Enclosure in the forest provoked a hostile reaction from the commoners in Queen Elizabeth's time and it did the same in James I's. It seems therefore reasonable to conclude that the same motive, fear of abridgment of common, was the explanation of the case of Adam de Walton's enclosure at le Westmose in the forest. Adam de Walton, King's sergeant at arms and steward of the forest, was granted licence to enclose 120 acres by the forest perch of waste land at the Westmoss (which looks like the Westmoor near Blue Bridge), with common of pasture, by the service of bearing the King's bow when he should hunt in the forest.[104] Licence to assart and cultivate the plot was granted on 3rd April, 1347.[105] A crowd of men from the surrounding villages came in the night, threw down the enclosure and burned the hedge. They included Hugh and Thomas Thorn, John son of Thomas Betrissone, William le Pynder, John son of Robert Maldeson, Nicholas his brother and John de Westerdale, all of Huby; William del Gappe, John Howery, John Belle, Roger Sourdevale, John del Halle, Robert Freman, Thomas Hudson and William son of Simon, all of Sutton on Forest; William le Smale, Nicholas Watson, Simon and Nicholas Prikhors, Thomas Joy, John Brok and John de Bradelaye, all of Shipton; Richard le Sutheren, Richard de Acklom, Adam Frere and Henry le Harpour, all of Newton-on-Ouse; William le Presteson and Henry de Overton senior, both of Linton-on-Ouse: Thomas son of Hamona daughter of Henry and John lately the servant of Simon de Burghbrigge, both apparently from Alne; and a number of others, including the rather oddly named Stephen

Hamondesheremyt of Hessay, who on the face of it had no possible interest in the matter since Hessay is well outside the bounds of the forest.

If, as seems likely, there had been a good deal of enclosure in the forest in the late thirteenth and early fourteenth centuries and then the local inhabitants were confronted with an enclosure of 120 acres, which moreover was to be cultivated, and this was an enclosure made by one of the officers of the forest, it is easy to see how tempers could become inflamed. Perhaps there is a similar explanation behind the incidents of 1315 referred to above, when an unofficial perambulation was made and foresters were warned out of the forest.

A good deal of information is contained in the Close Rolls about the economic side of Galtres as a source of food, fuel, building materials and other products for the crown. Gifts of venison were frequently made by the King and duly recorded by the royal chancery. Thus on 21st October, 1236, an order was given that, of six bucks without tails taken in Galteris, two should be given to the dean and chapter of York Minster, two to the Sheriffs of York, one to the Master of St. Leonard's and one to the preceptor of the house of the Templars at York.[106]

In January, 1282, six does were given to the Archdeacon of Newark and on 18th September, 1283, the keeper of the forest was ordered to supply Anthony Bek, Bishop elect of Durham, with 25 bucks.[107] (Anthony Bek appears to have had one of the earliest encounters with "le Gros Veneur" while hunting in the forest. The apparition appears to have been that of a man named Hugh de Pontchardin, who may have been known to the Bishop in life, since the latter addressed him by name.)

Sometimes the King's gift was of live deer as when he gave orders in 1237 for the Bishop of Durham to have four live bucks and ten live does from Galtres for his park at Creck (Crayke).[108]

Galtres was also on occasion used for the King's own provisioning. In October, 1239, the King ordered 50 hinds to be supplied for his use during the coming season. On 21st November, 1301, Edward I ordered venison from a number of his forests to be taken, salted, barrelled and conveyed to Berwick-in-Tweed, no doubt for the provisioning of his household and army. The quota from Galtres was fifty does and twenty roe does.[109] Again in 1315 the King sent three of his yeomen with three ventrers in charge of fourteen running dogs and a berner in charge of nine greyhounds to take fat venison in Galtres, with a team of nine lardeners to dress the venison, which was to be salted, barrelled and sent to Carlisle. The amount to be provided was twelve harts and twelve does. While employed in this work the yeomen were paid 12d. a day and the dog keepers (the three ventrers and the berner) 2d. a day as also were the lardeners. An allowance of $^1/_2$d. a day was made for each of the running dogs, but curiously enough not for the greyhounds. The latter were perhaps smaller beasts.

Richard I had, in his large way, given a charter to St. Mary's Abbey, York, entitling it to a tithe of all the King's venison taken in the County of York and in consequence the abbey claimed a tithe of the venison taken in Galtres. This was felt to be somewhat burdensome, since the resources of Galtres had been heavily taxed by frequent huntings for the King and others, and accordingly in 1328 it was arranged that for five years, instead of a tithe from Galtres, the abbey should receive all the venison taken in the forest of Spaunton in Blackhommore (Blackamoor) between the rivers Dovve and Syvene (Dove and Seven) [110] The arrangement was renewed for a further five years in 1331[111] and made permanent in 1335.[112]

Sources of fuel in the forest were the wood, charcoal and turf. On 23rd November, 1227, Henry III gave orders to the steward of Galtres to supply wood and charcoal for three days for the use of the Archbishop in his house at York during the King's intended visit at Christmas.[113] Again on 11th October, 1231, fuel was to be brought from the forest to York for the King before the feast of St. Martin.[114] Probably it was only the trees unsuitable for timber which were used as fuel. Thus on 29th August, 1300, the King wrote from Caerlaverock to order that fifty leafless oak stumps; from Galtres should be given to the dean of York for fuel.[115] St. Leonarrd's Hospital at the beginning of the 14th century had the right to take fallen oak branches for charcoal burning. They had this by long usage, but in general charcoal burning was not in favour because it tended to disturb the game and diminish the covert.[116] Adam de Walton, the steward, had a grant of all "stubbes" in the forest for charcoal or other purposes.[117] The term "stubb" does not seem to mean a stump, nor indeed does it seem to mean anything inferior to the complete tree, since in Sherwood Forest in 1334 vert fines were calculated on a value of 5d. or 6d. for an oak and 6d. for a stubb.[118] Perhaps it means a trunk which is sound, but trimmed ready for felling.

A third source of fuel in the forest was turf. What use, if any, the King made of the turbaries in the forest for his own purposes is not known. He did grant to Kirkham Priory in 1235 a turbary 50 perches long and 50 broad "on the moor of Traneberimose between our demesne wood of Mirescuh and the water of Fosse on the east."[119]

The King's gifts of timber from Galtres for building purposes were very numerous. They included gifts of four oaks to the Iceeper of Topeliffe Bridge for repairs because it had been broken (December 1227);[120] ten oaks to the prior of Marton for building his church (same date);[121] five oaks to the Master of the Templars at York for repairing their mill there (May, 1231);[122] twenty oaks for the rebuilding of the mills of St. Mary's Abbey at York, lately burnt down (September 1236);[123] forty oaks to the preaching friars of York for building purposes (September, 1237;[124] ten oaks to the Minorites (Friars Minor) of York (April, 1238);[125] six oaks to St. Clement's nunnery, York, and another six to the Franciscans of Scarborough (1280)[126]; six oaks to Wilberfoss nunnery for the repair of the dormitory (February, 1292)[127]; eight oaks to the Carmelites of York to build their church (June, 1300);[128] and four oaks to the Sheriff of York to rebuild a house in York Castle in which to hold the King's pleas (i.e. the assizes) (January, 1304).[129] All these are donations for public or charitable purposes and the King did not give so freely to individuals. There were however no less than three gifts of tim'ber to Anketill Malore, the first on 24th April, 1234, of six oaks to make posts and beams for his house at Tyverinton (Terrington),[130] the second of six oaks for his house at Mulethorp (Mowthorpe) on 7th April, 1238,[131] and the third of two oaks on 18th July, 1238.[132]

Probably the largest gift of timber ever made out of Galtres was ordered on 11th October, 1343, of five hundred oaks to the men of the town of Ravenserod in the Humber, to repair their quays, damaged by the sea.[133]

The King's licence was required for the felling of timber in the forest, as in 1294 when Robert of Hertford was allowed to fell 20 aqres of his wood of Flathewath (Flawith), within the metes of Galtres forest, so that he could pay his debts;[134] or in 1312 when Nicholas de Meynille was given permission to fell 200 oaks in his wood of Aldewark).[135]

Both the Patent and Close Rolls contain the names of many persons bailed or pardoned for trespasses of venison in the 13th and 14th centuries. They include not only local men but others such as John de Hothum, Bishop of Ely;[136] John de Hardeshuli, Edmund de Rye and Simon de Drayton knights; and Eustace de Hardeshull, William de Riseby, Mauger de Rye, Robert de Oreford, Ranulph de Parys, John de Drayton and Ralph Taillard[137]; all of whom were pardoned on 23rd June 1327 for hunting without licence in Galtres and carrying away deer. Venison offenders were of all classes — they included Master Robert de Rypplyngham, Chancellor of York Minster, pardoned in 1312 of trespasses both of venison and vert committed in the reign of Edward I (for which pardon he paid 100 marks);[138] Master Roger de Heselarton, King's Clerk, pardoned in the same year for taking a deer;[139] Richard de Ryvers, parson of Brandsby, pardoned in 1330 for a number of trespasses of venison;[140] John de Esby and Henry de Craven, canons of Newburgh priory, similarly pardoned on 3rd April, 1334;[141] Henry Chaufcire of Acomb, the chancery official, who had a grant of the forest of Ingolthwaite in 1328, and was twice pardoned of venison offences, in 1335 and 1336;[142] Richard de Myton, chaplain, pardoned on 4th October, 1335;[143] and Thomas de Blaston, baron of the Exchequer, pardoned in 1337.[144] On the other hand they included such persons as Nicholas le Venur (hunter) and William le Venur, bailed from the forest prison in November 1277;[145] John de Hustwait, bailed in March, 1316;[146] Robert Freman of Sutton on Forest, bailed the following August;[147] Henry le Serjeaunt of Easingwold, who was imprisoned in 1320 and was released on producing twelve mainpernors (sureties) for his appearance at the next forest eyre;[148] Richard de Paytefyn, probably of Easingwold, and Thomas de Bulmer, bailed from prison in October, 1329;[149] William le Milner of Styvelyngton (Stillington), bailed in March, 1331 ;[150] and Hugh son of John son of Hugh de Essyngwald, bailed in March, 1332.[151] Easingwold men were in trouble in this way fairly frequently. Pardons issued for venison offences included ones given to Hugh Gryvel (13th July, 1334);[152] and Roger and William Gryvel (9th October, 1335).[153] Richard Peitfyn, Paytevyn or Patevyn, of Huby was pardoned twice of venison offences on 9th October, 1335, and 13th February, 1336, and was in trouble again in 1342.[154] In November, 1370, John son of John Gregory, William del Bank, William Fleccher and Thomas Scot, all of Crayke, and William Day of Brandsby were all in "the King's prison of Davy" for trespasses in the forest.[155]

At least one case occurred of a woman being imprisoned in Davy Hall. In 1316 bail was ordered for Ellen, wife of Robert Cademan of Skelton, imprisoned for harbouring her son Thomas, who had been accused of trespass of venison in the forest.[156]

Davy Hall did not always hold those who were put there. On 18th October, 1389, John Vausour, one of the King's archers, was pardoned for having escaped from the custody of Robert Thornton,

174

goaler of Davy gaol, to which he had been committed by the Lord de Nevyll, justice of the forest.[157]

On one occasion Galtres was designated for the reception of "evacuees". On 24th October, 1345, the King in anticipation of an invasion by the Scots, ordered the Sheriff of Northumberland to cause the cattle of that county to be brought south to, among other places, Galtres, where they would be pastured without charge.[158] It does not appear whether this order was in fact put into operation. One can imagine a certain amount of objection from the commoners of Galtres.

A detailed picture of the administration of the forest in the time of Henry VIII appears from the proceedings of a court held on 23rd June, 1538, at Easingwold.

A number of customs recorded by the jury at this court have already been referred to. They also set out in detail fees and payments due to the various officers. The Justice had annual fees of 3/- each from Newton, Shipton and Haxby, 2/- from "Rocliffe" (Rawcliffe), 1/6 from Beningbrough, 6/8 from Husthwaite, 13/4 from Sand Hutton and 30/2 from Stockton on Forest. He also had a close called Justice Close, near Langthwaite Carr, worth 18/4 per annum. (Although the jury did not set them out he also appears to have had other rights including pasturage for twelve score cattle, waifs, strays and felons goods in the forest.)[159]

The Master of the Game had rights of herbage, pannage, browsing, cocking (which seems to mean netting woodcocks), pitting, windfalls, wood, fishing and fowling; the Laund House with the herbage of the Laund worth £10 per annum; and a close called Steward Close worth 13/4 per annum. He had annual fees of 12d. from the land of John Taylor of Beningbrough, 6/8 each from Easingwold Church, from the prebend of Stillington and from land at Shipton, and 13/4 each from the manor of Overton, from Pickering's lands in the manor of Wigginton, from the Vicarage of Sutton on Forest, from Holmes Land in the manor of Huntington and Ingleby Land in the manor of Rawcliffe. To these were added 20/- from the prebend of Alne, 25/8 from the manor of Beningbrough and 5/- for the fishing of Linton Beck. He had annual payments of 3/4 each from St. Leonards Hospital, Newburgh Priory and the Abbeys of St. Mary's York; Marton; Rievaulx; and Byland; and there was also due to him a payment of 38/8 on St. Thomas's Day, the last day of the fence month. This included payments of 12d. each for Beningbrough, Rawcliffe, and Strensall; 18d. for Huby; 2/- each for Newton and Shipton; 2/6 each for Clifton and Skelton; 3/4 each for Easingwold, Tollerton, Wiggington and Stillington; and 4/- each for Haxby and Alne.

"Gate law" (cheminage or wayleave payments) in the whole forest was due to the Master of the Game at the rates of 6d. for every 20 horses; 4d. for every twenty cattle; 2d. for every score of sheep; 3d. for every packhorse; and for the "whole geare of every wayne in fence monethe 4d. & every other tymes 2d."

The record of the court states: "The twelve men findeth that the gatelawe hath heretofore been leased for 26/8d. & hath been highly misused by the farmers" (lessees) "for reformacon whof. we think that the same farmers may take in fence moneth of all the bounders" (dwellers in the pulieus) "and foressters" (dwellers in the forest) "that carryeth there for every wayne 4d. & allso horse load — ob." (obolus i.e. a halfpenny). For a "wayne that carryeth merchandise or other stuffe being forryners to and from the Citye of York 4d.".

The Riding Forester had to ride the perambulations with the keepers and tenants and enquire of all who might be keeping enclosures which ought to be open in winter for the benefit of the deer; and to hunt the purlieus and outgrounds. His annual fees were 2/- each from the Master of the Commons at St. Mary's Abbey, from the Vicar of Sutton, from land at Shipton, from Newburgh Priory and from Byland Abbey; 2/6 from the King's tenants at Easingwold; 3/4 each from St. Mary's Abbey and from Holmes's land at Huntington; 3/6 each from St. Leonard's Hospital and from Newton; and 4/- "Tachmt." (attachment) money.

The Bowbearer was to watch as a keeper, by himself or his deputy. In winter and summer he was entitled by custom to all forfeit skins, all deer not warrantable and one tree per annum for firewood. He had fees of 1 2d. a year from each of St. Mary's Abbey, Byland Abbey and Newburgh Priory; "Tachment Money" of 3/- one year and 4/4 the next, alternately; £6 16s. 0d. from the King's auditors; and 40/- connected with the "Receevership".

The Bailiff of the South Bailiwick was paid £12 2s. 8d. a year by the King, 19/4 by St. Leonard's and 3/4 by St. Mary's. He also had payments from the towns in that bailiwick and claimed two bucks in summer and two does in winter, together with browsing and pannage and every seven years three trees "of the best" and to have a horse sold.

The office of Bailiff of the North Bailiwick seems to have been held jointly at this date by Francis Cockett and John Wighell. The

176

annual fee from the King, as in the case of the South Bailiwick, was £12 2s. 8d. with 11/- from Alne and Tollerton; 3/4 each from St. Mary's and Newburgh; 3/- from Byland; and "Tachment money" of 8/- in one year and 9/- in the next, alternately.

The Clerk of the Forest had annual fees including payments of 2/- from Rievaulx, 6/- each from St. Mary's Byland and Newburgh, 4/- attachment money and for "collyers horses from Ampleforthe every horse loade 2d." (This last may have been from surface workings on Ampleforth Moor or nearby). The clerkship of the forest was granted in 1510 to Edward Vaux, yeoman purveyor of the King's wines,[160] who was also made chief steward of the lordship of Raskelf in January, 1522.[161]

The jury at this court presented a number of matters which throw light on the life of the forest. They said that the Laund ought to be paled as it formerly had been down to the time of Henry VII, since when the paling had been allowed to decay. It was now largely "hedged with the King's wood, to the destruction of the same, and of the underwood called garsell". This seems to mean that vert was being taken to carry out rough and ready repairs. Edward Wood "12 years past did edyfye & build besyde the Lawne house one chapple on the King's comon". Unlicensed enclosures had been made by Lancelot Collins, Treasurer of York Minister; by the Prior of Newburgh in the first year of the King's reign (22nd April, 1509 — 21st April, 1510); by Sir Thomas Netherton, the farmer (lessee) of Strensall, of Strensall Ruddings; and by John Coop, Bailiff of Sutton, of Beck Close about 1535. Sir Henry Burton had taken common for twenty head of cattle for the past two years, which was beyond his entitlement. Thomas Kaye had for the past six years over-commoned with 40 head of cattle, had enclosed land called Coatburne, and had on 10th March, 1535, cut garsell in Coatburn and Gruntwayt to the extent of 5/- damage. The tenants at Raskelf ought not to have wood "on this side Raskall Beck" (i.e. the Kyle) or within the forest boundary. The keepers allowance of fuel should be kept to wood for one fire each.

Thomas (later Sir Thomas) Curwen of Workington held one of the foot forestership patents from 21st January, 1529, till about the middle of 1536,[162] and we find him complaining to the Court of Star Chamber that several tenants of Easingwold and Huby had pulled down his deputy's lodge in the forest, so that the latter was unable to spend the night there with his "lyeme hounds" or bloodhounds to prevent the King's deer being stolen.[163]

177

On 3rd July, 1557, Queen Mary made a grant of the offices of steward and master of the chace to Henry, Earl of West-morland, in consideration of his services in defeating and appre-hending the traitor, Thomas Stafford, and his accomplices in Scarborough Castle.[164] On the Earl's death Queen Elizabeth made a grant, dated 9th March, 1564, of these offices and that of keeper of the laund to John Vaughan.[165]

It appears that during Queen Elizabeth's reign a Mr. Barwicke was permitted to enclose land in the forest, but that this enclosure was later thrown open again on complaint from the commoners.

In 1608 a survey was made of the King's timber in the forest in the Manor of Easingwold and Huby. At Easingwold there were 378 timber trees valued at £121. 5s. 0d. and 1,970 other trees valued at £362. 15s. 0d., together with some ashes in the garths of the copyholders of no particular value. At Huby there were 2,048 timber and 8,118 other trees as well as 120 timber trees belonging to leaseholders and 534 "dottards", which seems to mean decaying or decayed trees.[166]

In 1611 Sir William Gascoigne and John Athye junior had a life grant of the offices of Steward and Master of the Game. This patent was assigned, no doubt for value, to Edward Stanhope of York, K.B., on 6th July, 1616, He later himself assigned it to Thomas Lumsden "one of the gentlemen of H.M. Privie Chamber" for £500 on 23rd March, 1620. Lumsden was a man with chronic financial difficulties. In 1619 he mortgaged his office of Keeper of Sheriff Hutton Castle to William Ferrers, father in law, and probably in this case nominee, of Sir Arthur Ingram, Secretary of the Council of the North. This mortgage was foreclosed in 1622.

Lumsden also had a patent of Sheriff Hutton Park, which he said in a petition to the King was worth £240 per annum to him. At the King's request, he said, he had surrendered this office, in order that it could be disposed of to Lord Sheffield, President of the Council of the North, on promise of a privy seal for the receipt of £1,500. He had made the surrender, but had not received the money and therefore petitioned for a pension of £200 a year. In view of the Crown's own difficulties at this period, it may be doubted whether he got it.

He borrowed a sum of £210 from Alderman Thomas Ather of York, his sureties being William Scudamore, Esquire, of Overton and William Tennant, yeoman, of Bootham, York. He had to give them a conveyance of his offices on 18th December, 1621, by way of indemnity. On 8th March, 1622, he assigned his offices to William Ferrers, perhaps by way of second mortgage. On 30th August, 1622, we find Lumsden, Scudamore and Tennant letting Lumsden's offices to Sir Arthur Ingram for six years from 7th December, 1621. Lumsden let the Laund, including the house known as the New Lodge, to William Tennant for a term of sixty-five years, but apparently also mortgaged it either to Sir Arthur or a Mr. Fenwick of London. Lumsden's affairs in fact seem almost insoluble. A petition by Tennant after Lumsden's death refers to the last mentioned transaction and an arrangement under which Sir Arthur was to pay Tennant £100, of which £80 had been paid.

On 16th December, 1623, Gascoigne and Athye surrendered the original patent, but it looks as if Lumsden had a new one. He certainly had Letters Patent dated 31st July, 1624, in respect of the fines and amercements in the forest, which would not have been much use to him unless he held the offices of Steward and Master of the Game. He had died by 13th June, 1626, when the foot forestership which he had also held was granted to John Rosse for life.

Sir Arthur is said to have been the principal creditor at Lumsden's death and to have acquired the offices of steward and master of the game.

It is also said that Lumsden had borrowed the money to pay for these in the first place. Other evidence of his difficulties is contained in a petition in the Temple Newsam Papers by twelve men for about two years wages for work done in the Laund. In addition to the offices above mentioned Lumsden in 1621 held that of Bailiff of the Manor of Sutton on Forest.

Whether Lumsden's financial weakness enabled Sir Arthur Ingram and his fellow business men to establish a foothold in the affairs of Galtres and work for its disafforestation is not clear, but it certainly was disafforested in 1630 and Sir Arthur picked up much of the land, together with quite a number of Lumsden's papers and 'letters relating to the forest. These are now deposited in the archives department of Leeds City Libraries. They are here referred to as "Temple Newsam Papers".

They give a remarkably detailed picture of the forest in the reign of James I. They appear indeed to show that the forest was not as decayed as is sometimes supposed, though it is true that there had been substantial enclosure and that trespasses of vert and venison were numerous. On the other hand the stock of deer was still substantial - 803 in 1625 - and the woodland was estimated in 1630 at 7,600 acres. What really seems to have killed Galtres was Charles I's need for money, combined with the powerful business interests which appear to have been gathering like vultures round the forest for five years or more.

It certainly seems clear that the forest was neither as profitable nor efficiently run as it had been in the past. A warrant of James I dated 8th August, 1620, authorised Lumsden to destroy all unlawful greyhounds within the bounds, on account of the great destruction of the deer by the local people and by the neglect of the forest officers. Several memoranda in the Temple Newsam Papers list matters which their maker, whoever he was, considered to be wrong with the forest at this period. The verderers neglected their duty through ignorance and the ranger is described as "mynding nothing but cherishing his house". The offices of bowbearer and ranger were unnecessary and burdensome to the forest and the former ought to make proper account to the clerk of the attachment court for fines collected. The purprestures and assarts (in particular Vicar Close) gave every advantage to deer stealers. Crossbows had been found concealed in "helmes" (sheds) in these nclosures. Persons working in the forest should riot be allowed to carry "geare" (which probably means nets) "for under pretence of working they kill hares and may allso kill his mats deere for ought that I knowe. . . . Swine were complained of as "the only means of the destruction of the underwood". James I himself gave orders to restrict the number of swine in the forest. His letter on the subject complains of the great numbers of swine "by means whereof the great part of the best herbage is digged up and made like a cornfield" and orders that swine be not agisted except by consent of the Master of the Game or his deputy, and then only when there is good store of mast. Officers of the forest are to shoot unauthorised swine. Other nuisances complained of by the writer of the memoranda in the Temple Newsam Papers were the graving of turves where the deer should feed and the steeping and washing of hemp in running streams, "whereby the waters are poysoned". It was also said that "Some persons doo wilfully catch partridges within the lymitte of the forest with netts and setting dogges" and that the inhabitants of Easingwold and others usually cut bracken a month or more before Holy Rood Day (14th September).

The verderers should both view and deliver wood for repairs. Much more was being taken than was allowed and much more allowed than was necessary. The hind at Kelthwaite (Kelsit) ought not to take firewood except from that enclosure, though he might take garsell elsewhere on view of the verderers. The occupiers of

180

the Kelthwaite and Grundthwait (perhaps Gunthwaite) enclosures were only entitled to common in those enclosures. The underwood ought to be carefully looked after, "being the speciall want in the forest". Fines for woodbearing ought to vary according to the amount taken and should not be arbitrary. Persons brought by the officers to the verderers to be committed to goal ought not to be allowed bail or mainprise except by the Justice or his deputy. What in fact was happening, apparently, was that the verderers merely took bond of the persons concerned to appear at the next swanimote. Persons who were committed to Davy Hall prison were being allowed by its keeper to walk about the streets of York and elsewhere at their pleasure.

However, although all this was doubtless very bad, the complaints or many of them are similar to those made in earlier centuries and it by no means follows that the forest had declined to the extent that the King was obliged to do away with it. There was as has just been said a reasonable stock of deer — 803, as compared with the figure of 800 for 1538-9 — and the commoners had just won a considerable victory over the enclosers by procuring the throwing open of the Howe enclosures near Easingwold, as described in Chapter II. The courts were still active, fifteen attachment courts being held in the period 11th October, 1619, to 25th August, 1621, with receipts varying from nil to £3 4s 0d.

Some of the complaints about the forest may have been exaggerated a little in any case. A note probably made in the 1620s of the number of "swyne driven" at one of the periodic drives showed 406 swine for Easingwold, Stillington, Crayke, Tollerton and Huby. Of these 250 belonged to 39 inhabitants of Easingwold, 92 to 29 inhabitants of Huby, 43 to 8 inhabitants of Tollerton, 19 to 6 inhabitants of Stillington, while one person from Crayke had two. This does not seem to be a very large number, although it is only fair to say that the drive may not have caught many swine which were habitually agisted in the forest, especially if their owners had some prior warning.

It is perhaps of interest that the writer of the memorandum states that the swine in Galtres "have caves made for them in hollow trees".

The Temple Newsham Papers contain many sheets of draft presentments for court for the years 1618-25. They include the following

(i)   6th August, 1618. Rafe Bake, woodward of Huby, lodged a buck in his barley close and fetched John Harcourt

181

(keeper of the Laund in the period December, 1621 - January, 1625, but perhaps not yet a forest officer in 1618) and his man from Sheriff Hutton, who killed and took away the buck. (Bake was also charged with cutting a timber tree in July, 1620 and also on another occasion with converting to his own use the timber of a bridge called Topham Bridge "overthrown by an inundacon", to the value of £10. He was also accused in a presentment dated 15th November, 1621, of having assarted a small close on Crayke Lane, formerly pasture, and cut and sold wood there. He had cultivated the land for eight or nine years, sowing one year rye and another barley.)

(ii)   9th April, 1620. A Stillington man in going through the forest 'hunted a doe with a greyhound bitch. The presentment adds that "the said greyhound bitch was hanged at the Lodge" (i.e. was put down by the keeper as an unauthorised hound).

(iii)   3rd September, 1620. "Mr. Wornam" (John Wirdnam, vicar of Sutton on Forest from 1605 to 1631) "parson of Sutton cut a faire tymber tree between the Eller Carr and the Laund hedge who was prohibited in his Mats name according to the lawes of the forest he notwithstanding carried away a wayne load thereof in a contemptuous manner and came 'two or three days after the Swanymote Court daie when all officers came to Court and with his draughte" (team) "carried the rest awaie. .'"

(iv)   8th September, 1620. "One George Bland Pynder of Styllington" (and) "Win. Hynson servant to Mr. Wilford in Stillington Diana Field did kill a deere with a goone". (Diana Field is actually in the township of Huby, but it lies towards Stillington and the mistake is natural).

(v)   14th October, 1620. Henry Bellasis and his man hunted in the forest with a black greyhound and took a doe.

(vi)   6th November, 1620. Walter Bethell, Esq., felled and carried away two timber trees below Dawney Bridge.

(vii)   10th November, 1620. "Richard Dunning" (actually Dunwell) "Ye Parson of nonmunkton shot a male deer with a goone and killed him with a mastiffe" in Newton Field. The deer was carried away on a bay mare and concealed in a barn till cut up and disposed of. Mr. Dunwell seems to have been in trouble on another occasion, since there is among the Temple Newsam Papers a letter dated

28th April, 1624, endorsed: "The minister of Nomunton his missive". In it Mr. Dunwell refers to a subpoena served on him that day by Mr. Clarke, one of the keepers, and prays that "the suit may surcease . . . My estate is meane, yea even in the lowest degree of Church service. Only a stipend & a poor one.. .". He has, he says, with landowners permission killed "one onelye deere which was not found till he was past eatinge",

(viii) 8th and 9th November, 1620. William Hampe of Tollerton cut two goodly timber trees near Dawney Bridge. Although dissuaded in His Majesty's name by Robert Cans, keeper of the High Walk, and previously warned in the swanimote, he persisted in "a forcible and contemptuous manner

(ix) 17th November, 1620. One Coleby of Crayke and his "mongrell" dog killed a fawn in Crayke Park.

(x) About Easter, 1620. William Driffield of Easingwold had three men working at the Howe, lopping and topping a large number of hawthorn, ash and elder trees for hedgebote.

(xi) About Lady Day, 1620. William Driffield and Thos Green of Easingwold had four labourers working at "Parke nooke and other places within and adjacent to the howe" to lop and top about 300 thorns and crabtrees.

(xii) "22 of August last", perhaps 1620 or 1621. Robert Caris the keeper found the skin of a buck in the house of John Trueman of Crayke and on further search the "cloute" in which the body had been concealed.

(xiii) Undated, perhaps 1621. Thomas Kirby and another Crayke man "did day and night with curres and greyhounds chase and disturbe the deer out of their grounds and being rebuked by Robert Cans said they would doe so still". Later Cans found Kirby "lurking about the ground with a greyhound in a slipp".

(xiv) Undated, perhaps 1621. A fortnight before Holy Rood (14th September) Thomas Gibson of Easingwold cut and carried away six loads of bracken in the forest.

(xv) Undated, perhaps 1621. On 2nd October last Thomas Browne of Easingwold cut and carried away two loads of garsell in the forest.

(xvi) 1st October, 1621. William Gibson of Easingwold cut two loads of whins at a place within the Howe.

(xvii)   Christmas, 1621. Robert Copland junior of Easingwold cut and carried away a load of oak wood in Longthwait Carr.

(xviii) 1621 or 1622. William Driffield senior, William Driffield junior and James Driffield were presented on the evidence of Robert Cans for sowing oats in the two closes called Stewart Closes "being a launde for the releife of the deere in winter".

(xix)   5th November, 1621. John Harrison of Easingwold and others coursed the King's deer in Greenthwaite Carr.

(xx)   6th May, 1621. Robert Wilson and Herbert How with others cut and carried away a timber tree in Havertwaite, despite the protests of Robert Caris, who was forcibly detained while they did so. Caris also charged How with cutting a fair timber tree "neare unto the Call Raines" on 6th April 1622, sawing it into boards and selling them.

(xxi)   1st June 1622. "Jas Dowthwaite of Newborough parke & William Dowthwaite of the same came into a place within the said forest called Browne Robin Hagg with a Bowe and thrin hunted to kill his Mats deere the next daie following a doe was found killed with an Arrowe which is very likely to have been killed by them".

(xxii)   10th June, 1622. "George Tomlynson of Birdforth, John Thornton of the same, Thomas Staveley of Thormanby, William Burnit of Bausker" (Boscar) "Grange, George Chambers of Baxby, George Roose of hustwyt", (Husthwaite) "Win Roose of the same gentleman, Thomas Potte of the same, James Millner of the same, about the time aforesaid, came into a place called hustwyt wood, and there wh hounds did hunt a Brace of his Mats deere and did backset them wh a brace of Greyhounds to defend them from the forest, and there in the said woods did kill a buck wth the said Greyhounds, the other Buck they did course to a place within the forest called how hill, and one harbart howe coming to ye Greyhounds tooke up one of them wh was Mr. Thornton's above name, wh Greyhound they did intreate for and told him they would inform what they had done".

(xxiii) Robert Caris, the keeper of the High Walk, was himself presented on the information of Thomas Pannet of Easingwold, woodward, for felling trees in the forest as follows:- three in October, 1624; one on 16th November,

1624; one on 19th November, 1624; for selling a tree to William Nightingale on 20th November 1624; for selling three loads of wood to Richard Stevenson; for felling a tree on 17th May "last" perhaps 1625); and another on 1st June.

Robert Caris, who is mentioned in many of these presentments, said himself that he had been keeper in the forest under "the Late Sovraign Lade Quene Elizabeth, as also to his moste Excellent Matie" James I). In 1608 timber at Huby is referred to as being in his walk. In 1619 his name was subscribed to a document entitled: "A viewe taken of the greatt spoyle of our kings maties woods in a place called the how wh is the lanterne of the forest of galtres, nere adioyning unto Easingwoulde the nynte day of marche in Anno dui 1619 . . .". (His walk therefore then clearly included Easingwold). Another document which Caris subscribed probably about the same time was: "A view taken of the great spoile of his Mats woodes and underwoods vizt Elders and Thornes by the rootes in a place called the Hyrne and Ladykar, for the fenceinge of a new Inclosure, which is a greate impoverishinge and an utter undoinge of his Mats game within his Mats Forest of Galtres, nere adioyninge the howe; vizt the quantitie of the said Elders and Thornes, in nomber Eleaven hundred and twelve for the fenceing of said now Inclosures." (The document goes on to say that the poor people had also carried away about a thousand elders. The Hurns and Lady Carr are to the south-east of Easingwold.)

Caris had the High Walk during the. period 1620-5 and there is a bond dated 27th November, 1619, among the Temple Newsam Papers given by him in respect of his office of keeper. In about 1623 he felt it necessary to make a statement to his superior, the Master of the Game, regarding complaints which had been made against him. He had a paper drawn up (he himself could not write) setting out the good service he had done in taking various offenders in the forest who were hunting with greyhounds and crossbows, sometimes by night. Thus he took "one John Watson, one of the greatest offenders on the forest side stalking in the night with his bow". He also took a number of other deer stealers, some at night in the Laund. "I tooke", he said "one John Troman" (probably of Crayke) "Ranginge through the Game Intendinge for to hunt . . . I tooke one of Mr. Chomleys men on the night wth greyhounds in Crak Lordshipp, and two other of the men Run from me"

Not content with this defence, he also wrote a letter dated from Easingwold on 30th January, 1623, in which he not only asserted that "my service hath bene honest & iust", but stirred things up by acquinting his worship of divers wrongs which were done in the low walks. He accused Harcourt, the keeper of the Laund, and Thomas Clarke, another keeper, of misconduct in killing in season and out of season, so that even their dogs could eat the venison, and remained "Your loveinge servant, to use to his power till deathe Robt. Cayrise".

No doubt the accusations of Pannett the woodward in 1625 did not do Caris much good. Honest and conscientious or not, he remains that very rare bird so far as Galtres records are concerned, the actual man on the job. He was almost certainly not himself the holder of a patent, but was deputy for the holder.

In 1622 the four walks in the forest were kept by Caris, Clarke and men name Faldington and Wetherill. Clarke was a Welburn man. In 1625 the walks were held as follows:— High Walk, Robert Caris; Lower North Walk, Robert Turner; Copers or Oopers Lodge Walk, Robert Fawdington; and Knackenthwaite or Lumley Lodge Walk, Thomas Clarke.

Another Easingwold forest officer was James Elimire or Elmore, yeoman, who was the deputy of William Gascoigne of Ruby, bailiff of the forest under a patent of 1608.

There are some detailed records of the deer in the forest in the period 1620-5. In 1621 36 bucks and 22 does were killed in the whole forest, only two being described as wounded by stealers. Of the bucks one was a pricket (second year buck), three were sorells (third year bucks) and four were sowes or soars (fourth year bucks). In the High Walk in the summer of 1622 thirteen bucks were killed, one after being wounded by stealers; and four does, one killed by stealers. During the winter a brace of "faundes morts" (dead fawns) was also found. In 1625 there were 164 deer in the North Bailey and 639 in the two southern Walks and the Laund.

Various persons were entitled to. bucks or does from the forest as fees. These included the Justice or his Commissioners, the Master of the Game, the Bowbearer, the Ranger, the Lander or keeper of the Laund, the four foot foresters or keepers, the two verderers, the steward of the swanimote, the clerk of the attachment court, the keeper of the Davy Hall prison and the regard jury. From a note made about 1620-5 it appears that they received between them forty-eight fee deer. The Lord President of the Council of the North and Sir Arthur Ingram, Secretary of the Council, received four each and it was usual to make a yearly allowance of four to the Dean and Chapter of York Minister, two to the Circuit Judges and two to the Sheriff as well as six to "bordering and well deserving neighbours". Frequently the receipients requested that their fee bucks should be delivered to friends as in June 1622 when the Earl of Rutland, who may have been entitled as a Commissioner or was perhaps a well deserving neighbour requested that a fee buck should be given to Sir Thomas Fairfax and another to Sir Oliver Cromwell. Special gifts were still made by the King as on 9th July, 1620, when he gave the Bishop of Durham a warrant for venison from various royal forests, including Galtres.

The Commissioners referred to were the Commissioners of the Justice of the Forests, Chaces and Parks beyond Trent. Towards the end of James I's reign this office was held by his favourite the Marquis (later Duke) of Buckingham. The Commissioners certainly included Sir Henry Constable (later Lord Dunbar), Sir Thomas Fairfax and Sir John Gibson of Welburn.

Deputy Justice about 1620 was Sir Richard Etherington, steward of the Honour of Pickering and of the Manor of Easing-wold and Huby. John Harcourt, as mentioned above, was Lander in the period 1622-5. William Scudamore of Overton had a patent for the offices of foot forester and ranger on 19th March, 1621, but later sold it to Cuthbert Pudsey, who was the holder in 1630. On 19th April, 1623, Robert Turner was appointed a keeper on the recommendation of the Earl of Rutland in place of Robert Jennings from whom he had bought the office, apparently despite the objection of the steward, Mr. Lumsden, that he was not a fit person.[168]

John Rosse succeeded to Lumsden's foot forestership on 13th June, 1626.[169] A document of 13th December, 1626, names Sir John Savile as "Maister of the sd. forest" and it looks as if he succeeded Lumsden as steward and master of the game.

The references in the list of fee deer quoted above to the steward of the swanimote and the regard jury seem to require explanation. The latter may be a new name for the regarders and the former is perhaps simply the steward of the forest.

The King had probably decided to disafforest Galtres by 9th September, 1629, on which date he made a grant of 14,178 acres of land in Galtres in socage at an annual rent of £40, in considera-tion of £200,000 paid into the Exchequer by Sir Allen Apsley. The grant was made to Sir Allen's nominees, Peter Lennarth, Thomas Austen or Augton and John Dullyn or Duling. An entry dated 17th

June, 1630, in the records of the King's Remembrancer's Office shows that Sir Robert Heath, the Attorney General, exhibited a bill in the court of Exchequer for confirmation of the arrangements for disafforestation. There were to be six commissioners for the allotment and enclosures of lands and for other matters. They were Sir Thomas Gower, Sir Richard Darley, Sir William Ingram, William Tankard, Esq., Robert Morley, Esq., and Alderman Thomas Lawne of York.

The Commissioners seem to have started work fairly quickly since a decree of the court on 19th November, 1630, confirmed their allotment of common to various townships in lieu of rights in the forest. The largest allotment was 1,776 acres to Easingwold at an annual rent of 13/4d. Next largest was that to Sutton-on-Forest of 1,500 acres at £1 per annum. The southern townships had large allotments, Haxby receiving 1,277 acres, Wigginton 1,232. Skelton 1,155, plus a special allotment in respect of the land of Thomas Atkinson, Shipton 1,029, Clifton and Rawcliff 734 and Strensall 537 at annual rents ranging from 6/8d. to £1 0s. 1d. Huby was allotted 888 acres at 6/8d. per annum and Stillington 694 at the same rent, while small allotments were made of 80 acres to Moxby, 58 to Tholthorpe and 20 each to Greenthwaite and Cornborough. Raskelf and Sheriff Hutton also accepted the commissioners award, the former receiving 250 acres of the Lund at 8/8d. per annum, the latter 600 acres at Myrescough Lund (laund) at 13/4d. Alne, Tollerton and Newton stood out and the court gave them until the first Thursday of the following term to accept, failing which they were to be left to their case at law. Exactly how the matter of the allotments of these townships was settled the writer does not know, but it must have been settled and allotments made to the commoners within the next year or two. The allotment for each landless cottager in the forest was four acres of good land in a convenient place, increased to six acres in the case of Huby and seven in the case of Easingwold "in pity and commiseration of the estate of the poorer sort of inhabitants".[169]

A list in the Temple Newsam Papers endorsed: "A coppie of the pticulers of Galtres Landes July 1640" gives details of former forest lands. There is no indication to whom they belonged, but their presence among the papers and a further note of 19th January 1641 suggests that Sir Arthur Ingram had the freehold of a moiety and an unexpired term of 19 years in the other moiety, with an option to give up the lease at Lady Day, 1642, in which case the lands would be partitioned between the owners of the two moieties. However, the ownership position is not really our concern. What is

188

of interest is the description of the lands concerned which seem to be pretty clearly lands allotted by the disafforestation commissioners. They include a house called Turner's Lodge with 764 acres of land, Farringtons Lodge with just over 60 acres, and Moubery's Lodge with just over 112. These look like former keepers lodges.[170] In December, 1640, there is a reference in the parish registers of Easingwold to "Robte Mowbrey of the lodg". Farrington's lodge may be that occupied on 1st September, 1625 by the keeper of one of the southern walks, Robert Fawdrigton, Fawdington, or Faldington. There is still a farm called Fawdington or Fordington Lodge a little to the west of Kelsit Grange. There was also a house called the Great Lawne with two parcels of ground on the north comprising just over 221 acres, and on the south side 62 acres of land called Black bushes and Burnt Oak. This could be the house occupied by John Harcourt, keeper of the Laund, in 1625. There were also "a ground called Oxmore" of just over 107 acres, the Stewards Closes of about 23 acres, grounds called Hawk-hills and the Shires of about 687 acres and "The Bourne and Mosse-Endes alias the Plaines" of 453 acres. Other substantial parcels were woods and wood grounds at Dodholm woods (460 acres), Westmoss and Newton Sleights alias the Stales (336 acres) and Sutton Waste alias Suet Carr, "Mirisque" (Myrescough) Lawn and Anchor Plain. There was also a parcel of ground adjoining the New Park.[171]

The New Park consisting of 995 acres of land was formed under the direction of Thomas Strafford, Viscount Wentworth, President of the Council of the North from 1628. On 30th July, 1630, a royal warrant gave instructions to him regarding the preservation of deer and timber in Galtres for the intended New Park.[172] A grant of the New Park appears to have been made to Strafford about 1633 and a letter written by him in 1635 refers to the New Lodge apparently in the New Park. By tradition the house known as New Parks is "a royal hunting lodge of James I". In fact this is not certain, but the tradition need not be wrong. A presentment dated 12th January, 1619, refers to "Mr. Lumsden's New Lodge". It has already been mentioned in the account attempted of Lumsden's tortuous transactions that he let the Laund and the New Lodge to William Tennant of Bootham for 65 years. The New Lodge does not appear to be the Laund House from which John Harcourt addressed a letter on 15th February, 1622. It seems very likely that the New Lodge mentioned by Strafford in 1635 was 'Thomas Lumsden's New Lodge of 1619. In 1637 "the New Lodge . . . within the demesne of the King, laitlie improved in the Forest of Galtres by Peter Leonardes, Tho. Austin and John Dewlinge" was occupied by John Gibbens, Esq., who appears also to have occupied land at Eller Carr, Laund House, Fawdington Lodge and "Mireskew" (Myrescough).[173]

Some of the deer in Galtres were no doubt transferred to the New Park in 1630. After Strafford's death in 1641 the New Park seems to have come into the custody of Thomas, First Viscount Savile, who let it from May, 1641 to Sir Arthur Ingram for £100 per annum. The latter made extensive alterations between September, 1641, and July, 1642. He died in August, 1642, and his son apparently gave up the lease.

A survey made in 1649 for the purposes of the Act for the sale of confiscated Crown lands recorded that the New Park had 270 fallow deer, 1,861 trees "of the better sort" and 3,492 trees fit only for firewood. Its buildings were then the Great Lodge, occupied by the head keeper, and the Little Lodge, occupied by the under keeper. At the date of the survey the lessee of the New Park was Sir Hugh Cholmley whose term was due to expire in Michaelmas next following.[174]

During the Commonweath the park was under the care of Col. Robert Lilburne. By 1660, when Captain Richard Harland of Sutton Hall replaced Lilburne, it was in decay and there were only twelve deer. The New Park seems never to have been restored as a deer park after this.

The disafforestation of Galtres led to the taming of the semi-wild landscape bounded by Easingwold, Huby, Sutton, Wigginton, Clifton, Skelton, Shipton and Tollerton, formerly without habitation apart from the New Lodge, Laund House, Kelsit Grange the four keepers lodges and one or two other houses at old enclosures. This landscape of bracken hills and old oaks, with its rustic landmarks of stones and trees and old crosses, was turned into enclosed farmland. The roads were improved and the old ford of the Fleet was replaced by a bridge, now called Blue Bridge.

As time went on many more farmhouses were built, though to judge by the evidence available for the township of Easingwold there does not appear to have been any excessive or very rapid movement of population into the forest lands. This is a matter for detailed research, but it was probably not till the end of the 18th century that the former forest was really assuming its modern aspect.

190

1   Cox : Royal Forests of England, 1905, p. 20.
2   ibid pp. 129-30.
3   Cox op cit.
4   Manwood : Treatise & Discourse of the Lawes of the Forest, 1598.
3   Cox op cit.
6   Thoroton Soc. Rec. Series Vol. XXIII.
7   Remembrances of the Forest, 1566
8   YAS Rec. Ser. Vol. XII, pp. 111-2.
9   Cal. Close Rolls (1302-7) p. 357.
10   Remembrances of 1566.
11   YAS Rec. Ser. Vol XXXVII.
12   ibid.
13   Holt : The Northerners: A Study of the Reign of King John, 1961.
14   YAS Rec. Ser. Vol. XII p.9.
15   Cal. Close Rolls (1227.31) p.6.
16   Cal. Pat Rolls (1232-47) p. 52; Cal. Close Rolls (1234.7) p. 140.
17   Cal Pat Rolls (1247-58) p. 76. YAS Rec. 5cr. Vol. XXXVII.
18   YAS Rec. Ser. Vol. XXIII pp., 117-9.
19   YAS Rec. Ser. Vol. XXIII p. 118.
20   YAS Rec. Ser. Vol. CXX p. 30.
21   YAS Rec. Ser. Vol. XXIII p. 13.
22   YAS Rec. Ser. Vol. XXXVII p. 88.
23   Cal. Close Rolls (1318.23) p. 150.
24   ibid p. 191.
25   ibid p. 192.
26   Cal Pat Rolls (1324-7) p. 195.
27   Cal Pat Rolls (1338-40) p. 422.
28   Cal Pat Rolls (1343-5) p. 52.
29   Cal Pat Rolls (1405-8) p. 21.
30   Cal Close Rolls (1374-7); & Cal Close Rolls Ric II, Vol. 1. p. 161.
31   Cal Close Rolls (1313-8) p. 187.
32   Cal Pat Rolls (1340-3).
33   Cal Pat Rolls (1330-4) p. 200.
34   ibid p. 265.
35   Cal Pat Rolls (1334-8) p. 46.
36   Cal Pat Rolls (1338-40) p. 463.
37   Cal Pat Rolls (1388-92) p. 111.
38   Cal Close Rolls (1435-4) p. 326.
39   Cal Charter Rolls (1327-41) p. 454.
40   Temple Newsam Papers.
41   ibid.
42   Cal Charter Rolls (1257-1500) p. 131.
43   Cal Pat Rolls (1338-40) p. 351.
44   Cal Pat Rolls, Henry VI, Vol. 2, p. 100.
45   Cal Pat. Rolls, Henry VI. Vol. 2. p. 100.
46   ibid.
47   Cal Close Rolls (1389-92) P. 201.
48   Cal Pat Rolls (1364-7) p. 383.
49   Cal Pat Rolls (1327-30) p. 257.
50   ibid p. 246.
51   Cal Pat Rolls (1324-7) p. 111.
52   Cal Pat Rolls (1364-7) p. 383.
53   Cat Pat Rolls (1485-94) p. 458.
54   Letters & Papers For & Dom. Henry VIII Vol. 1 p. 127.
55   ibid Vol III Pt. 1 p. 136.
56   ibid Vol. XVIII pt. II p. 184
57   ibid Vol. 1. p. 181.
58   ibid Vol. X p. 157.
59   ibid Vol. XV p. 293.
60   ibid Vol. XIX, pt. 1 p. 621
61   ibid Vol. 1 p. 58.
62   Cal Pat Rolls (1343-5) p. 101.
63   Cal Pat Rolls (1348-50) p. 143; & ibid p. 368.
64   Cal Pat Rolls (1364-7) p. 356
65   Cal Pat Rolls (1377-81) pp. 21 & 207.
66   Cal Pat Rolls (1388-92) p. 131.
67   Cal Pat Rolls (1405-8) p. 21.
68   Cal Pat Rolls (1436-41) pp. 63-364.
69   Cal Pat Rolls (1485-94) pp. 11. & 27.
70   Cal Pat Rolls (1494-1509) p. 566.
71   Letters & Papers For & Dom Henry VIII Vol. 1. p. 31.
72   ibid p. 873; ibid Vol. III pt. I, p. 1337.
73   ibid Vol. XVII p. 256.
74   ibid Vol. XVIII. pt. 1, p. 199.
75   ibid Vol. VI p. 132.
76   ibid Vol. XII, pt. II, p. 77.
77   ibid p. 410.

78   ibid Vol. XIV pt. II p. 32.
79   Cal Pat Rolls (1452-61) p. 544.
80   Cal Pat Rolls (1451-7) p. 151.
81   Cal Pat Rolls (1467-77) p. 263.
82   Letters & Papers For & Dom Henry VIII Vol. III, pt. p. 1337.
83   Cal Pat Rolls (1494-1509) pp. 120-1.
84   Cox op cit.
85   Cal Close Rolls (1302-7) p. 336.
86   Cal Close Rolls (1307-13) p. 45.
87   ibid p. 342.
88   ibid p. 564
89   Cox op cit.
90   Cal Close Rolls (1318-23) p. 211.
91   ibid p. 693.
92   Cal Close Rolls (1323-7) p. 526.
93   Cal Close Rolls (1327-30) p. 522.
94   Cal Close Rolls (1330-3) p. 555.
95   Cal Fine Rolls 39 Edw. III p. 310.
96   Rotuli Hundredorum temp. Hen. III and Edw. I. vol. 1, 1812.
97   Cal Pat Rolls (1232-47) p. 226.
98   Cal Charter Rolls (1257-1300).
99   YAS Rec Ser Vol. XXII p. 13.
100   YAS Rec Ser Vol. XXIII p. 117.
101   Cal Pat Rolls (1301-7) p. 206.
102   Cal Pat Rolls (1313-7) p. 165.
103   Cal Pat Rolls 1313-7 p. 391.
104   Cal Pat Rolls (1345-8) p. 217.
105   ibid p. 266.
106   Cal Close Rolls (1234-7) p. 325.
107   Cox, op cit.
108   Cal Close Rolls (1234-7) p. 325.
109   Cox op. cit; Cal Close Rolls (1296-1302) p. 506.
110   Cal Pat Rolls (1327-30) p. 316.
111   Cal Pat Rolls (1370-4) p. 177.
112   Cal Pat Rolls (1334-8) p. 190.
113   Cal Close Rolls (1227-31) p. 6.
114   ibid p. 569.
115   Cal Close Rolls (1296-1302) p. 226.
116   YAS Rec Ser Vol. XXXVII.
117   Cal Pat Rolls (1345-8) p. 477.
118   Thornton Soc. Rec Ser. Vol. XXIII.
119   Cal Charter Rolls Vol. 1. p. 213.
120   Cal Close Roll (1227-31) 681.
121   ibid p. 9.
122   ibid p. 510.
123   Cal Close Rolls (1234-7) p. 312.
124   ibid p. 498.
125   Cal Close Rolls (1237-42) p. 389.
126   Cox op. cit.
127   Cal Close Rolls (1288-96) p. 243.
128   Cal Close Rolls (1296-1302) p. 226.
129   Cal Close Rolls (1302-7) p. 118.
130   Cal Close Rolls (1231-4) p. 409.
131   Cal Close Rolls (1237-42) p. 40.
132   ibid p. 318.
133   Cal Close Rolls (1343-6) p. 184.
134   Cal Pat Rolls (1292-1301) p. 71.
135   Cal Pat Rolls (1307-13) p. 462.
136   Cal Pat. Rolls (1327-30) p. 133.
137   ibid p. 131.
138   Cal Pat Rolls (1307-13) p. 405.
139   ibid p. 448.
140   Cal Pat Rolls (1330-4) p. 16.
141   ibid p. 543.
142   Cal Pat Rolls (1334-8) pp. 172 & 224.
143   ibid p. 185.
144   ibid p. 392.
145   Cal Close Rolls (1272-9) p. 407.
146   Cal Close Rolls (1313-8) p. 272.
147   ibid pp. 361-2.
148   Cal Close Rolls (1318-23) p. 194.
149   Cal Close Rolls (1327-30) p. 455.
150   Cal Close Rolls (1330-3) p. 209.
151   ibid p. 444.
152   Cal Pat Rolls (1330-4) p. 560.
153   Cal Pat Rolls (1334-8) pp. 172-3.
154   ibid pp. 172-3 & 223 and Cal Close Rolls (1341-3) p. 423.
155   Cal Close Rolls (1369-74) p. 159.
156   Cal Close Rolls (1313-8) p. 363.

157   Cal Close Rolls (1377-81) p. 117.
158   Cal Close Rolls (1343-6) p. 600.
159   VCH NR Vol. II.
160   Letters & Papers For & Dom. Henry VIII Vol. 1. p. 156.
161   ibid Vol. III pt. 1, p. 865.
162   ibid Vol IV, pt. III p. 2311 & Vol. XI p. 157.
163   YAS Rec Ser Vol. XLI pp. 87-9.
164   Cal Pat Rolls (1555-7) p. 480.
165   Cal Pat Rolls (1563-6) p. 86.
166   Duchy of Lancaster Records Class XIX, Book V.
168   Cal State Papers Dom 1619-23 p. 562.
169   'The Agrarian History of England and Wales", Vol. IV, ed. Dr. Joan Thirsk,
       C.U.P. 1967. p. 37. quoting documents in the Public Record Office (LR 2, 194,
       f. 35; E 178, 5742.)
170   Moubery's Lodge seems to have been on the Hurns
171   Much of this land seems to have been later owned by Sir Miles Cooke and then
       Sir John Pole, Bart. of Shute, Co. Devon, before being conveyed to the Bethells of
       Alne in 1705.
172   Cal of State Papers, Dom 1629-31 p. 295.
173   NRQSR Vol. IV pp. 72 & 173.
174   YAJ Vol. XXXI art by T. S. William: The Parliamentary Surveys for the North
       Riding of Yorkshire.

INDEX OF PERSONS

195

196

199

INDEX OF PLACES

201

203

204

GENERAL INDEX

205

206

207

LIST OF SUBSCRIBERS

John Abell, Esq., York
Acomb County Junior School, York
Acomb Secondary Modern School, York
R.J. Agar, Esq. Dipi. Arch., A.R.1.B.A. York
Aireborough Public Library
A. Allen Esq., Easingwold
Mrs. T. M. Allenby, Helmsley
Ampleforth Abbey
Ampleforth College

J. W. Arnett, Esq., Easingwold
Miss G. M. Atkinson, Leeds
Dr. R. G. Balf, Easingwold
Chas. John Bannister, Esq., Easingwold
H. Bannister, E.sq., Easingwold
W. Bannister, Esq., Easingwold
The Bar Convent Grammar School, York
R. J. Barugh, Esq., Easingwold
E. J. Batchelor Esq., Harrogate
Mrs. E. Bailey, Leeds
R. D. Batty, Esq., Easingwold
Mrs. A. Beckwith, Easingwold
A. Beckwith, Esq., Easingwold
Bedale County Modern School
Mrs. A. C. Bell, Raskelf, York
Mrs. F. H. Bell, Uppleby, Easingwold
Ald. J. S. Bell, Thwaites Brow, Keighley
Miss E. Benten, Leeds 12
E. Bentley, Esq., Birkenshaw
Beverley Public Library
Bingley College of Education
Bingley Public Library
Birmingham Public Libraries
A. H. Boddison Esq., Easingwold
Boddy's Bookshop, Middlesbrough
Borthwick Institute of Historical Research, York
Rev. Dr. I. C. Bowmer, London EC1.
Bradford City Libraries
Bradford Historical & Antiquarian Society
G. Broad Esq., Easingwold
Jas. Brogan Esq., Sticklepath, Okehampton
G. E. Brooksbank Esq., Meltham
C. Brown, Esq. Kirkby in Cleveland
Mrs. Laura Brown, Easingwold
N. C. Bryning Eaq., Northallerton
Keith Burton Esq., Easingwold
Mrs. M. A. Burton, Easingwold
Geo. Burton Esq., Easingwold
W. A. Butler Esq., Grindleton, nr. Clitheroe, Lancs.
W. T. G. Byers Esq., Easingwold
Rt. Rev. H. de Candole, Harrogate.
Miss M. H. Cass, Wheldrake, York
G. L. Clark Esq., Easingwold
Mrs. Clarke, Bruton, Somerset
D. Clegg, Esq., Kearsley, Nr. Bolton
A. D. Cliff Esq., Crayke Manor, York.
Miss F. Close, c/o Newby Wiske Hall, Northallerton
Mrs. Margaret Coates, Easingwold
Mrs. H. Coleman, Four Oaks, Sutton Coldfield
A. W. Colligan Esq., Littleborough
J. M. Collinson Esq., Wyke, Bradford
The Convent Grammar School, Scarborough
T. L. Cooper Esq., Easingwold

F. B. Corner Esq., Thirsk
Rev. B. Crosby, Easingwold
R. Cresswell Esq., Easingwold
S. Curry Esq., Uppleby, Easingwold
Mrs. M. E. Curry, Easingwold
Miss R. Dancaster, Leeds 12
Mrs. R. M. Dawson, Easingwold
Derbyshire County Library

Dewsbury Public Libraries
S. B. Dobson Esq., Easingwold
Doncaster College of Education
W. Dooley Esq., Easingwold
G. R. Drake Esq., Easingwold
E. B. C. Driffield Esq., Helperby, York
Mrs. K. Driflield, Brafferton, York
Driffield County Secondary Modern SohooF
H. Duck, Esq., MB. Ch.B., Easingwold
G. W. Dunn Esq., Easingwold
H. Dunn Esq., Uppleby, Easingwold
A. W. Dyson Esq., Ashstead, Surrey
Easingwold County Primary School
Easingwold Grammar - Modern School
East Riding County Library
Dr. P. M. G. Eden, Dept. of English Local History, University of Leicester
Edward Pease Public Library, Darlington
Miss S. Elliot, Easingwold
Mrs. M. M. Elsworth, York
N. H. Elsworth Esq., Raskelf, York
Endsleigh College of Education, Hull
John C. English Esq., Husthwaite, York
Eskdale Modern School, Whitby
N. H. Essam Esq., Easingwold
L. L. Evans Esq., Easingwold
Dr. A. M. Everitt, Dept. of English Local History, University of Leicester
Mrs. E. M. Evers, Easingwold
F. Eyres Esq., Sunderland
Dr. Eric W. Fell, Tollerton, York
J. W. Fell Esq., Darlington
G. C. D. Fenwick, Esq., Easingwold
P. M. Fitchett Esq., Helperby, York
Robin Forbes, Esq., Helperby, York
Mrs. L. Foster, Easingwold
Mrs. M. Richmond Fox, York
Miss K. Frank, Easingwold
J. Freeman Esq., Easingwold
Mrs. G. Galloway, Easingwold
Gateshead Public Libraries
John Wm. Raymond Gibson Esq., Crayke, York
C. Gilbert Esq., c/o Temple Newsam House, Leeds 15.
A. D. Gollifer Esq., Wirral, Cheshire
J. E. Gollifer Esq., Uppleby, Easingwold
J. B. Goodfellow Esq., Uppleby, Easingwold
R. S. Goulding Esq., Halifax
Dr. H. Gray, Shillinglon, York
A. Green Esq., Easingwold
Guildhall Library, London E.C.2.
Mrs. F. M. Gunner, Summerbridge
Miss M. D. Haigh, Shipton by Beningbrough, York
Halifax Public Libraries
Mrs. D. A. Hallett, Kelfield, York
H. R. Hanson, Easingwold
C. W. Harmsworth Esq., Easingwold

208

Harrogate Public Library
Rev. R. S. Hawkins, Nether Poppleton, York
Haxhy Road Junior School, York
Miss J. Hey, Harrogate
T. M. Higham Esq., Crayke Castle, York
R. M. Hodgson, Easingwold
Mrs. W. Hodgson, Easingwold
H. W. Holey Esq, Knottingley
Michael F. Holloway, London S.E.26
Miss G. M. V. Holmes, Easingwold
The Holt Jackson Book Co. Ltd.,
    Lytham St. Annes
Horsforth Public Library
K. W. Houlston Esq, Fasingwold
Mrs. M. Hudleston, South Stainley,
    Harrogate
Huntington County Modern School
Miss M. E. Hutchinson, Easingwold
Ilkley Public Library
Mrs. Jackson, Myton-on-Swale, York
Joseph Rowntree Secondary Modern School,
    New Earswick, York
Dr. John A. Kay, Alne, York
Keele University Library
Keighley Art Gallery & Museum
Keightey Public Libraries
A. E. Knight Esq., Easingwold
The Misses Knowles, Crayke, York
D. Knowlson Esq., Easingwold
John Knowlson, Uppleby, Easingwold
K. L. Knowlson Esq., Easingwold
L. A. Knowlson Esq., Easingwold
"Kurts of Easingwold", Easingwold
Lancaster University Library
Miss U. M. Lascelles, Slingsby, York
A. Lawson Esq., Longnor, Buxton
Leeds City Art Galleries
Leeds City Libraries
Leeds City Museum
Leeds University, Brotherton Library
Leicester County Library
Lecester University, Dept. of English Local
    History
Leicester University Library
Liverpool University
P. M. Lumbard Fsq., Twickenham
Malton Grammar School
Mrs. MacDonald, Fasingwold
J. Madden Esq., Leeds
Mrs. P. B. Maclean, Faaingwold
M. G. Mandefield Esq., Thirak
Margaret Clitherow School, York.
C. Martin Esq., Husthwaite, York
Rev. P. J. McGee, Osbaldeston
Dr. W. McKim, Coxwold, York
John Michael Martin Esq., Southfield, Hessle
John Medd Esq., Easingwold
K. C. Medd Esq., Easingwold
Robert Medd Esq., Easingwold
Middlesbrough College of Education
Geoffrey Milner Esq., Uppleby, Easingwold
Lord Milner of Leeds, Leeds 8
Lady Celia Milnes-Coates, Helperby Hall,
    York
Lt.-Col. R.E. Milnes-Coates, Helperby, York
C. M. Mitchell Esq., F.S.A., F.M.A.,
    Leeds I
Mrs. M. K. Monkman, Wass, York
J. W. Moulds Faq., Shipley
Newcastle-on-Tyne City Libraries
Newcastle-on-Tyne University Library
North Riding County Library
North Riding County Planning Dept.
North Riding County Record Office
Norton Secondary School, Malton
Nottinghamshire County Libraries
Nottingham Public Libraries
Lt.-Col. J. R. Palmer, Husthwaite, Thirsk
W. Paragreen Esq., Crankley, Easingwold
R. C. Park Esq., Tollerton, York

G. A. Pears & Son. Crayke, York
H. G. Pearson-Adams Esq., Brandsby Hall
    York
E. W. Pick Esq., Pickering
R. Plowribgt Faq., Sheffield
A. R. Plunkett Esq., Easingwold
Public Record Office
Dr. C. N. Pulvertaft, Stillington, York
J. B. Price Esq., Manchester
Queen Anne Grammar School, York
F. Reynard Esq., Dringhouses, York
Richmond County Modern School
Ripon College
Ripon County Secondary School
Ripon Grammar School
G. P. Robinson Esq., Knaresborough
J. G. Robinson Faq., Linton-on-Ouse
    County Primary School
Mrs. G. C. Roper, Harrogate
Rothwell Public Library
Mrs. K. Rounthwaite, Newstead, Easingwold
Mrs. Dorothy C. Ryan, Easingwold
St. Hilds College, Durham
St. John's College, York
A. J. C. Salton Esq., Uppleby, Easingwold
Scarborough Public Libraries
Scawsby College of Education, Scawsby,
    Nr. Doncaster
Mrs. A. D. C. Scott, Easingwold
H. C. Scott Esq., Q.C., Crayke, York
Miss Segar, York
J. L. Sharper Esq., Alne, York
Sheffield City Libraries
Sheffield University Library
F. Skilbeck Esq., Easingwold
Skipton Public Library
W. Slinger Esq., Alne, York
C. Smith Faq., Easingwold
Clifford Smith Esq., Howden, Goole
D. H. Smith Esq., Easingwold
George Hudson Smith Esq., Easingwold
H. F. Smith Esq., Fasingwold
J. M. Smith Esq., Presteigne, Wales
J. T. Smith Esq., Easingwold
Miss M. M. Smith, Easingwold
Ronald Smith Esq., Howarth, York
R. J. Spilman Esq., Helperby, York
A. F. Spink Esq., Fasingwold
Dr. S. C. E. Spink, Easingwold
N. E. B. Stapleton Esq., Easingwold
Stockton-on-Tees Public Library
Miss A. Maxwell Stuart, Stillington, York
Miss Hilda Sturdy, Easingwold
W. A. Sturdy Esq., Easingwold
J. Swiers Esq., Thormanby, York
J. G. Swiers Esq., Helperby, York
J. W. F. Swiers Esq., Thormanby, York
Mrs. K. Swiers, Easingwold
Mrs. B. Sykes, Tibberton, Glos.
Miss M. Sykes, Leeds 8
F. Wilfred Taylor Esq., York
M. F. Taylor Esq., Harrogate.
Dr. Joan Thirsk, St. Hildas' College Oxford
Thirsk Grammar & Modern School
E. O'D. Thomas Esq., c/o Ripon Grammar
    School
Mrs. D. Tillott, Easingwold
H. Edwin Toothill Esq., Kilburn, York
R. W. Turnbull Esq., Easingwold
R. H. Turton Esq., M.P. Thirsk
Mrs. & Miss B. Tweddle, Roundhay, Leeds 8
Col. T. H. Twigg, Easingwold
Miss E. Vollans, London N.W.l.
Miss E. M. Walker, F.S.A., Ripon
Wakefield County Council
C. C. Warner Esq., Easingwold
Mrs. J. C. Warner, Fasingwold
Mrs. E. H. Watson, Aldwark, Alne
L. P. Wenham Faq., Dept. of History,
    Grays Court, Chapter House St., York

209

Wentworth Castle College of Education,
  Barnsley
Miss I. T. Westlake, St. Ives, Cornwall
West Riding County Library
Miss K. E. Whincup, Follifoot.
  near Harrogste
Mrs. E. M. Whitaker, Green Hammerton,
  York
Whitcliffe Mount Grammar School,
  Cleckheaton
Mrs. E. A. Whiteley, Alne, York.
M. E. Willis Esq., Easingwold.
Mrs. R. deV Winkfield, York
Mrs. Mary Wilkinson, Easingwold

G. J. Wilkinson Esq., Easingwold
Dr. F. P. Willis, Stillington, York.
Mrs. J. A. Wise, Uppleby, Easingwold
Mrs. E. B. Wombwell, Coxwold, York
Miss D. Wood, Easingwold
Woodhouse Grove School, Apperley Bridge,
  Bradford
Sir William Worsley, York
York City Libraries
York Minster Library
York University Library
Yorkshire Philosophical Society
Yorkshire Archeological Society

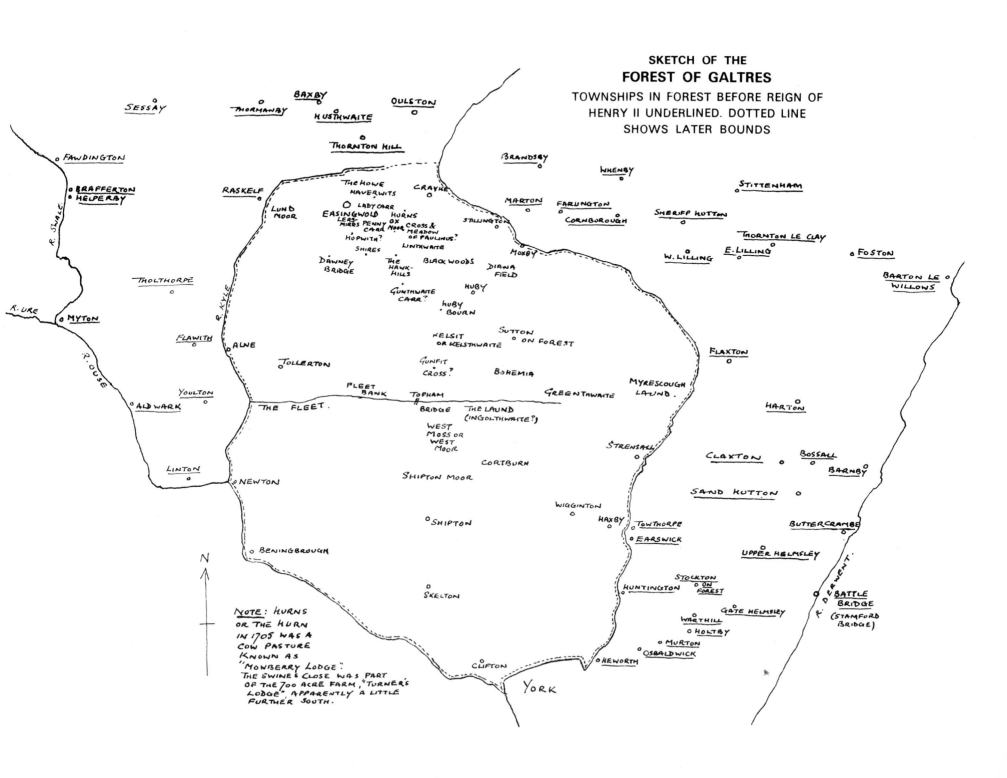

SKETCH OF THE
FOREST OF GALTRES
TOWNSHIPS IN FOREST BEFORE REIGN OF
HENRY II UNDERLINED. DOTTED LINE
SHOWS LATER BOUNDS

SESSAY

THORMANBY   BAXBY   OULSTON
HUSTHWAITE

FAWDINGTON

THORNTON HILL   BRANDSBY   WHENBY   STITTENHAM

BRAFFERTON
HELPERBY   RASKELF   THE HOWE   CRAYKE   MARTON   FARLINGTON   SHERIFF HUTTON
                HAVERWITS   CORNBOROUGH
                LADY CARR   STILLINGTON   THORNTON LE CLAY
LUND   EASINGWOLD   HURNS   OX   W. LILLING   E. LILLING   FOSTON
MOOR   LEAS-   PENNY   MOOR   CROSS &
        MIRES   CARR   MEADOW   BARTON LE
        HOPWITH?   OF PAULINUS?   MOXBY   WILLOWS
THOLTHORPE   SHIRES   LINTHWAITE
            DAWNEY   THE   BLACK WOODS   DIANA
            BRIDGE   HAWK-   FIELD
R. URE   HILLS
            GUNTHWAITE   HUBY
MYTON   CARR?   HUBY
                        BOURN
FLAWITH   SUTTON
        ALNE   KELSIT   ON FOREST   FLAXTON
                    OR KELSTHWAITE
        TOLLERTON   GUNFIT
R. OUSE   CROSS?   BOHEMIA
                                        MYRESCOUGH
YOULTON   FLEET   LAUND.
        BANK   TOPHAM   GREENTHWAITE   HARTON
ALDWARK   THE FLEET.   BRIDGE   THE LAUND
                    (INGOLTHWAITE?)
                WEST   STRENSALL
                MOSS OR   CLAXTON   BOSSALL
LINTON   WEST   BARNBY
                MOOR   CORTBURN
    NEWTON   SHIPTON MOOR   SAND HUTTON

                                WIGGINTON
                                        HAXBY   TOWTHORPE   BUTTERCRAMBE
                    SHIPTON   EARSWICK
BENINGBROUGH   UPPER HELMSLEY

N   SKELTON   STOCKTON
↑   HUNTINGTON   ON
                                                    FOREST   BATTLE
                                            GATE HELMSLEY   BRIDGE
NOTE: HURNS   WARTHILL   (STAMFORD
OR THE HURN   HOLTBY   BRIDGE)
IN 1705 WAS A   CLIFTON   MURTON
COW PASTURE   OSBALDWICK
KNOWN AS   HEWORTH
"MOWBERRY LODGE".
THE SWINES CLOSE WAS PART   YORK
OF THE 700 ACRE FARM, "TURNER'S
LODGE" APPARENTLY A LITTLE
FURTHER SOUTH.

R. SWALE
R. KYLE
DERWENT

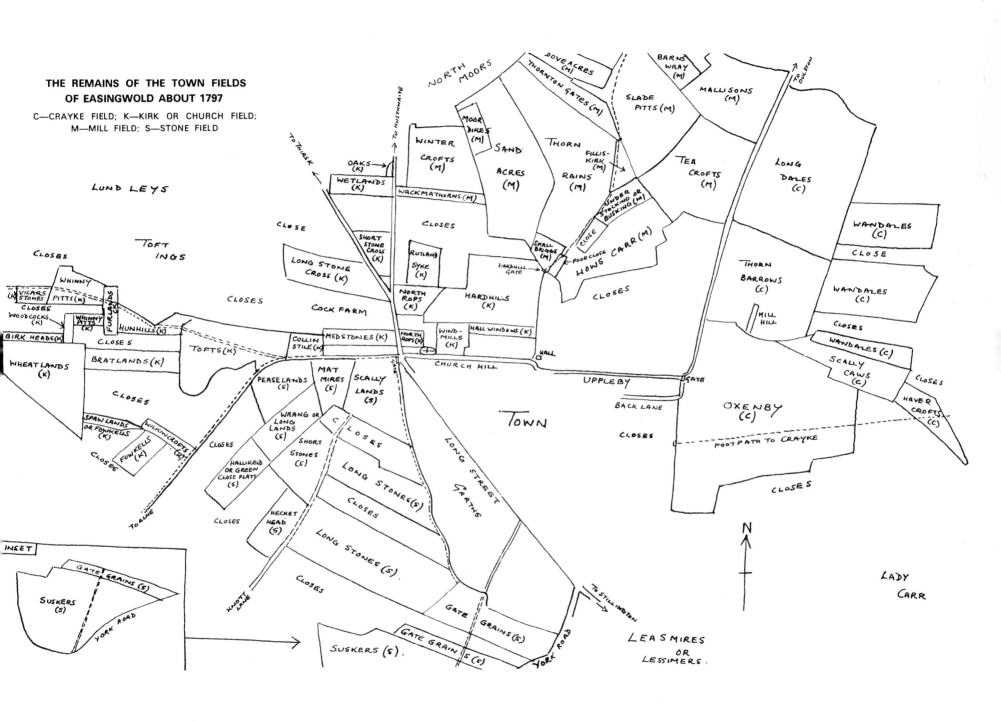

THE REMAINS OF THE TOWN FIELDS
OF EASINGWOLD ABOUT 1797

C—CRAYKE FIELD; K—KIRK OR CHURCH FIELD;
M—MILL FIELD; S—STONE FIELD

LUND LEYS

TOFT INGS

CLOSES

CLOSE

CLOSES

NORTH MOORS

TO THIRSK

TO HUSTHWAITE

TO CRAYKE

OAKS (K)

WETLANDS (K)

WINTER CROFTS (M)

MOOR DIKES (M)

SAND ACRES (M)

WACKMATHORNS (M)

CLOSES

DOVE ACRES (M)

THORNTON GATES (M)

BARNS WRAY (M)

MALLISONS (M)

SLADE PITTS (M)

THORN RAINS (M)

FILLIS-KIRK (M)

TEA CROFTS (M)

LONG DALES (C)

TO OULSTON

SHORT STONE CROSS (K)

LONG STONE CROSS (K)

RUTLAND SYKE (K)

UNDER STOCKING OR BUSKING (M)

CLOSE

SMALL BRIGGS (M)

POOR CLOSE (M)

HOWS CARR (M)

HARDHILL GATE

HARDHILLS (K)

CLOSES

WANDALES (C)

CLOSE

WANDALES (C)

THORN BARROWS (C)

CLOSES

WHINNY PITTS (K)

VICARS STONES

CLOSES

WOODCOCKS (K)

WHINNY PITTS (K)

FURLANDS

HUNHILLS (K)

NORTH RODS (K)

COCK FARM

CLOSES

BIRK HEADS (K)

WHEATLANDS (K)

BRATLANDS (K)

TOFTS (K)

CLOSES

COLLIN STILE (K)

MEDSTONES (K)

NORTH RODS (K)

WIND-MILLS (K)

HALL WINDOWS (K)

MILL HILL

CLOSES

WANDALES (C)

SCALLY CAWS (C)

CLOSES

HAVER CROFTS (C)

HALL

CHURCH HILL

UPPLEBY

GATE

BACK LANE

OXENBY (C)

CLOSES

FOOTPATH TO CRAYKE

CLOSES

TOWN

PEASELANDS (S)

MAT MIRES (S)

SCALLY LANDS (S)

WRANG OR LONG LANDS (S)

SPAN LANDS OR FOWKELLS (K)

WILKINCROFTS (K)

FOWKELLS (K)

CLOSES

CLOSES

CLOSES

CLOSES

HALLIKELD OR GREEN CLOSE FLATT (S)

SHORT STONES (S)

CLOSES

HECKET HEAD (S)

CLOSES

CLOSES

LONG STONES (S)

LONG STONES (S)

LONG STREET GARTHS

TO LANE

KNOTT LANE

CLOSES

GATE GRAINS (S)

GATE GRAINS (S)

TO STILLINGTON

YORK ROAD

LEASMIRES OR LESSIMERS.

LADY CARR

N

INSET

GATE GRAINS (S)

SUSKERS (S)

YORK ROAD

SUSKERS (S).

GATE GRAIN S (S)